Skin

Second Edition

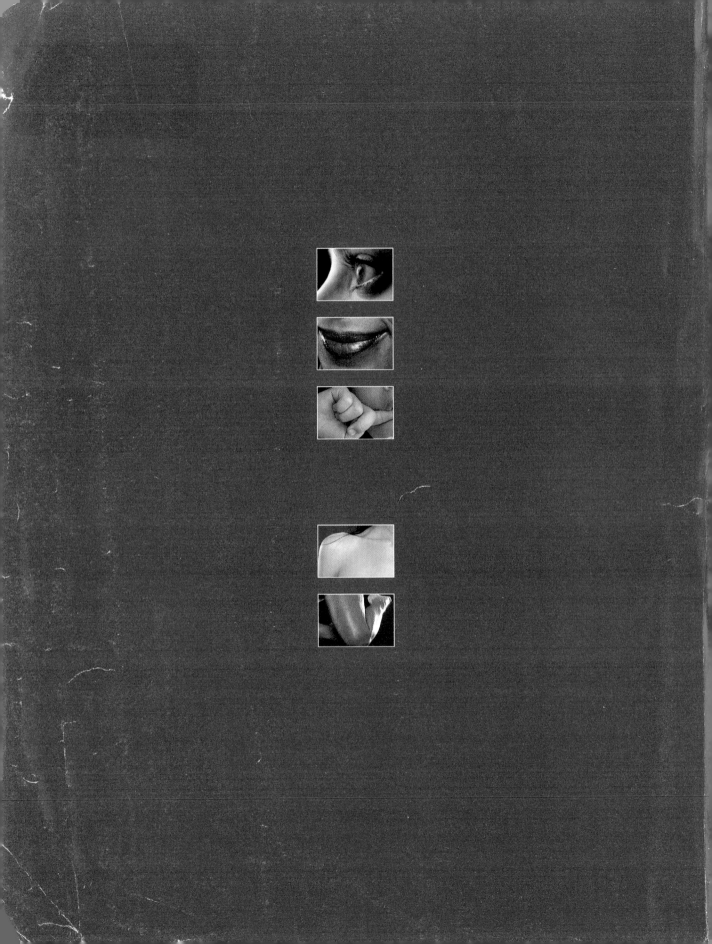

Skin

The Complete Guide to Digitally
Lighting, Photographing, and
Retouching Faces and Bodies

Second Edition

Lee Varis

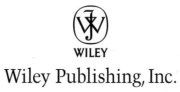

Wiley Publishing, Inc.

Acquisitions Editor: Mariann Bsrsolo
Development Editor: Mary Ellen Schutz
Technical Editor: Doug Nelson
Production Editor: Elizabeth Ginns Britten
Copy Editor: Kathy Grider-Carlyle
Editorial Manager: Pete Gaughan
Production Manager: Tim Tate
Vice President and Executive Group Publisher: Richard Swadley
Vice President and Publisher: Neil Edde
Book Designers: Franz Baumhackl, Lori Barra
Compositor: Kate Kaminski, Happenstance Type-O-Rama
Proofreader: Nancy Bell
Indexer: Ted Laux
Project Coordinator, Cover: Lynsey Stanford
Cover Designer: Ryan Sneed

Copyright © 2010 by Wiley Publishing, Inc., Indianapolis, Indiana

Published simultaneously in Canada

ISBN: 978-0-470-59212-0
ISBN: 978-0-470-90661-3 (ebk)
ISBN: 978-0-470-90663-7 (ebk)
ISBN: 978-0-470-90662-0 (ebk)

For general information on our other products and services or to obtain technical support, please contact our Customer Care Department within the U.S. at (877) 762-2974, outside the U.S. at (317) 572-3993 or fax (317) 572-4002.

Wiley also publishes its books in a variety of electronic formats. Some content that appears in print may not be available in electronic books.

Library of Congress Cataloging-in-Publication Data is available from the publisher.

10 9 8 7 6 5 4 3 2 1

Dear Reader,

Thank you for choosing *Skin: The Complete Guide to Digitally Lighting, Photographing, and Retouching Faces and Bodies, Second Edition*. This book is part of a family of premium-quality Sybex books, all of which are written by outstanding authors who combine practical experience with a gift for teaching.

Sybex was founded in 1976. More than 30 years later, we're still committed to producing consistently exceptional books. With each of our titles, we're working hard to set a new standard for the industry. From the paper we print on, to the authors we work with, our goal is to bring you the best books available.

I hope you see all that reflected in these pages. I'd be very interested to hear your comments and get your feedback on how we're doing. Feel free to let me know what you think about this or any other Sybex book by sending me an email at nedde@wiley.com. If you think you've found a technical error in this book, please visit http://sybex.custhelp.com. Customer feedback is critical to our efforts at Sybex.

Best regards,

Neil Edde
Vice President and Publisher
Sybex, an imprint of Wiley

For my many students who have inspired me to share my experiences in the world of digital photography.

Acknowledgments

I could not written this book without the help and support of many people. First, I need to thank my wife, Gila, for putting up with me these past several months—she is always ready to listen to and encourage me. Thanks also to my kids, Aaron and Erika, for being an inspiration to me and for being such great subjects for my example images. A special thanks also goes to my sister Yvonne, who besides being a gracious subject for the retouching chapter has provided many years of creative inspiration through her music.

I must thank my contributors—Aaron Rapoport, Ken Chernus, Anthony Nex, Audrey Stein, Paul Blieden, Michele Eve Sanberg, Mark Harmel and Erin Manning; Erin was also the subject for the basic portrait-lighting examples. This book would not be anywhere near as good as it is without the great photographs contributed by these fine artists.

I must also thank my technical editor, Doug Nelson. Doug made sure I didn't slip up, and he caught the tiniest errors in screenshots, captions, and descriptive text. He made numerous suggestions for clarifying technically dense text—and made sure this old timer got the updated application terms correct. I can't forget to thank the many subjects of all the photos whose humanity is on display in these pages; few of them are mentioned by name, but all are deeply appreciated for their contributions.

Of course, this book wouldn't be possible without the Sybex team: acquisitions editor Mariann Barsolo, production editor Liz Britten, developmental editor Mary Ellen Schutz from Gentle Editing LLC, copyeditor Kathy Grider-Carlyle, proofreader Nancy Bell, indexer Ted Laux, and compositor Kate Kaminski from Happenstance Type-O-Rama.

A special thanks goes to my agent, Matt Wagner, who has been watching my back in more ways than one (thanks for the insights on tattoos).

I could not have accomplished anything in digital photography without the many teachers I have had over the years: Tony Redhead, Kai Kraus, Ed Manning, Dan Margulis, David Biedney, Al Edgar, Daniel Clark, Jeff Schewe, Bruce Fraser, Chris Murphy, Katrin Eismann, Eric Magnusen, Bryan Allen, and many others who have helped me surf the bleeding edge of digital imaging technology.

Of course, no book on digital photography should fail to acknowledge the Knoll brothers, Thomas and John, who created Photoshop and let the genie out of the bottle to the delight of digital artists everywhere. And no book on photography techniques could begin to repay the debt owed to Ansel Adams, who established the great technical foundation for the art and craft of photography. I stand on the shoulders of giants to make my very modest contribution to the vast world of digital imaging.

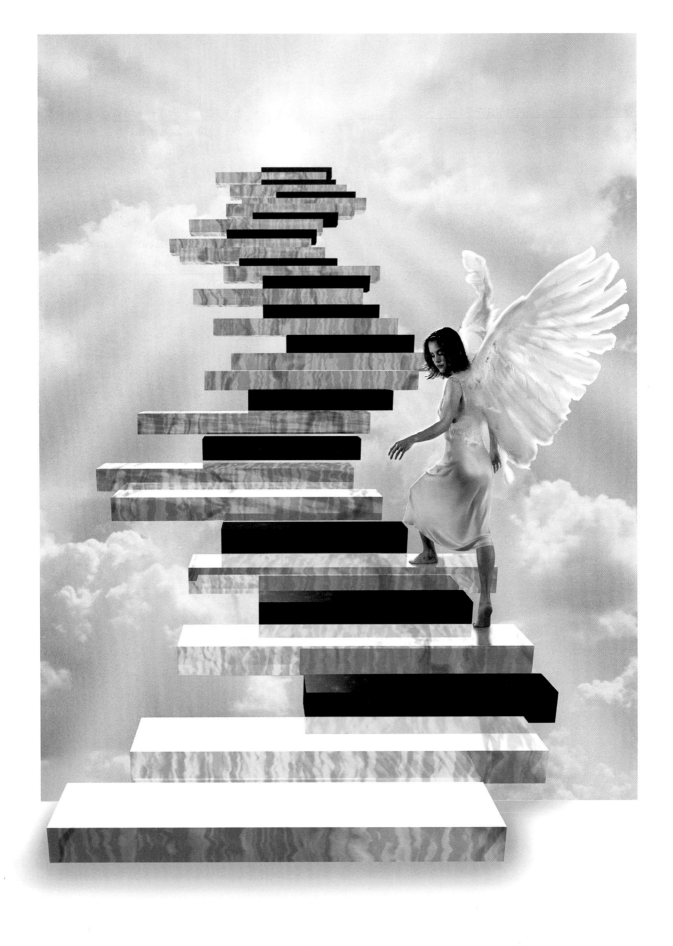

About the Author

Lee Varis, who has been involved in commercial photography for the past 30 years, is a photo-illustrator working in Hollywood. He began working with computer imaging two decades ago, after one of his clients took him to see what they were doing to his photography on the Quantel Paintbox. Lee was hooked and spent many hours hanging out at Electric Paint, one of the first creative imaging services to utilize the new technology for movie posters and album covers. His first imaging computer was a Macintosh SE—a tiny computer with a B+W monitor that could process RGB color files. Lee began exploring digital photography using some of the earliest systems available, and he helped Dave Etchells (of Imaging Resource) conduct the very first comprehensive tests of digital camera systems in his photo studio back in 1990. Lee currently works with digital as well as conventional photography in conjunction with computer graphics to create images for print advertising.

Lee's work has been featured on movie posters, video box covers, CD covers, and numerous brochures and catalogs. His creative imaging has been featured in *National Geographic, Newsweek,* and *Fortune* magazines as well as trade journals such as *PDN, New Media, Micro Publishing News, Rangefinder, Design Graphics, Photo Electronic Imaging,* and *PC Photo.*

Lee has also been involved with consulting and training activities for numerous corporate clients. He conducted two series of imaging seminars for Apple Computer that took him to most of the major metropolitan areas in the United States. He is currently active in seminar programs with APA, ASMP, PPA, Santa Fe Photographic Workshops, Maine Media Workshops, and Julia Dean Photographic Workshops, as well as ongoing *Photoshop for Digital Photographers* workshops in Los Angeles. He is one of the founding fathers and current president of the Los Angeles Digital Imaging Group (LADIG, a chapter of the USDIG). Lee also serves on the board of the Digital Image Marketing Association (DIMA), a division of PMA, the Photo Marketing Association.

Besides his work in digital photography, Lee is an amateur musician with a passion for collecting and playing unusual instruments. His current favorite instrument is the *oud,* a Middle Eastern lute that was popular with his Greek ancestors. You can usually find him playing music while his computer is processing multiple RAW digital camera files.

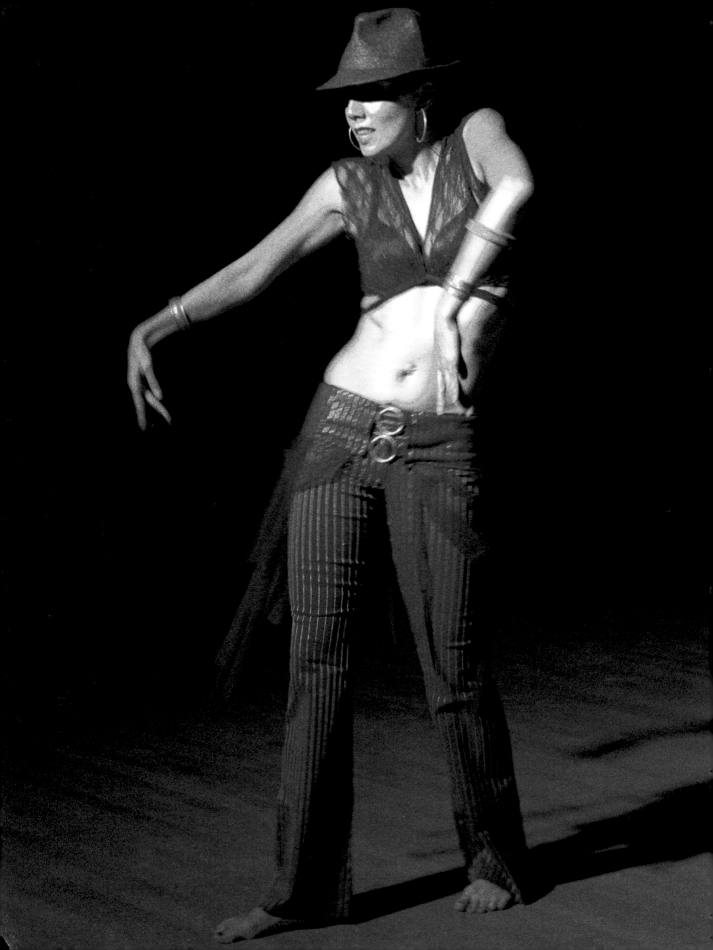

Contents

Foreword   *xv*

Introduction   *xvii*

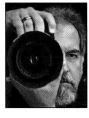

Chapter 1   **Digital Imaging Basics, Workflow, and Calibration**   **1**

Chips and Pixels 2

Your Monitor and Calibrator 6

Basic Digital Capture Workflow 7
Setting Up a Lightroom Catalog   8
Calibrating for Digital Capture   10
Building a Camera Calibration   22
Using Camera Profiles   29
Editing Camera Profiles for Better Skin Color   32
Working with Your Calibration   34
Calibration Review   36
Testing Procedure Overview   36

Putting Color Management in Context 37

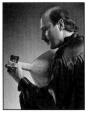

Chapter 2   **Lighting and Photographing People**   **41**

Lighting Technology 42

Basic Portrait Lighting 47
Rembrandt Lighting   53
Natural Light   57
On-Camera Flash   60
Breaking the Rules   63

Advanced Lighting Techniques 65
Ring Light   65
Combination Lighting: Daylight Plus Flash   68
Controlling Natural Light   71
Action Stopping Lighting   78

Experimenting with Light 83

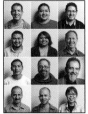

Chapter 3   **The Color of Skin**   **87**

White Points, Black Points, and Places In-Between 88

Zone System: Contrast and Tone 89

Neutral Color: Using Balanced Numbers 91
Curves: The Basic Color and Tone Tool   93
Contrast Control: The Basic Curve Shapes   94
Info Panel: Reading Basic Numbers   99

White/Black Point Correction 100

Adjusting the Numbers for the Color of Skin 103

The Family of Man: Cultural and Psychological Issues 108

Cultural and Personal Color Bias 113

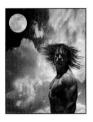

Chapter 4   **Tone and Contrast: Color and B+W**   **117**

Converting to B+W 118
The Channel Mixer   119

Split Channels: Layer Blending 123

Luminosity Blending. 127
Instant Tan   128
When Color Overwhelms: Look for the Good Channel   131

Hue/Saturation Toning Effects 138
Split-Toning   141
Gradient Map Colorizing   145

The Power of B+W 149

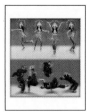

Chapter 5   **Retouching**   **155**

Basic Image Repair 156

Hue/Saturation Color Repair 165
Skin Smoothing   170

Beauty Retouching 178

Subtle Retouching. 204

Figure Thinning Techniques 210

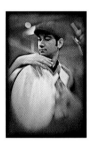

Chapter 6   **Special Effects**   **219**

Soft Focus 220
Basic Diffusion Effect   220
Screen Diffusion   225
Multiply Diffusion   228
Overlay Diffusion   230
Depth of Field Effects   232
Lens Tilt Effect   242

Film Grain and Noise 251

Cross-Processing. 258

Grunge 265

Tattoos 270
Enhancing Existing Tattoos   270
Faking Tattoos   276

Final Notes 280

Chapter 7   **Preparing for Print**   **283**

Sharpening 284
Unsharp Mask   284
Smart Sharpen   289
Multiple Sharpening Layers   292
Octave Sharpening   295
Overlay Sharpening and High-Radius Effects   300

Color Management for Print. 308
Translating from RGB to CMYK   308
Profiles and Look-Up Tables   308

Soft Proofing. 310

Desktop Printing. 312
Print Options   312
Output Simulations   315

Creative Print Finishing 315
Background and Canvas Options   317
Edge Treatments   317
Last Minute Fixes   323

Chapter 8   **Parting Shots**   **329**

The Creative Workflow. 330

Future Developments 331

Index   *335*

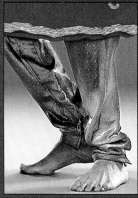

"Though the focus is on skin, the concepts and techniques apply in all types of photography."

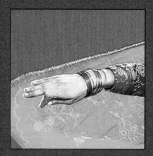

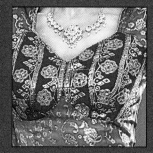

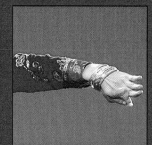

Foreword

I usually don't buy or recommend new digital photography or Photoshop books, for two main reasons: One, there is a ton of free how-to information on the Web; two, just about everything that can be said about every possible digital photography subject has been said in many books.

This book is one of the few exceptions, which is why I put this thought in its own separate paragraph; it's *that* important.

If you are in a bookstore, I recommend that you proceed to checkout with the book in hand. If you are reading this post on my blog, or if you have already purchased Lee's book, you, as well as the person in the bookstore, are in for a real educational treat, because Lee will take you on a complete journey into the magical world of digital imaging. In a nutshell, you will learn digital imaging from start to finish—from one of the best of the best.

Obviously, Lee sent me all the chapters in advance of the publication of this book. In reading through the chapters, I found, as you will find, that Lee, who is a highly acclaimed master of digital photography and retouching (among other talents, including musical) presents high-tech, how-to techniques in a way that we can all understand.

I've been in this game for about 30 years. HDR expert Trey Ratcliff calls me, "One of the godfathers of photography." Still, I learned more than a few tips and tricks from Lee while reading his text and looking at his exquisite images. What's more, I picked up a few tips, including tips on sharpening and the Channel Mixer (to name a few), that I will share with my audience. I know that will be okay with Lee, because he is all about sharing and teaching. Plus, he is one heck of a nice guy, which you will experience firsthand if you ever attend one of his workshops or seminars.

The book's introduction and table of contents (don't skip these two items!) give you a very good idea about what's in this book and how to use it, so I don't think I need to go into that stuff. What I would like to impart to you is this: You have found a friend and advisor in Lee Varis, a person who will help and guide you in your quest to improve your digital images—a friend you should follow on this site, blog, Twitter, Facebook, and so on.

RICK SAMMON
www.ricksammon.com

P.S. I first met Lee at the Palm Springs Photo Festival in 2010. He always had a smile on his face. (He was also the best dressed.) You may "feel" Lee's happiness while reading this book, because Lee writes as he speaks. Obviously, Lee is one happy guy—someone who loves what he does, which is good news for all of us.

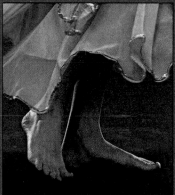

"*In wisdom gathered over time, I have found that every experience is a form of exploration.*"

—*Ansel Adams*

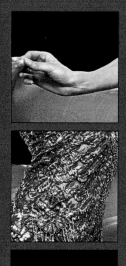

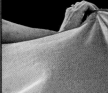

Introduction

The book you are holding is the result of over 30 years of experience capturing photos with film and digital technology. I have tried to distill all my experiences with people photography into a short volume that concentrates on the technical and creative aspects of digital photography of human subjects. This second edition updates many techniques and adds new ones to take advantage of new software and improvements in hardware.

The biggest problem for me was figuring out what to omit. If I had included every little detail, the volume would have swollen to well over 800 pages. Therefore, I tried to concentrate on information that is not readily available elsewhere and still cover enough basic information to provide some foundation for the more advanced concepts in the book.

The title of this book is *Skin,* but the tutorials contained herein cover much more than just the surface material of the most popular subject for photography. There is skin here, to be sure—just perhaps not the type of "skin" that such a title might suggest. In these pages, you will find valuable information about digital photography and retouching skin—skin that belongs to real people, all kinds of people: young, old, and of all ethnic types. You will find out how to use lighting for portraits, action, outdoors, in-studio, and on location. You'll learn several techniques to make dark skin reproduce better. Although the focus is on skin, the concepts and techniques this book explores have broad application in all types of photography.

I've attempted to address the rather large holes found in most other books on the subject of people photography, where it seems that the photo-universe is populated by exclusively by white middle-class people or skinny, young, beautiful women. I've included examples from other photographers shooting in different styles that range from Gen-X advertising to lifestyle stock, as well as more straightforward portraiture. Much of this work is very contemporary, shot recently, and, as such, it represents current trends in photography rather than legacy work of an author who hasn't shot a real job in years.

Above all, this is a technical book about professional digital photography. Although it is oriented toward commercial, stock, and professional shooters, the technical content is perfectly applicable to fine art photography. You won't find pages and pages of philosophical ramblings about art and psychology, but you will find loads of practical techniques that you can use in any context. Many of these techniques have never been published before now, and all of them are presented in great detail with variations so that you can better adapt these methods to your own specific needs.

Who Should Buy This Book

I've made certain assumptions regarding the reader:

- You are familiar with basic computer functions.
- You know basic photographic principles such as f-stops and shutter speeds.
- You have used a digital camera to capture images, at least as JPEGs.
- You are familiar with basic Photoshop functions.
- You have a rudimentary understanding of layers and masks in Photoshop.

This book is not intended as a basic text on digital photography or Photoshop, but it can be used in conjunction with a basic text to take you to the next level in digital photo mastery. The tutorials herein, with the associated digital files provided on the companion website (www.varis.com/skinbook), will allow you to learn professional techniques for capturing and enhancing images of human subjects. You will not find the usual simple brightness/contrast or red-eye–reduction techniques that are more than adequately covered in every other book on digital imaging; *Skin* is about *professional* techniques for creative photography.

On the other hand, don't let me intimidate you. There is plenty of material here that can be put to good use by serious beginners. You might need to invest some time and energy, but you'll definitely be rewarded if you follow along with the step-by-step instructions. So roll up your sleeves and let's begin!

What's Inside

Here is a glance at what's in each chapter.

Chapter 1: Digital Imaging Basics, Workflow, and Calibration begins with a basic explanation of digital capture technology: the hardware and software we photographers have to manage in order to capture and improve our images. Then it moves into a thorough examination of testing and calibration techniques that allow you to build idealized camera profiles to use when processing images in Adobe Camera Raw and Lightroom.

Chapter 2: Lighting and Photographing People shows basic lighting techniques, gives examples of more elaborate lighting, and provides diagrams illustrating the placement of lights and reflectors

Chapter 3: The Color of Skin covers color correction specific to skin tone and shows how to achieve the best possible color rendering for a wide variety of subjects.

Chapter 4: Tone and Contrast: Color and B+W introduces you to the best methods for grayscale conversion and explores the concept and techniques for luminosity blending. It also demonstrates how to tone or colorize B+W.

Chapter 5: Retouching shows how to do basic as well as more advanced retouching for men and women. Special techniques are presented for rebuilding skin texture, minimizing skin defects, smoothing skin, and even slimming figures.

Chapter 6: **Special Effects** covers advanced Photoshop techniques with creative methods specifically suitable for people photography, including a section dealing with tattoos.

Chapter 7: **Preparing for Print** provides tutorials for print preparation with sharpening and other print-enhancing techniques.

Chapter 8: **Parting Shots** presents some ideas about the creative workflow and the future of imaging technology and its impact on the practice of photography

The Companion Website

To help you with the material presented in this book, I've provided the image files for most of the tutorials on the book website:

www.varis.com/skinbook

These image files are copyrighted; they are intended for your private use in learning the techniques presented in this book. You are permitted to manipulate them and print them to check how well you did. You may not publish them in any way, including posting them online, sharing them, or allowing any reproduction beyond what you need for your own private use.

The website allows me to provide updated information in a more timely manner—the first edition of this book was prepared over four years ago, an eternity in the world of digital photography! For the current edition, some things have changed and others remain more or less the same, but I cannot guarantee that much of the content won't become obsolete in the next few years or even the next few months! So . . . to build on the relationship that I've established with you, the reader, I have created a website to support your continued involvement with photography.

The ideas I've presented here are a true work in progress. I will be uploading new content, example files, additional tutorials, videos and other materials that relate to the ideas presented here. While this is not meant to replace the book, it is a place where I can provide further support, correct errors, and build a community where we can come together to develop the ideas further.

This is my promise to you—I will continue to support your development as a photographer in whatever capacity I can.

How to Contact the Author

I welcome feedback from you about this book or about books you'd like to see from me in the future. You can reach me by writing to varis@varis.com. For more information about my photography, visit my website at www.varis.com.

Sybex, an imprint of Wiley Publishing Inc., strives to keep you supplied with the latest tools and information you need for your work. Please check their website at www.sybex.com.

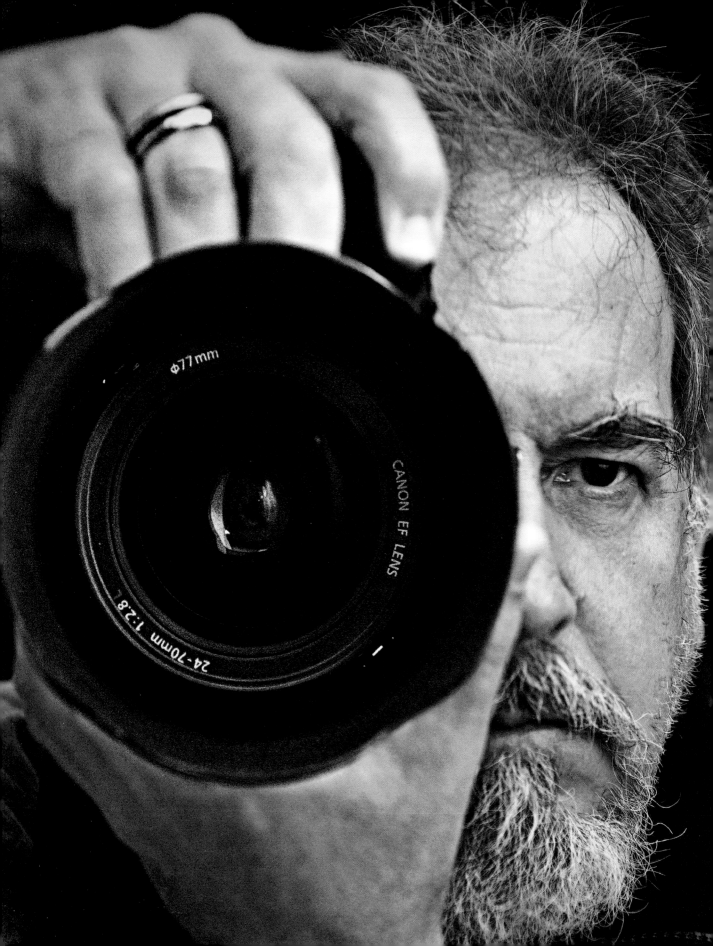

Digital Imaging Basics, Workflow, and Calibration

Every journey begins with the first step. Unfortunately, for many, the temptation to skip the first step is enhanced by the belief that they already know how to take pictures. After all, we've been snapping photos since we were kids, haven't we? Modern cameras do everything automatically, don't they?

For consistent success, you need to predict the outcome of the image capture with certainty—and for professional results, you can't rely on the display on the back of the camera. Before you begin, you need to learn how digital photography works and develop an image capture workflow; then you need to test and calibrate your equipment. Only then can you take the first tentative steps to digital photo mastery.

1

Chapter Contents

Chips and Pixels
Basic Digital Capture Workflow
Calibrating for Digital Capture
Color Management in Context

Chips and Pixels

All cameras function like human eyes (Figure 1.1). In both, a lens focuses light through a small hole (iris) onto a receptive surface (retina/film/chip) that translates the varying intensities and colors of the light into meaningful information. The main distinguishing feature between different cameras and the eye has to do with the receptive surface. The eye's retina is a receptive surface comprising two different structures (rods and cones) with three basic color sensitivities (red, green, and blue). Film is made of silver salt grains suspended in gelatin in three different layers to receive color. Digital camera chips contain photoreceptor sites on a silicon chip; each photoreceptor site has one of three different colored filters to record light.

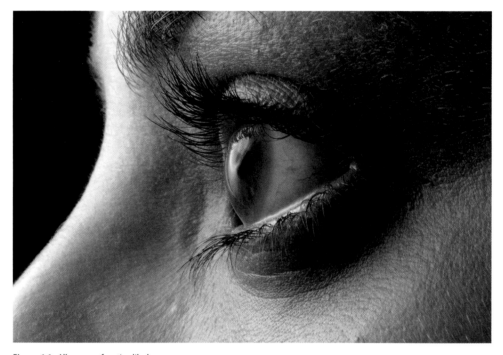

Figure 1.1 All cameras function like human eyes.

Digital cameras are similar to eyes in that the camera's chip translates the light into information (electrical signals) directly. Much as the eye translates the light falling on the retina into nerve impulses (electrical signals) that travel to the brain for processing, the electrical signals from a digital camera require processing in a computer "brain" before they can be used to create photos.

The actual process is rather more complex, but a few things are important to understand. Most digital cameras capture images using chips with receptor sites that have red, green, and blue filters arranged in a regular pattern on the surface of the chip. Light intensity is the only thing captured at a receptor site. During the processing phase, the color of light hitting a receptor is determined by calculating differences in intensities between adjacent sites that have red, green, or blue filters. This process produces an RGB bitmap image. A *bitmap* is a regular grid of square units of color. These units are called *pixels*. Color is determined by the relative values of red, green, and blue for each pixel. We, therefore, think of these pixels as being in three "channels" (Red, Green, and Blue) simultaneously so that the complete image is recorded as three different black and white (B+W) images that form the full-color version. This concept will be important when we get to color correction.

The number and density of receptor sites on the chip determine the resolution of detail. This *pixel count* is given as either dimensions, such as 4992×3228, or as a total, such as 16 megapixels, where "mega" means million (totals are usually simplified to the nearest decimal). Therefore, an 8-megapixel chip has less resolution than a 12-megapixel chip. Professional-quality people photography can be done with cameras delivering 8 megapixels or more of resolution. Pixel count can be manipulated after the fact through mathematical calculations that *interpolate* new pixels from existing ones, but the amount of image detail can never exceed the original *resolution* of the chip. That being said, there is no reason for you to obsess over the number of pixels available as a standard of quality. Movie posters have been made from images with fewer than 6 megapixels, and the quality of those pixels in terms of lack of noise and fidelity of color information is more important than the quantity used for photographing people.

Bayer Pattern Chips

The usual arrangement of red, green, and blue photoreceptors across a digital camera chip surface is called a *Bayer pattern*. This regular pattern alternates green with red and blue so that there are twice as many green pixels as there are red or blue. There are more green pixels because green holds 60 percent of the overall image luminosity (lightness-darkness) in an RGB image. The signals from adjacent pixels are averaged together using complex algorithms to determine the overall color and interpolate this into each pixel in the image. Skin colors sit right between the red and green filter frequencies used in most chip designs, and as it turns out, calculating skin color correctly is difficult. In digital photography, skin color can end up being a little too red. You'll learn how to compensate for this later.

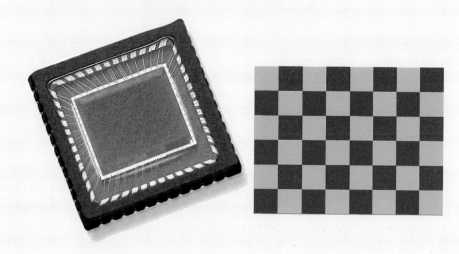

The dynamic range of a captured scene is an important yardstick for quality (Figure 1.2). This is the brightness range from dark to light that affects how much detail can be rendered in the darkest and lightest portions of the scene. Dynamic range is often represented in f-stops. Digital cameras can often capture a range of 11 f-stops from black to white, whereas a paper print from a desktop inkjet printer might have, at best, a range of five f-stops. Regular offset lithography, such as magazine printing, has even less dynamic range—typically four f-stops or even less. This disparity between capture and output is at the heart of reproduction problems because we often have to determine how we are going to compress the range of an image to fit the output. You will often hear about "bit depth" in the same breath as dynamic range. *Bit depth* refers to the number of steps between black and white that are encoded in a digital capture. Higher bit depth captures have a finer density of steps and yield a smoother ramp from black to white; however, bit depth does not determine dynamic range. It is certainly better to have higher bit depth with wider dynamic range, but the two are not necessarily interdependent.

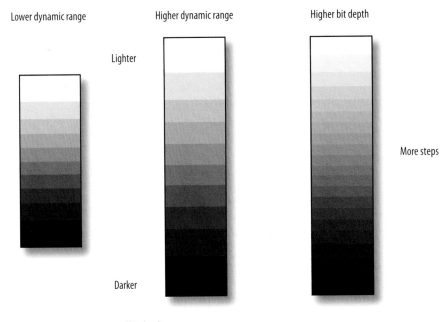

Figure 1.2 Dynamic range and bit depth

The RAW signal from the camera chip can be processed either in the camera firmware or later in software under user control. There is some debate over the merits of both approaches. Generally, if you opt to have the camera do the processing, you will be shooting JPEG files to the memory card or directly to a computer.

 Note: JPEG stands for Joint Photographic Experts Group, the organization that developed the file format.

JPEG is a file format that was developed to reduce file size by using mathematical algorithms that simplify the pixel structure in the bitmap image. This process is considered *lossy* because some image detail is "lost" during the process. Digital cameras apply a conservative level of compression or size reduction, and this is generally considered visually *lossless*. This does not mean that there is *no* loss—just that the loss is not apparent at first glance. Even the best JPEG file does not carry the same amount of information or image detail as a noncompressed or unaltered version.

The main advantage to shooting JPEGs is that by compressing the file size, you can fit many more images onto a memory card (so you don't have to change cards as often). Because the files are smaller, they also write faster and enable faster shooting speeds. This can be important for shooting wedding candids, news, sporting events, and any other fast-breaking action. The disadvantage to shooting JPEGs is that you have to accept the camera's interpretation—of color, contrast, etc.—and you limit the potential quality of the image. You give up some flexibility and quality for speed and convenience.

JPEG Compression Artifacts

JPEG compression works by simplifying adjacent tones; similar tones are assigned the same value. This can cause distinctive "blocky" artifacts and "messy" edges, which are most noticeable in extreme magnifications. JPEG artifacts can become a problem when image files are sharpened for print output or scaled up from smaller sizes. For most work destined for offset lithography (magazines and newspapers), JPEG artifacts don't pose a problem because they are obscured by the printing linescreen.

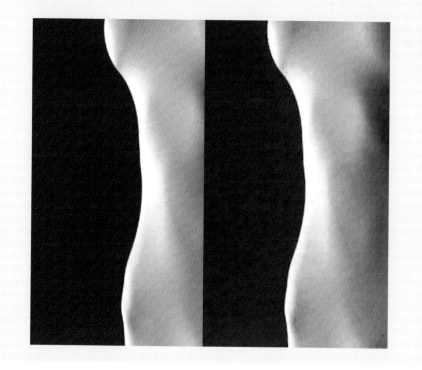

If you are concerned with the best possible quality, then you probably will prefer to record the camera's RAW signal and process this data using your computer software in a *RAW file workflow*. Doing so complicates the process slightly by adding an additional post-processing step to your photography workflow. The main advantage to a RAW file workflow is that you can postpone final decisions on color rendering, tone, and contrast until after the shoot, when you have fewer distractions and you can concentrate on basic photo elements such as lighting, composition, and exposure. You also gain a considerable amount of control over color rendering, tone, and contrast. The disadvantage is that you have to take extra time after the shoot to process your RAW files into a useable format.

Your Monitor and Calibrator

After pixels are captured and assembled into images, those images need to be viewed and interpreted. Every image-creation system must include a monitor to view the captured images. A good monitor is an absolute necessity for any serious photographer. However, a good hardware calibrator is even more important (Figure 1.3). You'll need to purchase a calibrator with the necessary software and use it regularly to keep your display in good working order. Even a mediocre display can be serviceable if it is properly calibrated, but an expensive display is almost useless if it lies to you! Calibrate your display every two weeks to be on the safe side.

Note: Many hardware calibration devices are on the market. Some popular systems are the i1Display (X-Rite), the ColorEyes Display Pro (Integrated Color), and the BasICColor Display (Color Solutions).

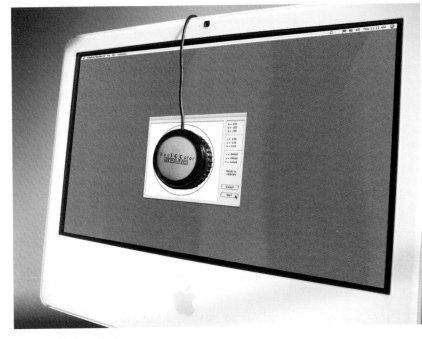

Figure 1.3 Monitor calibration

I highly recommend that you choose a simple, gray desktop color and select a gray interface option for the overall color scheme for your computer. The idea is to eliminate as many color distractions as possible for the environment in which you will be making color decisions. If the background behind your images is bright blue, you will tend to see everything as warmer than it is because of the *color contrast* with the blue background. You probably will have a tendency to make your colors too cool as a result. A neutral gray background is the safest choice because it will not bias your judgment one way or another.

Basic Digital Capture Workflow

You need to develop consistent procedures for capturing, saving, and working with your images. Each picture-taking situation will demand a slightly different series of steps depending on your specific hardware, software, and working preferences. At the most basic level, you will be

- Capturing images
- Downloading image files to a computer
- Adjusting the files (cropping, color correcting, retouching)
- Delivering images (printing, uploading, saving)
- Backing up files (saving and storing)

The basic steps can change slightly depending on whether you are shooting RAW or JPEG, tethered to a computer or to memory cards, archiving original RAW data, or converting to DNG format. Many of the repetitive tasks can be automated in certain software or by using scripts. Look for more details on workflow automation on the www.varis.com/skinbook website.

> **Note:** DNG (Digital Negative) is an open-published RAW file format developed by Adobe to address the need for a standard format for digital camera data. Currently, most camera manufacturers use proprietary file formats unique to their particular cameras. This is equivalent to Nikon cameras using only Nikon film, which would be an unacceptable situation with the photographer at the mercy of the manufacturer to support his images. A big push is underway in the industry to move toward an openly supported file format that will work with all cameras, and most photographers see DNG as becoming that standard.

Most of the *digital workflow* occurs after the photo shoot because that is where you work with the captured digital data. A professional workflow maintains a backup protocol from the beginning, always maintaining duplicate copies of files at every step. A typical progression of steps might look like this:

1. After filling your memory card, place it in a card reader and mount the drive on your desktop.

2. Copy the image files to a folder on your computer, rename them, and duplicate the files onto a separate hard drive as a backup.

3. Verify the integrity of the backup. (This automatically verifies the first copy.)

4. Once you are satisfied that the files are OK, you can reformat the card in the camera before shooting more images.

Of course, you might not have enough time to copy, duplicate, and verify while you are shooting, so you might need to have multiple cards on hand. Always strive to have two copies of every image file at any one time. Cards can be downloaded to the computer unattended, so you can always have one copy on the computer and one copy on the card at the very least. Some cameras have the capability to shoot to two separate cards in camera (usually a CF card and an SD card), so you'll have backups automatically as you shoot. Having a computer on hand can be inconvenient for many photographers. In that case, consider using one of the portable, self-contained card reader/hard drives (Figure 1.4) as a temporary backup solution.

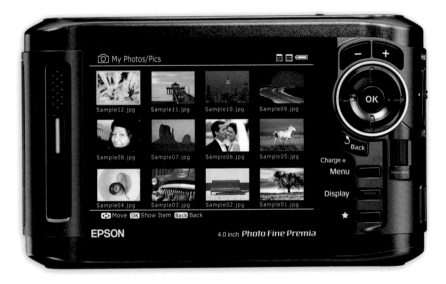

Figure 1.4 A typical card reader

After all the images are shot and backed up, they will have to be evaluated and worked on in some fashion. Professional photographers tend to generate a high volume of images, and file management can become a real issue. Fortunately, modern software tools, specifically designed with the photographer's needs in mind, have become available. I recommend using an integrated image processing and cataloging application such as Lightroom or Aperture. My own preference is Lightroom, so I will use it in the rest of this chapter.

Setting Up a Lightroom Catalog

Lightroom is an image cataloging system that stores information about images in a separate catalog file. It is beyond the scope of this book to provide full step-by-step instructions for using Lightroom, but I will cover certain features that pertain to the various tasks under discussion in the following chapters. Here we are concerned with getting started with an image catalog. There are a number of different ways to use Lightroom to organize your images—I prefer to have Lightroom mirror the file organization I have on my hard drives. To accomplish this, you need to begin with some organizational structure. This is how I set up my hard drives (Figure 1.5).

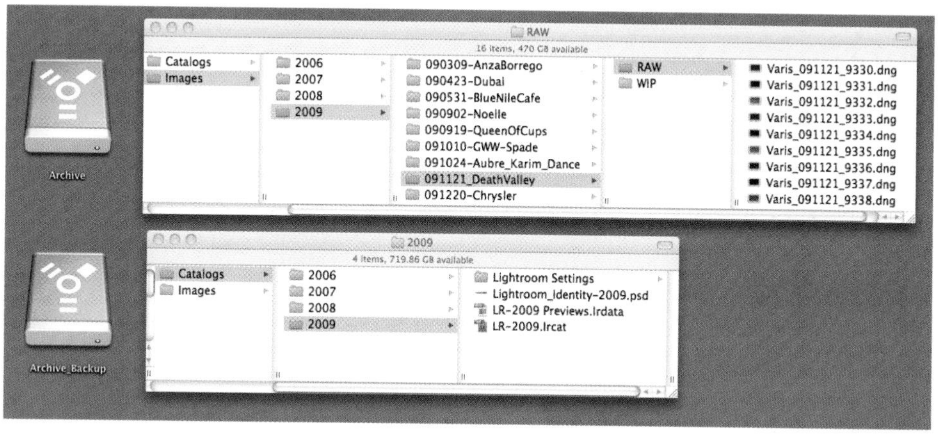

Figure 1.5 Dual external hard drives set up as Archive and Archive_Backup

I keep all my images on an external hard drive—this is my image archive that I duplicate onto a second hard drive. This backup drive gets updated every day or whenever I have made any changes to my images or my image catalog. Once a week this duplicate is moved off site and a third hard drive is brought in and updated to the current state of the image archive—this now becomes my new backup and is maintained every day in the same fashion. After a week of activity, the third drive goes off site and the second drive is brought back and updated. The two backup drives are continuously cycling on- and off-site so I always have a disaster insurance copy in the event of a fire, flood, meteor strike, or other such event that would render both my archive and backup unuseable.

The root level of the archive contains two folders—one for the images and one for the Lightroom catalogs. Images and catalogs are organized by year—I make a new catalog every year to correspond to the image folder for that year. Inside the year catalog folder is the Lightroom catalog file, previews file, settings folder and the identity plate file that I use to "label" the open catalog with the date so I know at a glance which catalog I'm working with. Inside the year image folder are the individual jobs folders, all labeled with the date (year, month, day) and a descriptive name. Inside the job folder is a "RAW" folder that contains the RAW captures, as well as a "WIP" folder that contains work-in-progress PSD files. When images are finished for delivery or printing, I make a "Finals" folder for them. Inside the "RAW" folder, the images files are named with my name, followed by the date, followed by the camera's unique file identifier number.

I download images from shooting sessions directly into this structure. Once that is done and the images are renamed, I am finally ready to import the files into Lightroom. This way the folder structure of the image archive is exactly reflected inside Lightroom so I can always find images from specific shooting dates without having to search, filter, or otherwise perform any catalog gymnastics. The folder structure is clearly visible in the "Folders" pane of Lightroom's "Library" module (Figure 1.6).

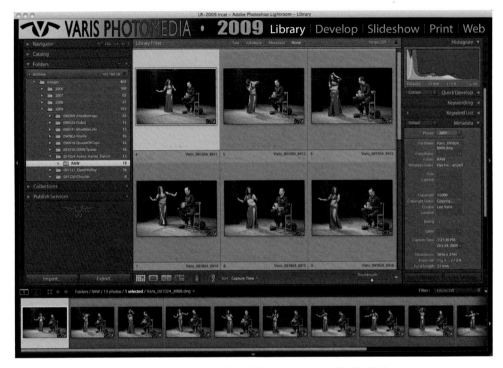

Figure 1.6 The Lightroom Library module shows the hard drive folder structure at the left in the "Folders" pane.

Lightroom has become my software tool of choice for organizing and processing my growing image collection. Just about every imaging task—short of retouching—can be accomplished with it. Its functions include making slideshows, printing, and making web galleries. These functions are also expandable using third-party plug-ins.

Calibrating for Digital Capture

Back in the old days, serious photographers tested their equipment and film to establish the best working methods for their particular gear. Ansel Adams developed the Zone System for his work with black-and-white film. Commercial photographers shot tests through different color gels to determine the color bias of a particular emulsion as processed through their particular labs. Testing was an ongoing process that photographers used to stay on top of their game. Modern digital capture has opened up new possibilities for accuracy and color quality, but the need for testing still exists. We'll explore one approach to digital testing and calibration (with a special emphasis on skin tones) that I have used with my equipment and readily available software and hardware. There are as many testing methods as there are cameras and software packages, and the following is presented more to illustrate concepts than anything else.

I've already mentioned monitor calibration; this is a relatively straightforward process with a hardware colorimeter. You must calibrate your monitor before doing anything else. The next step is to calibrate your camera with your RAW processing software. We will look at how to do this using Lightroom or Adobe Camera Raw (ACR) as a system that works with the widest range of digital cameras. There are other approaches, but none of them currently offer as much control in a convenient and relatively inexpensive manner.

To calibrate your camera, you must shoot a test. The test shot will need to include some kind of standard target (Figure 1.7).

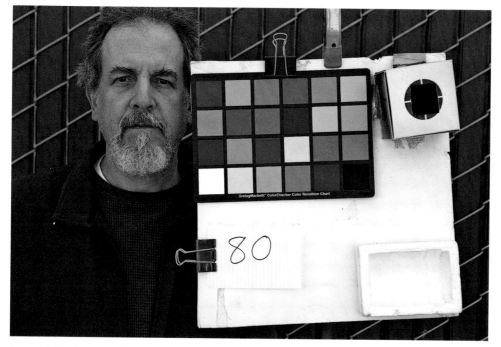

Figure 1.7 Sample test setup

The most widely used target is the X-Rite ColorChecker 24 Patch Classic. Originally known as a *Munsell chart*, this target has been in widespread use for at least 50 years in the motion picture and television industries. You should be able to purchase one at any camera store. An ideal test will include this target, a human subject (for *real* skin tone), and some written reference for the exposure.

My test setup includes a black trap, shown in the upper right. This is a small cardboard box with a hole cut on the top: the inside is lined with black velvet. I like to include this for a real black reference because the black "patch" of the ColorChecker target is not very black. My test target also includes a highlight reference (some Styrofoam lens packing is in the lower-right corner). The curved form creates a soft ramp from near white into a "clipped-to-white" tone and allows you to see just how much detail is preserved in extreme highlights. These additions are not critical for calibration purposes, but they help to visualize the dynamic range of the capture in highlights and shadows.

Note: The skin color patch on the ColorChecker target is intended to represent average Caucasian skin. Real skin comes in all different colors, and it is practically impossible to represent every kind of skin. Try to have some real skin that you feel is representative of your cultural average in your shots, but don't obsess over it. A real person in the test shot provides a visual reference to balance the technical nature of the target.

The testing procedure involves a series of steps, which are summarized here:

1. Establish lighting that mimics the conditions for 6500° K and 2850° K—open shade and tungsten lights indoors.

2. Shoot a range of exposures to determine your camera E.I. (exposure index, ISO, or ASA rating).

3. Import RAW files into Lightroom or ACR, and white balance to the light-gray patch.

4. View the series of exposures in Lightroom or ACR and apply "Zero slider" settings.

5. Identify the best exposure by comparing the exposures and reading numbers from the mid-gray patch.

6. Convert the best exposures to DNG.

7. Open the two DNGs representing 6500° K and 2850° K color temperatures into Adobe's DNG Profile Editor or X-Rite's ColorChecker Passport software and build camera profiles.

8. Save your settings and create a new "camera default" setting for your camera.

Establishing Lighting

You should shoot your test exposures under conditions as close as possible to 6500° K (open shade) and 2800° K (regular incandescent or halogen lights) color temperatures—two complete test sequences. If you shoot mostly outside, you'll also want to set up and test outdoors using direct sunlight as well. To cover all your bases, you might want to calibrate for other unusual lighting conditions. Here are some considerations for various lighting conditions.

Outdoor Daylight   Try to set up in broad daylight under clear sky conditions. Make sure that no shadows hit your target—especially the ColorChecker. Stay away from buildings as much as possible to minimize the effect of reflected light on your test—if you set up near an orange-colored wall, it *will* affect the color.

Outdoor Open Shade   Set up your test subject in open shade in an area that is illuminated by a broad expanse of blue sky. Try not to set up under trees because light filtering through green leaves will pollute the color temperature.

Indoor Incandescent Lighting   If possible, use a single light positioned at a 45-degree angle to the target and about 10 feet away. Make sure you're in a room with white or neutral colored walls. Aim for as even illumination as possible—again, make sure no shadows hit the target. You can use a higher ISO setting on the camera to bring the exposure within range, but try not to go above an E.I. of 800.

Studio Flash Lighting   This is very similar in character to daylight, but here you want to simulate your most common lighting. Use the lighting you normally use for your subjects: use the same umbrellas or other light modifiers. Don't do anything special just for the test. If you use two lights, make sure they are the same type or make. You can skip any hair lights and just concentrate on your front lighting.

Fluorescent Lighting   Shooting a test under fluorescent lighting is almost not worth the effort, because each uncontrolled situation you encounter will be different. Also, fluorescent lighting is a really unbalanced spectrum with big gaps and spikes in the frequencies represented. These situations almost always require some selective color correction in Photoshop after processing, so the kind of calibration you achieve here will be of limited use. If you frequently must shoot under a specific fluorescent lighting condition, then you can test for that—similar precautions against shadows and uneven illumination will apply.

Shooting to Bracket the Exposure Range

The idea is to shoot a wide bracket around the expected best exposure to determine the actual best exposure. Set your camera on manual and, if possible, change only its shutter speed to shoot the bracket.

> **Note:** As you may remember, back in the days of film we were told to bracket using f-stops because shutter speeds were not as accurate. Digital capture works differently. The exposure is timed electronically not by a mechanical shutter; in fact, there is no curtain shutter—just a mirror that has to move away. Lens f-stops will vary slightly from lens to lens and also, just slightly, across their range. So, the shutter speed is the most consistent way to bracket a continuous light source—you only need to use f-stops for flash.

Use the lowest default ISO setting for your camera. A hand-held light meter works best; a spot meter would be ideal. I use a combo meter that is capable of incident and spot reading in continuous as well as flash lighting (Figure 1.8). The spot meter has the advantage of being able to measure the value of the mid-gray patch (third from the right in the bottom row of patches) from the camera position (Figure 1.9).

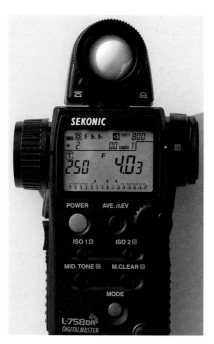

Figure 1.8
Sekonic L-758DR Digital Master meter

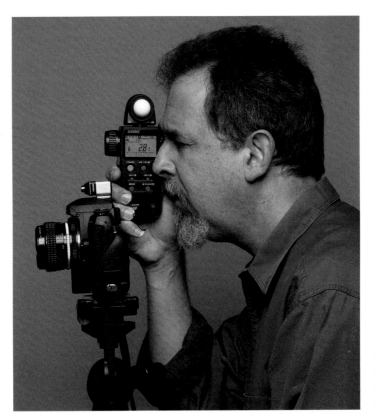

Figure 1.9
Spot meter readings are taken from the camera position.

The Mysterious "K" Factor

The mid-gray patch is calibrated to 18 percent reflectivity; this is supposed to match the 50 percent luminosity that light meters are calibrated to—but, in fact, it is off by roughly ⅓ to ½ stop. Why this is so is unclear. Many reference "gray cards" are referred to as 18 percent gray. In the printing industry, 18 percent reflectivity is considered halfway between the white of paper and the black of printing inks. However, actual scene luminance is a bit different than the brightness of printing ink on paper. Light meters are calibrated to an ANSI standard of 12.3 percent reflectivity, which is a closer match to 50 percent luminosity or L=50 (in Lab colorspace).

For some unknown reason, reference cards in use for photography—if they are calibrated at all—choose 18 percent to represent medium gray. This may come from Kodak who continues to manufacture and market an 18 percent gray card. Kodak's cards are produced using printing ink on an offset litho press and 18 percent gray actually refers to a printing specification. Presumably, this makes it easier to manufacture.

The bottom line is that the 18 percent Kodak gray card is a bit "lighter" than the 12.3 percent reflectivity that light meters are calibrated to—and so, if you expose at the reading you get from the Kodak card, you will be underexposing by about ½ f-stop. Ansel Adams was aware of this and made reference to a mysterious "K" factor in his book *Camera and Lens*. His instructions there had you opening up by ½ stop from the reading off the card. In general practice, I prefer the exposure precision afforded by adjusting exposure in ⅓ stop increments—therefore, to avoid overexposing, I only open ⅓ stop from readings taken off 18 percent gray cards.

A spot meter can read directly from the mid-gray patch (third from the right on the bottom of the ColorChecker); open up ⅓ stop to get the base exposure. If you don't have a spot meter, use an incident meter and take a reading from the subject position, pointing the white dome at the main light source (Figure 1.10). The ideal way to take exposure readings, at least for the test, is to use a hand-held light meter. A hand-held meter is better than relying on the camera meter for a number of reasons. If you have to use your in-camera meter, get yourself a large reference card like the Lastolite EZYBalance (Figure 1.11). You can move in close enough to fill the frame with the large gray field. Remember to open up ⅓ stop from any reading off any 18 percent gray reference.

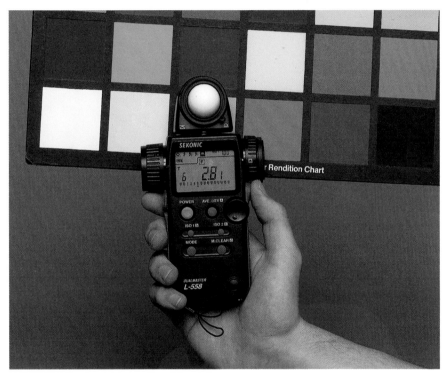

Figure 1.10 Point the incident meter "dome" at the light source.

Once you've determined your starting exposure, you will shoot additional exposures, incrementing the f-stop value by ⅓ f-stop using the manual controls on your camera. Shoot two stops on either side of the starting exposure and keep track of the exposures as you go along. I find it convenient to indicate the exposure change on the target itself by writing on a paper attached to the target. I write down the difference in exposure as a change in ISO. In other words, if I stop down one-third from the ISO 100 reading, I write 125: ⅔ = 160, 1 stop = 200, and so on. The beginning of the sequence would go: 100, 80, 64, 50.

Whatever you do, don't base your exposure off the appearance of the LCD on the back of the camera! (See Figure 1.12.) Not only do most viewing conditions prohibit accuracy, but the LCD will only show you how the camera would generate a JPEG—it can't show you what is in the RAW file. Typically, the histogram is only a composite histogram—and even when you can display separate RGB histograms, they are not accurate except as a rough approximation of the camera JPEG. We are looking for better than JPEG performance; otherwise, it's not worth shooting RAW. In practice, I find that relying on the LCD almost always causes you to underexpose the shot. Of course, with a lot of experience, you can learn how *overbright* the image on the LCD needs to be to arrive at the correct exposure. I personally prefer a more controlled approach.

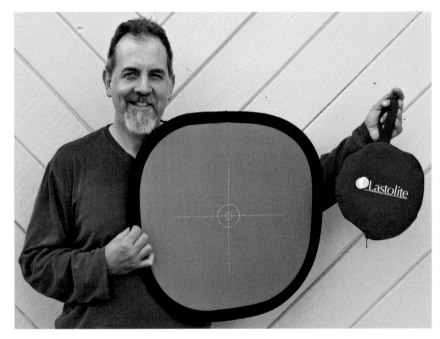

Figure 1.11 The Lastolite EZYBalance

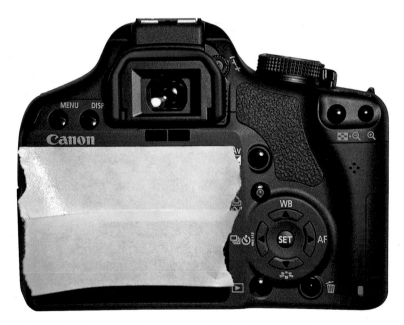

Figure 1.12 Do not be tempted to base your exposure decision on the built-in LCD.

Importing Shots and Evaluating Exposure

Now, you have to evaluate the shots to determine the best exposure. I will first look at how this is accomplished in Lightroom.

Import the image files into Lightroom (Figure 1.13). Use the General – Zeroed develop preset to get everything set up with no adjustments. Make sure you are using the "Camera Neutral" calibration preset to get as unbiased a rendering as possible (Figure 1.14). Once your sequence is imported, you can survey the images for a quick fix on the best exposure (Figure 1.15). Before you start making serious evaluations, do a white balance—click on the light-gray patch (second from the left) with the White Balance tool (the Eyedropper in the Basic panel of the Develop module). The images will appear very flat, and this can bias your judgment, so it is best to evaluate the images using numerical readings off the mid-gray patch.

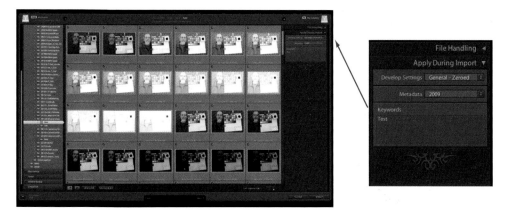

Figure 1.13 Set the Develop Settings to General – Zeroed and import the test images into Lightroom.

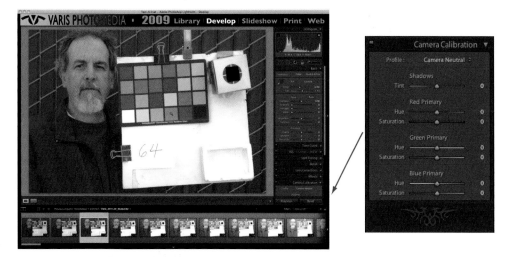

Figure 1.14 In the Develop module, select Camera Neutral in the Camera Calibration pane.

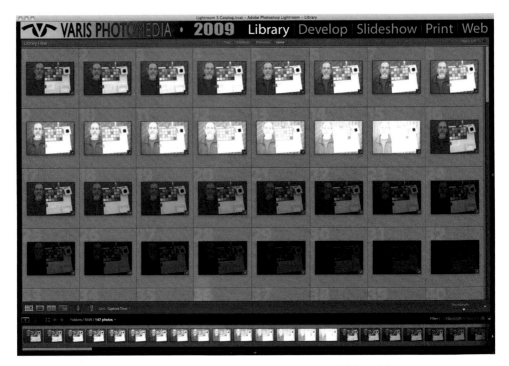

Figure 1.15 Evaluate the exposures for the best overall exposure and zoom into the most likely candidates.

Look for the exposure that gives you a reading close to 51 percent and, very importantly, without having the white patch go over 90 percent. Move the cursor into the image and look at the numbers that show up right under the histogram display, as shown in Figure 1.16. In my example, the gray patch is closer to 51 at the ISO 64 exposure where it reads 53 percent; however, the white patch is 100 percent, clipped. The next exposure down would give me an ISO of 80, and here the gray patch is at 48 percent. This one still doesn't quite work because the white patch is 93 percent (Figure 1.17). So, in the end, I'm back to ISO 100 where the gray patch now reads 43 percent but the white is at a safe 85 percent (Figure 1.18). Once you have found the ideal exposure, you can calculate what kind of compensation you will need—plus ⅓ to plus 1 stop are common.

It is also common for this compensation factor to be different, depending on the color temperature of the light. For my Canon 5DmkII, the compensation for direct sun is +⅔, for open shade it is 0 (no compensation), and for tungsten it is +1. Most of the time, you can enter this compensation into your camera settings if you rely on your in-camera meter. I will typically enter an average exposure compensation across all three lighting types for my in-camera meter settings and just leave it there. Another thing to consider is that you can often recover up to one stop of highlight detail without suffering image degradation, but using Fill Light or something similar to recover shadow detail will result in extra noise. So... if you are going to err, err on the side of over exposure. In my case for this camera, I would use an exposure compensation in camera of +⅔ even though that would be overexposing in open shade lighting. I only need to put the Recovery slider at 20 to get the white patch to read 89 percent (Figure 1.19).

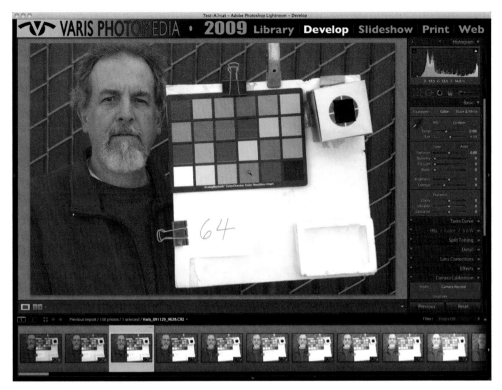

Figure 1.16 This exposure has a good mid-gray patch reading, but the white patch is clipped.

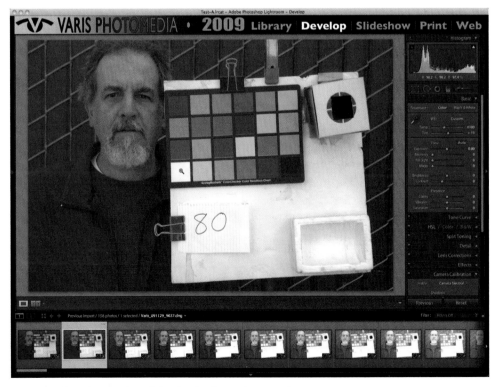

Figure 1.17 The mid-gray patch is still close, but the white patch goes past 90 percent.

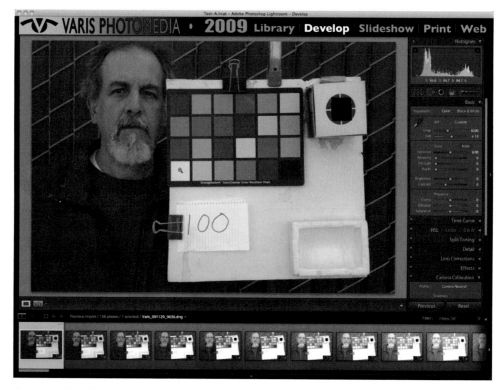

Figure 1.18 The mid-gray patch is somewhat low, but the white patch is now in a safe range at 85 percent.

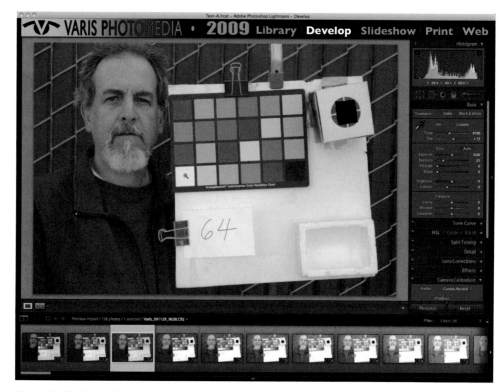

Figure 1.19 Highlight detail can be recovered with the Recovery slider.

The shooting procedure for ACR is the same. Once you have shot the exposure sequence, open the RAW captures in ACR, either from Photoshop or Bridge. Make sure you have all your slider settings at "zero" and your tone curve set to "linear," and then do a white balance and synchronize all the captures before you start looking for the best exposure. ACR does not display the same Linear ProPhoto feedback numbers that Lightroom uses. (The engines are identical, but the RGB numbers are not.) Instead, it displays RGB numbers according to the workflow settings. I recommend using Adobe RGB as your preferred workspace (Figure 1.20). This is the best compromise between working with the ludicrously wide ProPhotoRGB and the gamut constrained sRGB. It is not so narrow that significant printable colors fall outside of its color gamut, but not so wide as to make editing in Photoshop difficult.

After you set your workflow preferences, the RGB numbers display will exhibit numbers that represent the chosen workspace in standard RGB from 0 to 255. In Adobe RGB, you will look for the exposure that renders the medium-gray patch closest to 121 without pushing the white patch past 245 (Figure 1.21). Once you identify the exposure, you can calculate your exposure compensation much as in Lightroom.

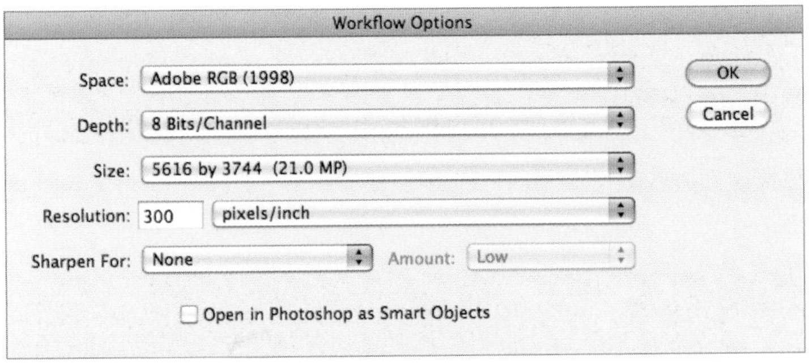

Figure 1.20   The Workflow Options dialog in Adobe Camera Raw

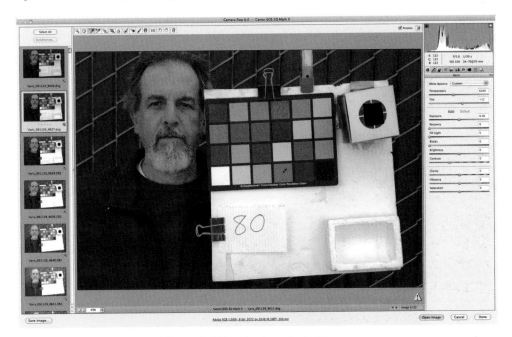

Figure 1.21   Evaluate the exposure in ACR using the RGB numbers just under the histogram.

Building a Camera Calibration

RAW processing software is designed to interpolate color information from varying brightness of pixel sites that have a colored filter of red, green, or blue. In essence, there is no color in the RAW data—color is inferred by measuring the brightness of pixel clusters. The colored filters covering the tiny pixel sites are not perfect and, manufacturing processes being what they are, there is some variation from camera to camera even from the same manufacturer. Some RAW processing software is set up to allow for a certain amount of adjustment to calibrate the camera's color to a known target. Adobe's processing software offers this capability though sliders in the Calibrate tab in ACR; Lightroom offers the same capability on the Camera Calibration panel. There is also a stand-alone application, DNG Profile Editor from Adobe (in public beta at the time of this writing), that simplifies the process.

DNG Profile Editor

DNG Profile Editor is an application designed to modify the lookup tables that Adobe software uses to convert the raw data from the digital camera into a standard color workspace. Every camera supported by Adobe Camera Raw or Lightroom has a lookup table associated with it to enable the raw processor to de-mosaic, or render color from the brightness data recorded under the red, green, or blue pixel sites on the chip. The DNG Profile Editor uses various controls to manipulate the color result generated by the lookup table and regenerate the table, and it has a straightforward calibration process that utilizes the X-Rite ColorChecker 24 Patch Classic. The software will do an automatic analysis of an image capture of the target and generate a table that can be saved and used by Lightroom or ACR. For our purposes, I will use the target analysis function to build an idealized color calibration.

First, select the ideal exposures from your test shots under the different color temperatures and convert the files into DNG format. In Lightroom, go to the Library module and select Library > Convert Photo to DNG from the menu bar. The DNG Profile Editor only works with DNG files, so you will need to convert all the good exposure shots before opening them into the software. ACR requires that you save the files as new DNGs.

Launch the DNG Profile Editor application, and you will be presented with a simple color editor (the first tab at the top of the interface) and the helpful instruction, "Tip: Start by opening a DNG Image from the File menu" (Figure 1.22).

Open the shot from the open shade test and then click the Chart tab (Figure 1.23). The image should open with the white balance you set in Lightroom or ACR. If for some reason it doesn't, simply click on the light-gray patch to reestablish a white balance. Four small colored dots will appear in the image; they are referred to as "colored circles" in the on-screen instructions.

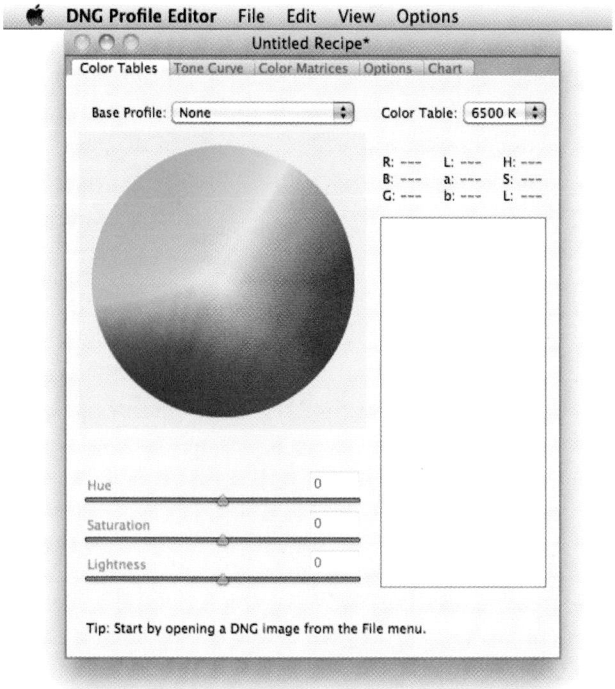

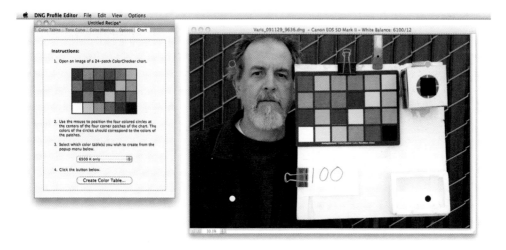

Figure 1.22 The DNG Profile Editor opens with the Color Tables tab active.

Figure 1.23 Open a test shot and click on the Chart tab.

Follow the instructions and position the four colored circles (dots) over their respective patches on the target. You can zoom in on the chart image to make it easier to position the dots in the middle of the patches (Figure 1.24).

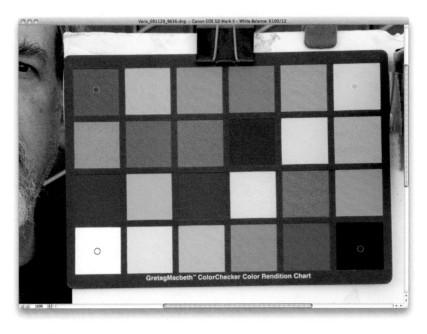

Figure 1.24 You may need to zoom in to position the colored dots accurately.

Select 6500 K only from the drop-down to identify the color temperature of the table you will create. Click the Create Color Table button, and you will be brought back to the Color Tables tab with all the patch colors mapped onto the Color Wheel. The table is created (Figure 1.25). If the test was shot correctly and you chose the appropriate exposure, there will be no problems. If, however, the white patch is too bright (clipped), the program will throw up a warning and you'll have to pick another bracket or reshoot.

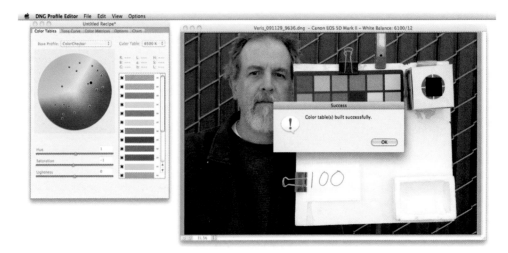

Figure 1.25 After creating the table, you will receive a confirmation, and the Color Tables tab will open with the values fully populated.

Next, you will create the table for 2850° K. Open the tungsten test shot. This is more likely to be at 3000° K to 3400° K, depending on the lights you actually used, but it will be close enough for this purpose. Once the tungsten test shot is open, click the Chart tab, select 2850 K only as the table to build, and position the dots (Figure 1.26).

Again, click the Create Color Table button and you'll be back at the Color Tables tab, this time with the 2850 table created (Figure 1.27).

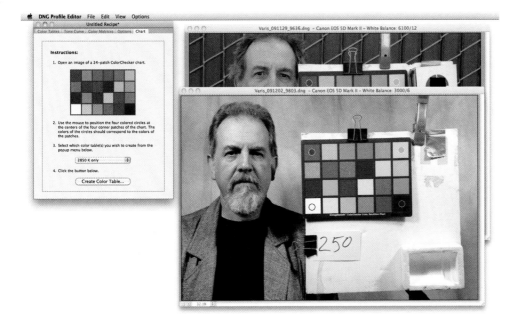

Figure 1.26 Open the second test shot.

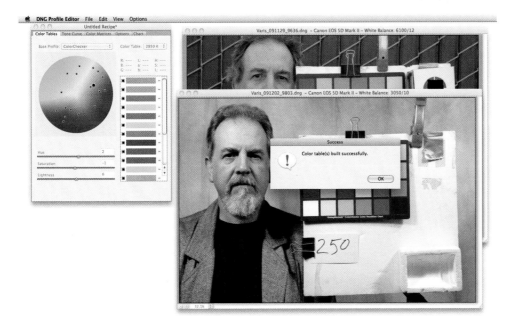

Figure 1.27 Create the second table and you will have a complete dual temperature set waiting to be saved.

At this point, all you need to do is select: File > Export *your camera name* profile and give the file a meaningful name (Figure 1.28). The DNG Profile Editor finds the correct location for the profiles so that they can be used in ACR or Lightroom.

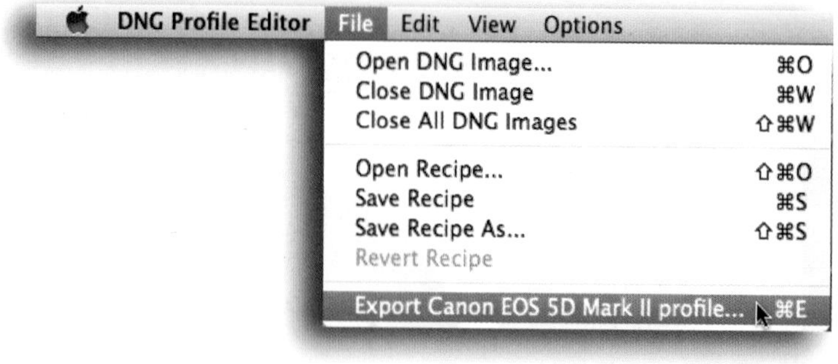

Figure 1.28 Save the complete camera profile from the File menu.

Note that to create the profile you opened two test images, one for 6500° K and one for 2850° K, and you built individual tables for each. The RAW processing engine that Adobe uses interpolates color values between (and beyond) these common color temperatures to arrive at a correct interpretation of color in a wide range of different lighting conditions.

Creating a Custom Lighting Profile

There is a third choice for building the color tables for a camera profile: both tables. If you select both tables, the DNG Profile Editor will build both the 6500 and the 2850 table from whatever *single* image is open. This is less than ideal for a general-purpose table, but it can be useful for a specific lighting condition that might otherwise be problematic. For instance, you might shoot a test target under stadium lighting conditions to build a more accurate color table for the unusual sodium vapor lighting (and get a better color rendering for the athletic teams' jerseys). Of course, you would use this table to build a profile you would use only for this specific lighting condition (more on using the profiles later).

X-Rite ColorChecker Passport

The X-Rite color calibration system utilizes a special version of the ColorChecker target that comes in its own self-enclosed carrying case and includes some extra warming-cooling white balance patches for portraits and landscapes (Figure 1.29). I prefer to use a full size Gretag Macbeth ColorChecker for the exposure tests, but this little target is very convenient for quick color calibration shots. Shoot the target in the lighting you want to test, but simply aim for a good exposure—no need to do more than a narrow bracket sequence—just to make sure you have a good exposure with which to work. The ColorChecker Passport system comes as a stand-alone application, as well as a plug-in for Lightroom, that almost completely automates the creation of DNG camera profiles within Lightroom. There are very good instructions with the software, but it almost doesn't need any because it is very easy to use. Launch the ColorChecker Passport application and you will see a wizard interface with instructions that walk you through the process (Figure 1.30).

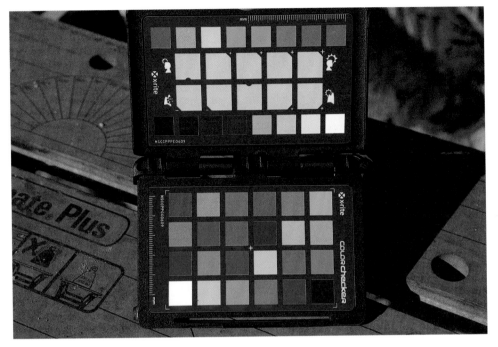

Figure 1.29 The X-Rite ColorChecker Passport target

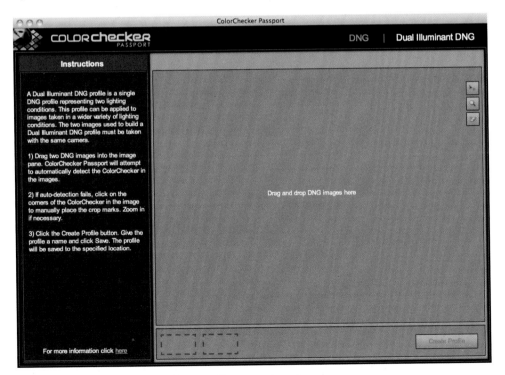

Figure 1.30 The ColorChecker Passport software provides on-screen instructions.

Drag two different test shots (preferably under shade and tungsten light) into the image window. The software will automatically locate the patches for each shot. Then simply click the Create Profile button, name the resulting file, and you're done. (Figure 1.31)

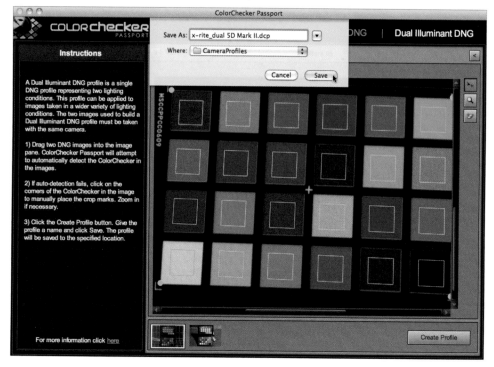

Figure 1.31 Once you drag the test images in, you can create and save a camera profile.

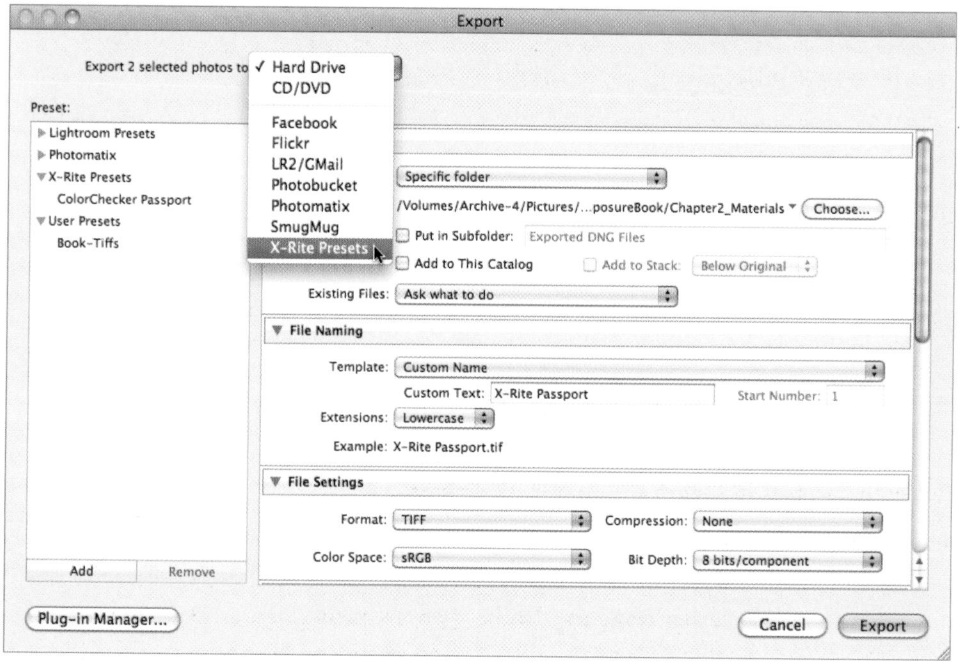

Figure 1.32 The X-Rite ColorChecker plug-in is accessed through the Export dialog in Lightroom.

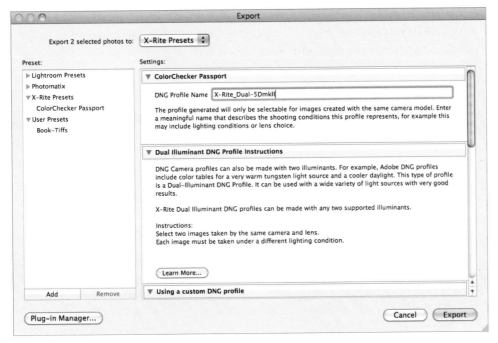

Figure 1.33 Select the X-Rite presets, and the dialog changes to accommodate the creation and saving of camera profiles.

The Lightroom plug-in is particularly easy to use, because you never have to leave Lightroom. The plug-in is invoked from the Export dialog; select X-Rite Presets from the Export To drop-down menu (Figure 1.32). The dialog changes specifically to accommodate saving DNG Profiles (Figure 1.33). The resulting file is automatically saved to the correct location.

Both Calibration systems work well to provide customized camera profiles for your specific camera. The X-Rite software seems to generate slightly more saturated color, is a bit easier to use, and comes with the very handy target. I personally prefer the less-saturated results I get with Adobe's DNG Profile Editor, and the Adobe software offers the ability to manually tweak the color of the profile—something I often find necessary with skin tone. More on this later...

Using Camera Profiles

As I mentioned earlier, these profiles are not industry standard ICC (International Color Consortium) profiles but special Adobe-formatted color lookup tables that can be used in ACR or Lightroom. Both color calibration applications save the camera profiles in the appropriate place on the computer.

In Lightroom

To use the profiles in Lightroom, follow these steps:

1. Select an image.
2. Go to the Develop module and, in the Camera Calibration pane, select the profile you saved earlier using the Profiles pop-up menu (Figure 1.34). You can save this camera profile along with any Develop setting preferences as a new Camera Default.

3. After applying the camera profile, go to the Basic pane, set your white balance to As Shot using the WB list box, and then select Set Default Settings from the Develop menu (Figure 1.35). You'll receive a warning and a confirmation of the camera model and serial number.

4. Click the Update to Current Settings button. Now every time you import a RAW file from this camera, it will appear with these settings and camera profile.

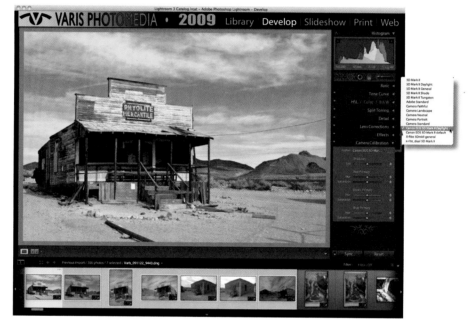

Figure 1.34 Apply a camera profile in Lightroom.

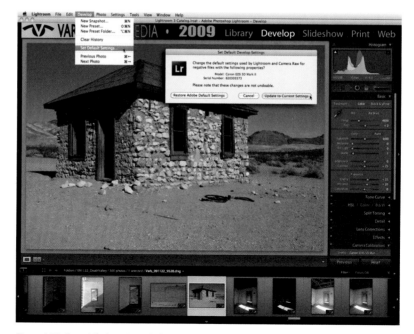

Figure 1.35 Set a default setting in Lightroom.

In Adobe Camera Raw

Similarly in ACR, to apply the profile, follow these steps:

1. Open the images in ACR.

2. Select them, click on the Camera Calibration tab, and select the profile you saved earlier from the Camera Profile pop-up (Figure 1.36).

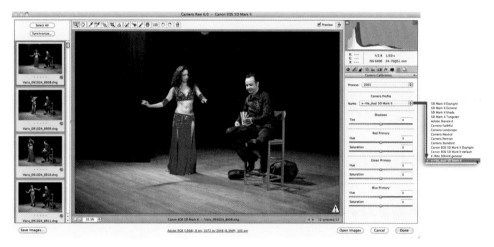

Figure1.36 Apply a camera profile in ACR.

3. To save a new Camera Raw Default, apply the profile and then go to the Basic pane.

4. Set the white balance to As Shot, and set any additional adjustments you prefer.

5. Select Save New Camera Raw Default from the settings drop-down (Figure 1.37).

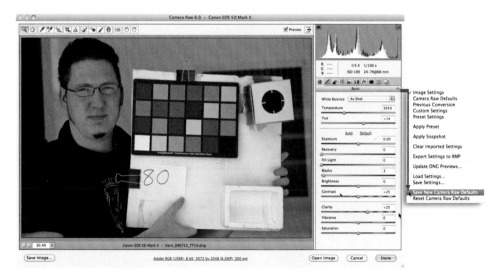

Figure 1.37 Save a new Camera RAW default in ACR.

Editing Camera Profiles for Better Skin Color

One common issue with digital capture is that any red component in the skin color can be overemphasized, and people often complain that the skin color turns out too red! If you find this to be the case with your files—even after you've built a calibration—you can tweak the red out in the DNG Profile Editor.

First, you must arrange to shoot a test with a subject that exhibits the red skin defect in your digital captures. Once you have tested and identified the ideal exposure, open the DNG in the DNG Profile Editor application. Build the tables as usual, but before you save the camera profile, zoom in on the subject's face. (The same keyboard shortcuts you use in Photoshop apply: Command+space or Ctrl+space. See Figure 1.38.)

Now, find an area on the face that has that overly pink look to it. As you scroll over the image, look at how the color values (as displayed in the region above the color patches to the right) change. Good skin color will have Lab values with the "a" and "b" numbers equal or the "b" value slightly higher. In the example here, a=17 and b=9. This area is too red! Click on the spot, and a dot will appear in the Color Wheel where that color lives.

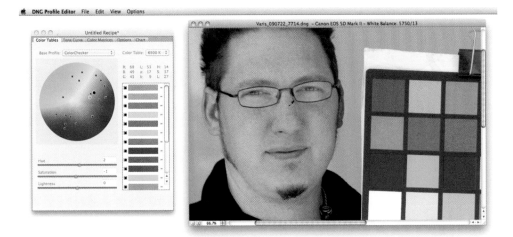

Figure 1.38 Zoom in and locate an area of red skin.

Now, take the Hue slider and move it to the right, toward yellow—the last patch in the column of patches will show the before and after of the color you are now editing (Figure 1.43). You may want to reduce the saturation of the color as well. The beauty of editing the one problematic color in the Profile Editor is that it leaves more saturated versions of that particular hue alone, so it won't damage lip color as much as it would if you were editing hues in Lightroom, ACR, or Photoshop.

When you are done editing, save the camera profile as before and give it a descriptive name such as *Camera Name-Skin*. The profile can be used as a special-purpose profile for those situations where you might have trouble with overly red skin color. There are times when even this specialized profile cannot automatically render an ideal skin color, so it won't eliminate post-process color editing altogether, but it will help when you are working up a large volume of images for approval before doing fine-tuning on final selects.

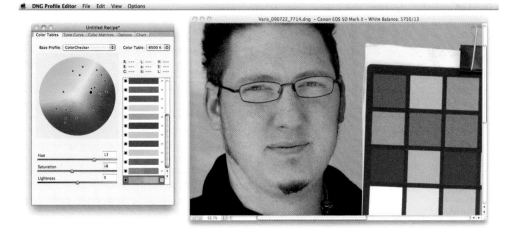

Figure 1.39 Edit color using the Hue and Saturation sliders.

When you calibrate this way, you maintain the best possible quality and retain the most flexibility for processing your RAW files. Establishing a calibration with Zero slider positions ensures that the RAW data is recorded at the highest signal level without encountering serious white point clipping. This is pretty much like "exposing to the right of the histogram" but with greater precision. The only drawback is that the previews on the camera LCD might seem a little bright. Adobe Camera Raw is the only RAW processing software I'm aware of that allows for true zero or linear defaults in all its settings, so this calibration strategy won't work with your camera software or something like Phase One's Capture One software.

Exposing to the Right

You might have heard that it's a good idea to "expose to the right of the histogram." Experts often recommend doing so when you evaluate the exposure based on the histogram display on the LCD on the back of the camera (see the accompanying graphic). The idea is to open the exposure enough that the main peak in the histogram is right of center but not slammed against the right edge, thereby placing the captured data where most of the useable bits are.

The idea is good in theory but bad in practice because the histogram cannot tell you where you are placing your tones with any precision, and it can't tell whether the histogram is appropriate for the subject. (What picture goes with this histogram?) The camera's histogram is only a general indication of the distribution of values in the camera-generated JPEG. It is usually a composite of all three channels. The RAW data has a much wider distribution of tones that will vary in each channel, so you may not know if you are clipping important data in the Red channel simply by looking at the histogram display on the camera.

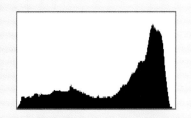

Working with Your Calibration

Although a full exploration of Adobe Camera Raw or Lightroom is beyond the scope of this book, I can offer the following general breakdown for RAW file processing using Adobe products.

Ideally, you should shoot a gray card in the same lighting as the bulk of your subject matter. Have the subject hold the ColorChecker or a gray card. (For the test shown in Figure 1.40, I stood in for the subject and had an assistant shoot for the gray card. The remaining shots were taken of the real subject, and this shot was used to white balance only.) Most often, this can be a simple test shot done at the beginning of a shoot.

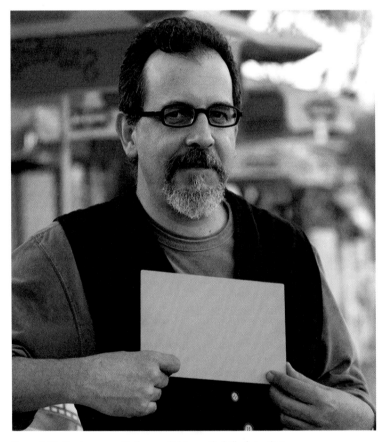

Figure 1.40 Shoot a gray card in the same lighting as the bulk of your shots.

When you are ready to process the shots, simply use the White Balance tool on the gray card in the first shot, adjust any other sliders you like, and apply the settings to the rest of the images. After applying White Balance, select all the images; and then in Lightroom, click the Sync button located in the lower-right corner of the interface and click OK in the dialog box that opens (Figure 1.41).

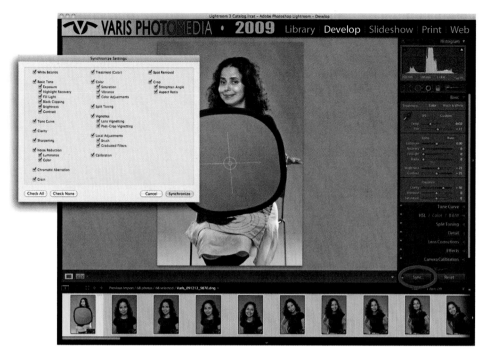

Figure 1.41 Sync the files in Lightroom.

Similarly, in ACR click the Synchronize button (located in the upper-left corner) and click OK in the resulting dialog, as shown in Figure 1.46. If you've done a good calibration and you've exposed properly, you seldom have to do more than slight brightness and contrast adjustments to "cook" the image to taste!

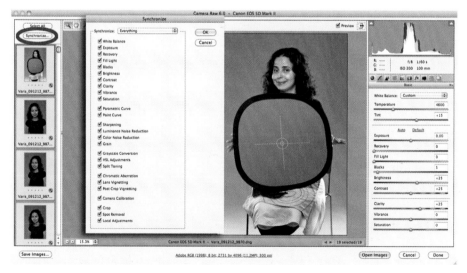

Figure 1.42 Synchronize the files in ACR.

If you do not have the opportunity to shoot a gray card, you can select a default from the White Balance drop-down in the Adjust tab (ACR) or the Basic pane (Lightroom) or you can accept the As Shot settings; however, a gray card takes all the guesswork out of the color and can save a lot of post production, especially if you are working with a large volume of images.

Calibration Review

The testing procedure consists of shooting the test target in a controlled manner, capturing a wide range of under-, normal-, and overexposures to see exactly the limits of the camera capturing capabilities. Ideal exposure is determined with numeric precision so that the maximum amount of useable data is available for post-capture manipulation in software. Under- and overexposure limits are similarly determined so that you know how far you can go with a particular important tone in an image. The goal is to be able to give the maximum useable exposure and thus ensure that you have the cleanest, most noise-free information in the captured image.

Once you have a good exposure of the test target, color calibration is accomplished using software in an automated fashion. Remember that color is not nearly as critical as value or tone. Ideal color is fairly subjective, and the photographer will be compelled to interpret and adjust for creative effect after the image is captured. However, it makes sense to start from a neutral unbiased point and so the color calibration step should be included—just don't lose sleep worrying about how accurate your color is.

Testing Procedure Overview

The testing procedure breaks down into the following items:

- Shoot an X-Rite ColorChecker 24 Patch Classic target in shade and tungsten lighting.
- Measure a mid-gray reference of 18 percent and open $\frac{1}{3}$ to determine base exposure.
- Bracket around the expected normal exposure—two stops under and two stops over.
- Increment exposures by $\frac{1}{3}$ stop, using shutter speed if possible.
- Change the E.I. reference on a card in the shot to reflect the change for exposure (100, 80, 64, 50 for $+\frac{1}{3}$ exp).
- Import files into Lightroom or ACR with Zero slider settings.
- Evaluate the exposure sequence for the ideal exposure.
- Use this information to enter an exposure compensation factor in the camera or as an E.I. setting in a hand-held light meter.

- Open the ideal exposures from the shade and tungsten lighting shots in the color calibration software (X-Rite or Adobe), build a camera profile, and then save it.

- Set this calibration profile as a camera default in either Lightroom or ACR.

I encourage you to tweak your calibrations to suit your personal preferences. You shouldn't necessarily accept the numerically accurate renderings of the color patches—most of us don't sell pictures of ColorChecker targets. Think about how you prefer your color. More contrast? More saturation? Put these into your camera default settings so you don't have to tweak every file every time.

Remember, you are calibrating a complete capture system that includes the lens. You can usually count on lenses from the same manufacturer to have the same color bias, but as soon as you switch to a different manufacturer (a third-party lens), you will likely affect the subtle color bias and you'll need a different calibration. For that reason, I recommend staying with your camera manufacturer's lenses whenever possible.

Finally, calibration is no substitute for creativity. Feel free to break away from rigidly accurate color renderings to suit your creative needs or the needs of your clients. Your calibration settings are only a starting point from which you are obligated to depart on a journey to your personal vision. You should also save creative renderings as presets that you can call on for different purposes. The calibration method outlined here should be considered a tool to allow you control over your photography and not an end in itself.

Putting Color Management in Context

Color management is a relatively new discipline that is still evolving. The goal of color management is to control color appearance in various input and output devices so we can achieve better agreement between the different renderings of the same image viewed in different media. Notice that we are specifically *not* talking about color matching. Real color matching is currently impossible, and some level of difference has to be tolerated. There is considerable disagreement about what differences are tolerable under what conditions, so talking about color management in absolutes is difficult. Control over color *is* highly desirable, however, whether or not we agree on how that control is applied.

Color management starts by attempting to define color in an unambiguous way. Not too long ago a group of manufacturers in the graphics industry got together and developed the ICC profile as the foundation for a digital color definition. An ICC profile references the color appearance of a particular device (camera, monitor, printer) to a numerical representation that is independent of any specific device. This numerical representation is currently CIE L*a*b* (CIELAB, essentially the same as Lab in Photoshop). Profiles are generated by capturing the color rendering of specific devices and mapping the results to the numbers required to generate colors on that device. As an example, your monitor uses a certain set of RGB numbers to generate a color that can be defined as a specific shade of red in Lab. When you want to display that shade of red (as defined in Lab) on another monitor, you will likely need a different set of RGB numbers. If the other monitor has been profiled, you can derive the new set of RGB numbers by running the Lab numbers through the profile for that monitor. As such, profiles allow for some method of translating colors for different devices by referencing into and out of Lab.

Profiles are also used for generic color-editing environments called *workspaces*. Adobe RGB, Colormatch, and sRGB are examples of standard RGB workspaces. An RGB workspace is defined in a way that allows for easier color editing, and one unique property of this is that neutral gray is always defined with equal values in red, green, and blue. One of the common activities in color management is transforming color numbers from a capture device into workspace numbers for editing and then transforming those numbers into numbers appropriate for a printer or display device for viewing.

Most of the problems associated with color management concern the mismatch between color spaces with different gamuts. *Color gamut* is the volume of colors defined in a given color space. The real world represents a huge volume of possible colors. Digital cameras are capable of encoding a somewhat smaller volume of colors. The Adobe RGB workspace is smaller still, and almost every output device can represent a smaller volume than Adobe RGB. Overall volume is not the only factor. There are other mismatches. Some possible colors in one workspace don't exist in another, even if the overall volume in the second space is greater. Imagine trying to fit a square peg in a round hole—color spaces can be thought of as having 3D shapes based on different regions of colors. The graphics industry has adopted various methods of translation or gamut mapping between the different color space shapes using ICC profiles in an attempt to mitigate the problems.

Most of the time, photographers make a bigger problem out of this than is necessary. People photography is mostly concerned with the color of skin. As it turns out, skin color is easily defined in just about every color space with which we can work. Conservative color spaces such as sRGB are perfectly adequate for people photography, and translating between sRGB or Adobe RGB and any type of output we need is not a problem. Problems typically arise with attempts to match garment colors or other products that may be of primary interest to an advertising client. Some products might contain colors that are outside the range of Adobe RGB but just inside CMYK for a magazine ad. Sometimes the dyes and colorants used to manufacture these items do not reproduce accurately no matter how well the system is color managed. Most of the time, the solution involves color correction in the final output space and not color management. The odd color mismatch in a manufactured product can usually be tolerated; however, if you can't get good skin color, you are in trouble.

For our purposes, color management simply involves calibrating the monitor, choosing an appropriate workspace, and utilizing printer profiles at output. You do not *absolutely* need anything more exotic than Adobe RGB as your workspace. If you shoot RAW, as you should, then there really is no *absolute* need for a custom camera profile because the RAW data can be processed into a standard workspace in ACR. The calibration steps we've just gone through determine how your color is rendered into the workspace. You can think of the workspace as the color definition that determines what the various RGB number values look like. Once a file is *tagged* with a workspace definition or profile, you can track the colors in the image through editing and finally into a print.

We will examine various color management issues as they come up throughout the rest of the book.

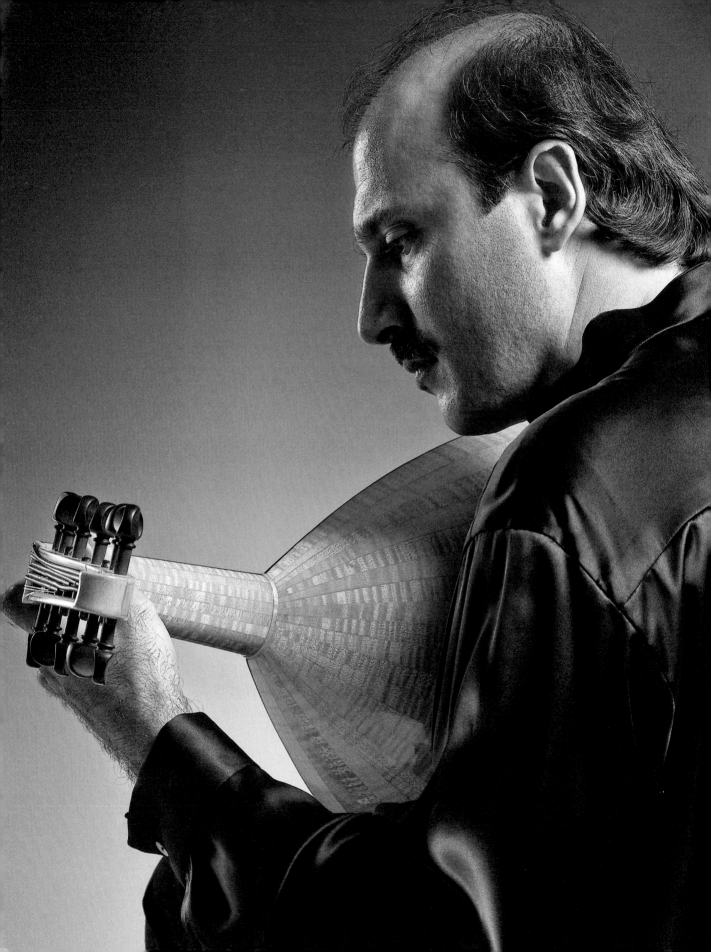

Lighting and Photographing People

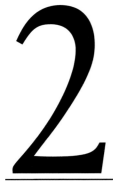

Digital photography is the process of recording focused light that falls on the image sensor in a camera. This recorded light is the essence of photography, and control over lighting is one of the core disciplines in the art. We are going to explore various approaches to lighting as they pertain to digital capture and human subjects. I will also go over different shooting scenarios and how to deal with people in your photographs.

Chapter Contents
Lighting Technology
Basic Portrait Lighting
Advanced Lighting Techniques
Experimenting with Light

Lighting Technology

Many different types of light, both artificial and natural, can be used with human subjects. Natural light originates with the sun, but it can have many different characteristics depending on the time of day or weather. Artificial light can be generated in a number of different ways, and it is mostly categorized by color temperature. (Table 2.1 lists the temperatures of the most common artificial sources.) Light control remains the most important element for the photographer regardless of the light source. Light must be directed and the intensity controlled. Shadows must be balanced against highlights, and their edges must be softened or sharpened.

Table 2.1: Common Artificial Light Sources

Light Type	Typical Color Temperature (degrees)
Incandescent/household bulb	2800 K
Photoflood	3200 K
Tungsten (halogen)	3400 K
Fluorescent	3800 K (approximately)
Electronic flash (strobe)	5500 K

Note: Flash is usually the most desirable light source to use for photographing people because it provides the most light with the least heat. Regular fluorescent lights are the worst light source because their spectrum is very spikey or uneven, and this makes it difficult to fully color correct for good skin color.

The most basic light controller is a simple board that can block or reflect light. This simple tool has evolved into a wide variety of specialized reflectors and flags—white, black, silver, and gold. The most recent innovation is the spring-frame reflector that can be folded into a relatively small disk and unfurled into a larger disk or panel (Figure 2.1). Most often these panels are double-sided or have reversible fabric covers that allow an assortment of surfaces to be employed as the situation demands. These panels are particularly convenient to use outdoors for available light control. Panels can be used as translucent diffusers to soften harsh direct light.

Large 4-feet × 8-feet sheets of foamcore can be used to create *V-flats* (Figure 2.2). These are great bounce-light reflectors that provide a large diffused-light source that is particularly well suited to rim lighting a subject (more on this later).

Another classic variation on the simple black card is the fabric *flag*, which is a wire frame with black fabric stretched around it (Figure 2.3). These flags come in all sizes and are utilized extensively in movie production. Flags are made to be used with C-stands and fit into the jointed knuckles of the stand, which allows them to be easily and precisely positioned.

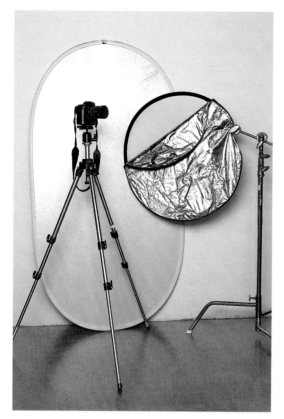

Figure 2.1
The large panel folds into a disk half the size of the disk at the right. The smaller light disk is a translucent panel with a removable cover that can be reversed to show a white, gold, or silver side. It is essentially four panels in one.

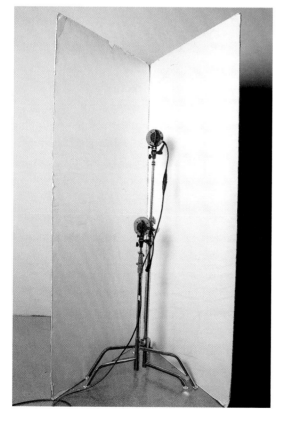

Figure 2.2
Two bare flash heads aimed into the V-flat provide a broad diffused-light source.

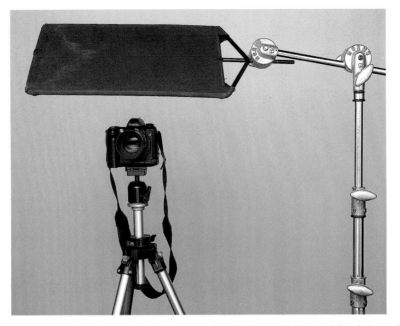

Figure 2.3 This flag is being used to shade the camera from light that would otherwise fall on the lens and possibly create flare.

Reflectors and flags can be universally applied in all lighting scenarios—outdoors, in-studio, and with all kinds of available light. The remaining lighting equipment that we'll cover is utilized with electronic flash lighting. Flash is usually the lighting of choice for people photography because it produces a lot of light with very little heat. This cool lighting is much more comfortable for the subject, and its use minimizes perspiration and makeup problems. A number of specialized reflectors and diffusion systems, as well as different flash heads for on-camera and off-camera applications, are available.

Besides the usual polished reflectors, the most common flash lighting accessory is the umbrella (Figure 2.4). The umbrella is just that, an umbrella with an inner surface that is lined with reflective material. A flash head is commonly made to accept the rod-end of the umbrella so that it aims into the parabolic reflector dish made by the open umbrella. Umbrellas usually have a removable black backing that controls any light spilling through the back. By removing the black backing, you can *shoot through* the translucent umbrella and use it as a light diffuser rather than a reflector.

The *softbox* is another common flash lighting controller (Figure 2.5). The flash head shines into one end of this tent-like enclosure; the inner surfaces are reflective, and the other end opens to a diffuser panel. The softbox acts as a portable window light and creates a nice, soft light source that is especially useful with portrait photography.

There are many specialized lighting units that incorporate unique reflectors, but perhaps the most exotic light used to photograph people is the *ring light* (Figure 2.6). This light is most commonly an electronic flash in the shape of a ring that can be fitted around the lens. It is used to create a unique light that manages to preserve some sense of sculptural modeling while eliminating shadows. We will see some examples of its use in the following pages.

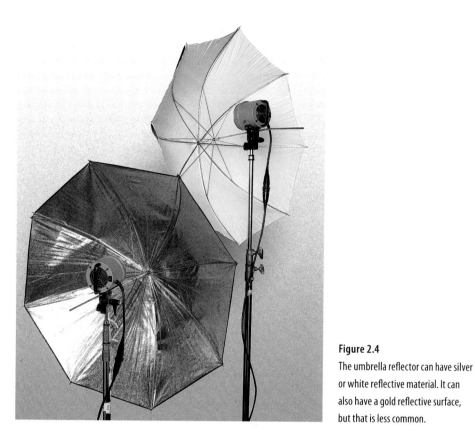

Figure 2.4
The umbrella reflector can have silver or white reflective material. It can also have a gold reflective surface, but that is less common.

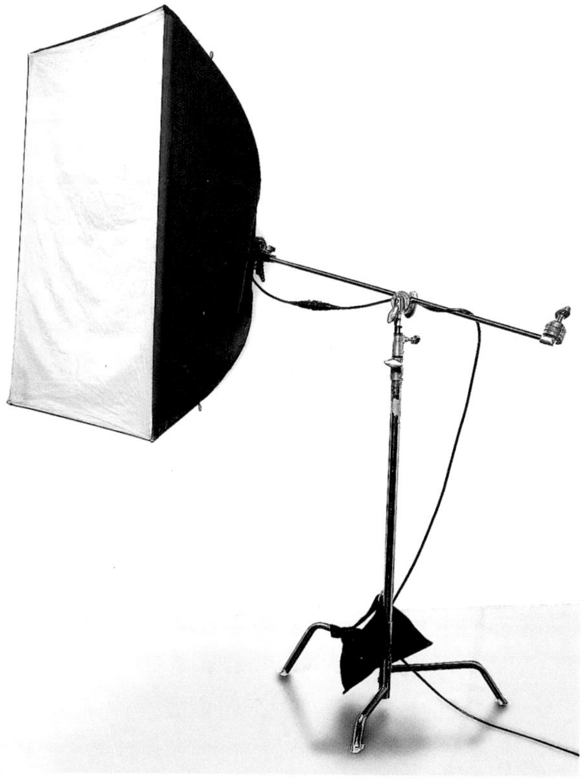

Figure 2.5
Softboxes can be found in all sizes. The one pictured here is a medium-sized box that is appropriate for portrait photography.

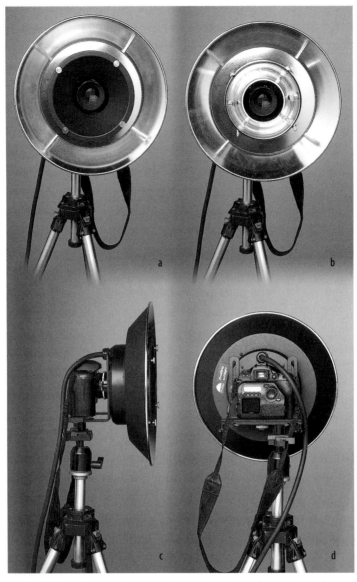

Figure 2.6 (a) The ring light with an inner reflector mask hiding the direct ring flash tube (lens is in the center); (b) the mask removed to show the flash tube; (c) a side view showing the camera; (d) a rearview

A *radio slave* is an absolute must-have accessory for the digital photographer working with studio flash lighting (Figure 2.7). It is a radio-remote that consists of a transmitter and a receiver that can trigger a flash unit without directly connecting the camera to flash through a sync cable. Although modern flash units pose less of a problem than older units, the high voltage of most studio flash equipment will degrade the sensitive electronics inside a digital camera with repeated flashes through the sync contacts on the camera. The radio slave separates the camera from the flash source, and the signal generated by the radio transmitter is very low power; therefore, repeated flashes are no longer destructive.

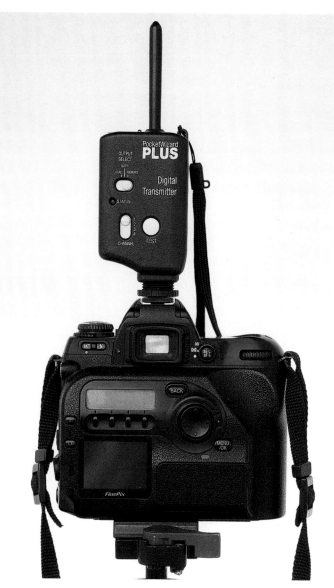

Figure 2.7 The transmitter of the radio slave fits in the hot shoe of the camera and synchronizes the flash unit through radio signals.

Basic Portrait Lighting

Two basic light qualities are applied to most portrait photography. Light, as used in photography, is normally thought of in terms of softness or hardness, qualities that relate to the character of the shadows created by the light. A large diffused-light source will have a soft shadow. A small, directional light source will have a hard shadow. The art of lighting is involved with the creative manipulation of these two extremes.

In addition to the hard or soft nature of light, the direction of the light hitting the subject is important. We will examine the basic elements of portrait lighting with the assistance of Erin Manning, a talented photographer who is normally found on the other side of the camera. Each of the following examples will show a lighting diagram as an overhead schematic, along with the resulting image. Each lighting style is presented in its most basic form and also in more enhanced versions with additional lights and reflectors.

Beauty or glamour lighting usually places the light source centered on the planes of the face directly above the camera and evenly lighting the face (Figure 2.8). Sometimes called *butterfly lighting*, after the shapes of the highlights on the face, this even light is considered the most flattering for women. The essential element of this style of lighting is that the light source is oriented in line with the center of the face regardless of the direction the subject is looking (Figure 2.9). Most of the time beauty light utilizes a large diffused-light source such as a softbox or umbrella.

It is common to use a reflector, placed in front of the subject just out of frame, to fill the shadows under the chin and nose. This reflector, which is sometimes referred to as a nose light, also helps smooth skin texture and wrinkles. Figure 2.10 shows what the subject sees; the white card reflector here is clamped in a low C-stand directly below the softbox and angled to bounce light back up at the subject. The result gives a softer, more open look (Figure 2.11).

Do not underestimate the effectiveness of a single light source with a simple reflector for fill. This shot of Noelle was accomplished with a single umbrella beauty light with a white reflector disk on her lap (Figure 2.12). Notice how she has turned just slightly to her right—this places a shadow along the nose giving it a little more dimension. Slight changes in position can have a subtle but important impact on the lighting.

Next, you might want to add a *hair light* above and directly behind the subject (Figure 2.13). Many lighting manuals simply suggest using a flash head with reflector; however, using another soft light source will spread the highlight into the hair and prevent hot *sparkles*. This is especially important to keep blond hair from looking dirty. It is best if you can place this hair light close to the subject, so I recommend using a softbox rather than an umbrella. (I find an umbrella more suitable for the front light.) The result places attractive highlights along the shoulders as well as hair; this helps to separate the subject from the background and creates a nice dimensional effect (Figure 2.14).

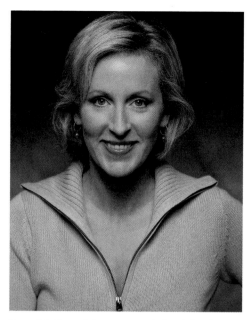

Figure 2.8 Beauty light creates even shadows below the nose and chin.

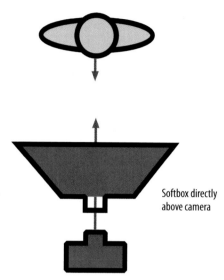

Softbox directly above camera

Figure 2.9 The softbox is placed above the camera in line with the center of the face.

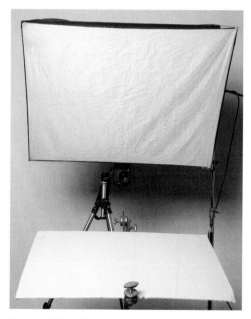

Figure 2.10 The subject's view of the lighting setup shows the softbox with a white card reflector directly below the light source.

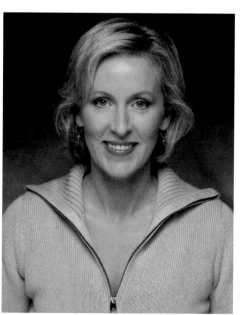

Figure 2.11 The reflector fill creates a softer look.

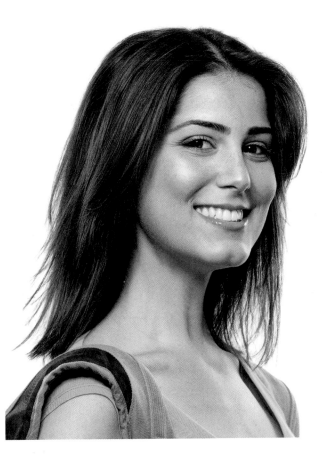

Figure 2.12
Turning off center can
give a little more shading
to one side of the face.

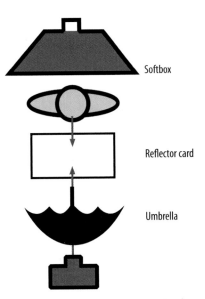

Softbox

Reflector card

Umbrella

Figure 2.13 All the lighting elements are placed
in line with the subject and camera.

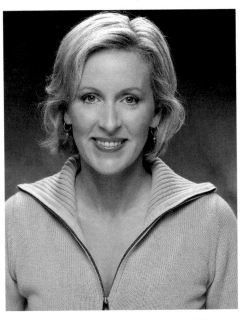

Figure 2.14 The classic beauty light includes a hair light to
create the soft highlights in the hair and along the shoulders.

Shoot a Card

For color calibration purposes, it's always a good idea to take a shot with a neutral gray card so you have something to use to white balance. It is equally important to make sure that your light sources are balanced. This means that you use the same color-temperature flash heads for your lights and test for consistent color when using any light modifiers such as umbrellas or softboxes. You don't have to get too carried away with this. Just be aware that if you are using two umbrellas and one of them is much yellower than the other, the color of the light will not match.

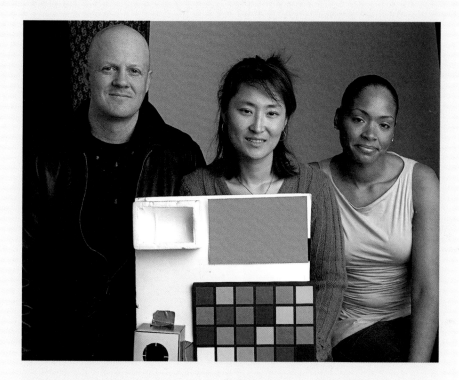

Regardless of any color-matching issues, you should always white balance to the main light. You can also use the card to judge exposure. I use the Robin Myers Digital Gray Card, which has a documented brightness of RGB = 150, 150, 150 in Adobe RGB. When I'm shooting men, I aim for RGB = 155, 155, 155. When I'm shooting women, I aim for RGB = 170, 170, 170. I've found that shots of women almost always look better if they are overexposed just a little, in most cases by $1/2$ to $2/3$ stops.

Beauty Light Variations for Dark-Skinned Subjects

Normally, with fair-skinned subjects, I try to avoid having shiny highlights on the skin. Shadows formed by the natural fall-off of the light delineate the shape of the face and details of the features. Makeup is "powdered" to eliminate moisture that creates hot reflections because the skin is already light and more shadow is needed.

The opposite is desirable with darker complexions. Baby oil is sometimes applied to create extra moisture for hotter highlights. Very dark skin benefits from light sources placed near the axis of the lens to maximize reflections off the moisture in the skin. The beautiful woman in this portrait by Ken Chernus has a well-developed "shine" (Figure 2.15). Ken has placed additional lights at the sides just to the rear of the subject. This creates additional highlights that lighten the skin without changing the overall impression of a beautiful "chocolate-toned" complexion. You can count the number of light sources in the reflections in the apple. Ken placed the main light just above the lens with a large umbrella fill light directly behind the camera. All this on-axis light forms nice reflected highlights on the young woman's face (Figure 2.16).

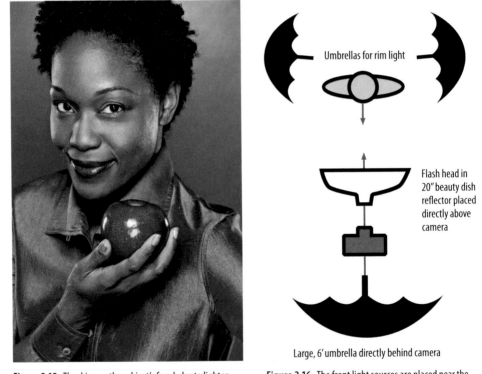

Figure 2.15 The shine on the subject's face helps to lighten her skin and delineate her features. (Photo by Ken Chernus)

Figure 2.16 The front light sources are placed near the lens axis to maximize reflections off the skin.

This extra "skin shine" effect can work wonders for body shots as well (Figure 2.17). This "Tarzan Torso" utilizes almost the same lighting setup (Figure 2.18). Strong rim lighting is achieved with umbrellas placed to the right and left rear. Black cards flag this rear light from the lens, and a flash in a big dish reflector right over the camera provides the front light. The model was sprayed with water right before the shot to give the illusion of sweat and help shine up the highlights on the muscles. In this case, the shot is deliberately underexposed to put more distance between the highlights and the average skin tone, effectively increasing the contrast and sense of dimension.

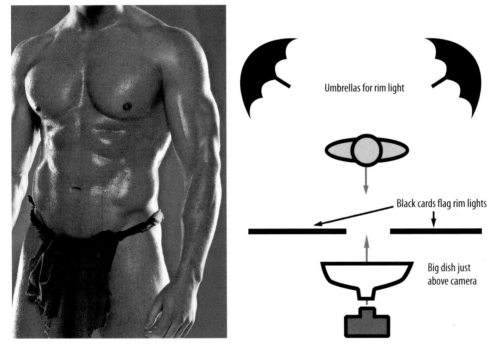

Figure 2.17 Strong rim lighting and "sweaty shine" combine to delineate the muscles in this figure shot.

Figure 2.18 Similar to Figure 2.16, the umbrellas provide the rim light and a big dish reflector pops the reflections on the moist skin.

Rembrandt Lighting

Rembrandt lighting is a classic style of lighting named after the famous Dutch master. The main light is off to the side, creating a distinctive triangle highlight on the shadow-side cheek (Figure 2.19). More commonly used for men, this lighting emphasizes shape and texture. The result is often more dramatic and dimensional (Figure 2.20).

The effect is softened considerably with the addition of a fill card and hair light (Figure 2.21). The direction of light is preserved, but the harsh shadows are filled with light reflecting off the fill card (Figure 2.22). If you move the fill card very close to the subject, the shadow side can be opened up even more to mimic the open quality of beauty light.

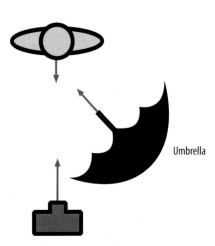

Figure 2.19 Rembrandt light comes from the side, about 45 degrees off-axis.

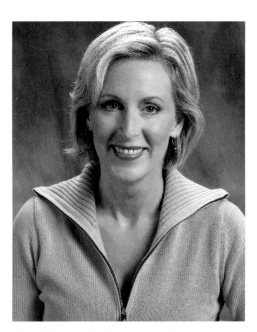

Figure 2.20 Notice the triangular highlight on the left cheek under the eye.

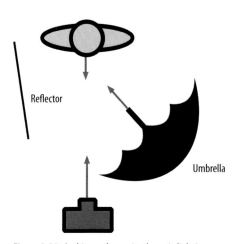

Figure 2.21 A white card opposite the main light is used to fill the shadows.

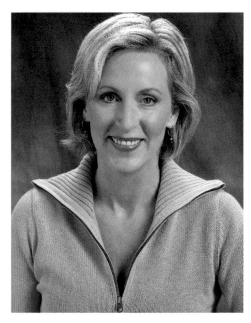

Figure 2.22 The fill creates a softer effect.

A variation of the fill effect is to turn the fill into a rim light by moving it to the rear of the subject (Figure 2.23). This shot of Munir Beken utilizes a basic Rembrandt light position and incorporates a small umbrella placed to the rear-left well behind the subject. This adds that little "kiss" of rim light to the dark side of his face (Figure 2.24).

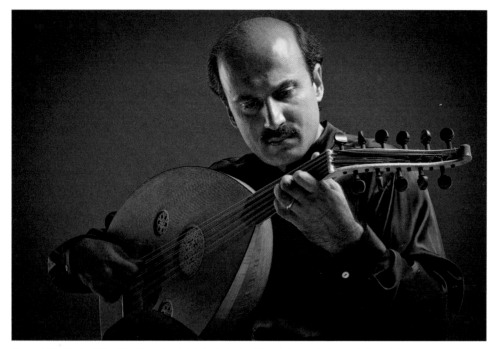

Figure 2.23 The rim light adds a dramatic relief to the dark side of Munir's face and lights up the face of the instrument, which is turned away from the light.

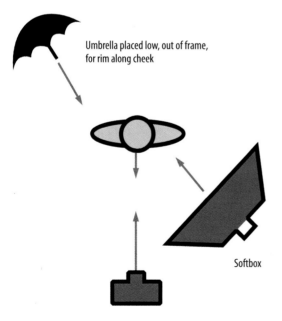

Umbrella placed low, out of frame, for rim along cheek

Softbox

Figure 2.24
A small umbrella placed to the rear provides the rim of light on the dark side of the subject.

Another interesting variation of this lighting technique is something I call "Reverse-Rembrandt." Here the shadow and highlight areas are reversed. The main light is a little hotter and occupies the area normally held by the shadow. The fill light is now the main light with the filled shadow falling across most of the face, creating a darker triangle shape in the highlighted half of the face (Figure 2.25). To create this effect, bring your main light around more to the side so that the far side of the face is completely in shade. Use a larger reflector card or another light to fill in the main planes of the face (Figure 2.26). The main light is now an accent. You should increase the intensity, but be careful so that it doesn't *blast* to white. The shadow side is filled with enough light to bring the exposure to ideal for the skin.

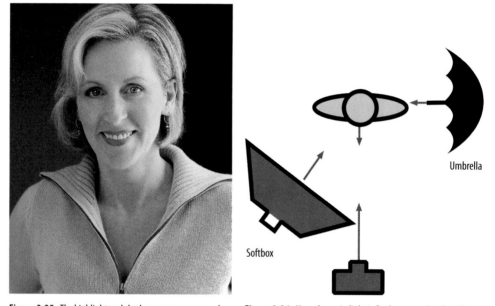

Umbrella

Softbox

Figure 2.25 The highlight and shadow areas are reversed. The fill now occupies the main planes of the face, and the area that would normally be shaded in traditional Rembrandt lighting is highlighted.

Figure 2.26 Here the main light is farther around to the side, and an additional light is used at lower intensity to fill the face.

Rembrandt lighting lends itself to strong dramatic effects. Instead of fighting the harshness of unfilled shadows, Aaron Rapoport emphasizes them by using a small, focused Fresnel spot light in this dramatic portrait of a boxer (Figure 2.27). The light is high and to the side to emulate the look of a bare bulb fixture in the gym. No fill was used, allowing the shadows to go inky black. The harsh direct light brings out the texture and at the same time reflects strongly off the moisture of baby-oiled skin, which helps to lighten the dark complexion and increase the contrast. Very simple, one-source lighting is used to great effect in this powerful portrait.

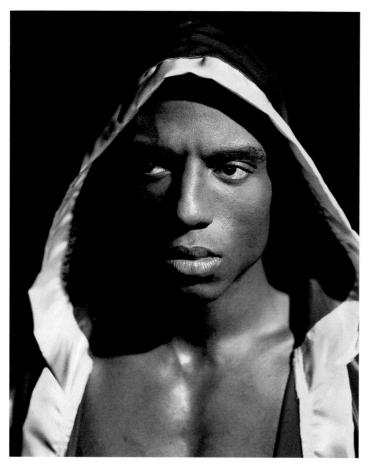

Figure 2.27 Harsh lighting complements the strong features in this powerful portrait. (Photo by Aaron Rapoport)

Natural Light

When photographers work with lights in the studio, they usually aim for a naturalistic feel. The lighting used in these examples attempts to emulate natural light. However, the studio can offer many opportunities to use real natural light in portrait settings. One of the most obvious applications of natural light is window light. With this technique, the subject is placed next to a window, re-creating a true Rembrandt lighting effect (Figure 2.28). Because the camera can't be positioned inside the wall, we are a little more constrained with the direction of the light; therefore, it is sometimes necessary to have the subject turn into the light a little, as you see here. Move a fill card in toward the subject, and you can lighten the mood (Figure 2.29).

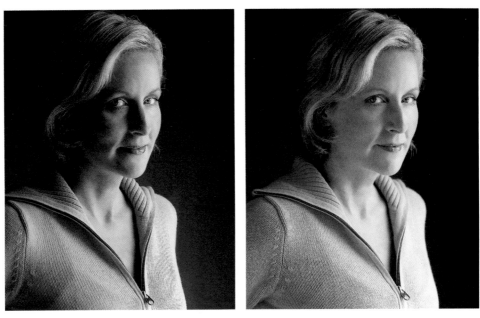

Figure 2.28 Erin is posed next to a window for a classic Rembrandt look.

Figure 2.29 To lighten the mood, add a fill card.

Natural beauty light can be created by placing the subject where the face can be evenly illuminated by a broad expanse of sky. Here Erin is standing in an open doorway facing out into the backyard (Figure 2.30). The sun is on the opposite side of the building, and all the illumination comes from open sky. She is actually holding a large fill card at her waist. The result is soft and open.

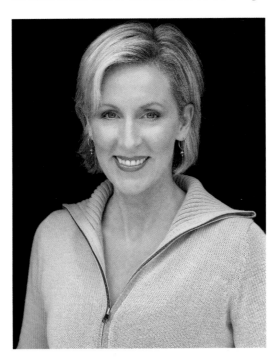

Figure 2.30
The sky makes a perfect large diffused source for this flattering, natural beauty light.

One of the problems with all this natural light is that frequently it is too intense for comfort. Subjects frequently squint at the bright light, especially if you use a white fill card. To remedy the situation, have the subjects close their eyes and open them only at the moment of exposure. Another subtle problem has to do with *catch lights* in the eyes. The extra-broad expanse of sky creates a great soft light, but the spectral highlights in the eye (the catch lights) are diffused so that the effect is a less-lively glazed look. Notice how simply adding some bright catch lights livens up the eyes (Figure 2.31) and enlarging the pupils during retouch makes her appear friendlier.

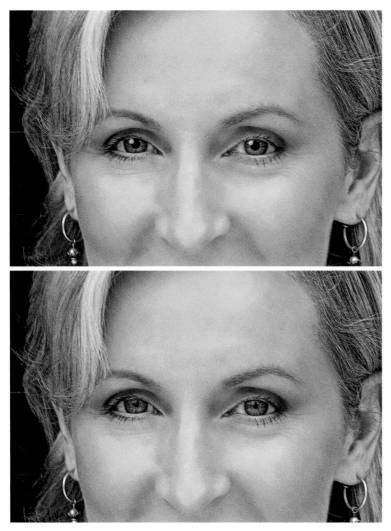

Figure 2.31 Compare the original eyes on the bottom with the retouched version on top.

Years ago, a university psychology study examined people's responses to photos of other people. Test subjects were shown two sets of photos. In one set of photos, the eyes had been retouched to have larger pupils. That was the only difference between the sets. The subjects consistently reported that the people with larger pupils seemed to be warmer and friendlier, even though they were not aware of the difference between the shots. For this reason, I often enlarge the pupils if I am retouching the eyes. You can see the difference in Figure 2.31.

Note: Catch lights in the eyes are the reflection of the light source. However, this reflection is not 100 percent white. When you paint these spots, do it in a new layer and reduce the opacity to 50 to 60 percent. You can enlarge the pupils by painting with black in another layer; this layer can be at full opacity, but place the Pupil layer beneath the Catch Lights layer.

Notice how the retouched version of this shot (Figure 2.32) has so much more life and sparkle in the eyes. When your lighting doesn't create nice catch lights, retouch them. Don't be too heavy handed with the technique, and it will go a long way to enhance your portraits.

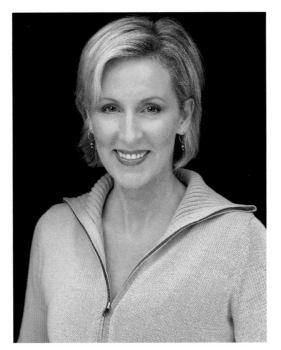

Figure 2.32
Compare this retouched version with the original in Figure 2.30.

On-Camera Flash

Although photographers like to avoid it, there are times when we have to use on-camera flash. The small light source attached to the camera right above the lens does not have the most flattering quality (Figure 2.33). It's hard to avoid the "deer in the headlights" look with this kind of police mug-shot lighting.

Anything you can do to broaden and soften the light source will make an improvement. A number of bounce reflector gadgets are available for the small, hot shoe camera flashes. These lights are often set up with swiveling heads to facilitate bouncing the light. You can make your own bounce reflector from a piece of white cardboard as shown here (Figure 2.34). In a pinch, you can even tape a small business card to the flash.

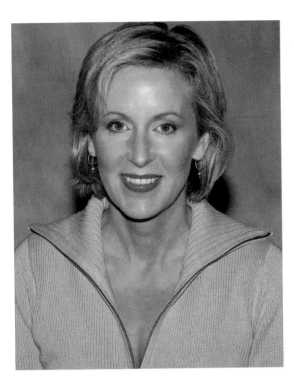

Figure 2.33
On-camera flash tends to emphasize shiny highlights and creates a strong edge shadow under the chin. Close backgrounds show a strong black shadow behind the head.

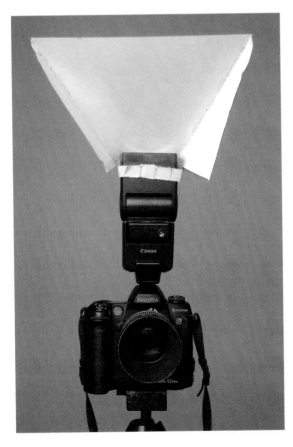

Figure 2.34
This reflector was made from an 8.5-inch × 11-inch cardboard shirt stiffener.

The bounce reflector moves the light farther away from the lens and spreads it to soften the light considerably. This becomes, in effect, a small beauty light setup. You can get very nice lighting without giving up the portability that an on-camera flash affords (Figure 2.35).

The catch lights are still likely to be small and positioned in the middle of the pupils, so you might consider retouching to put some sparkle in the eyes (Figure 2.36).

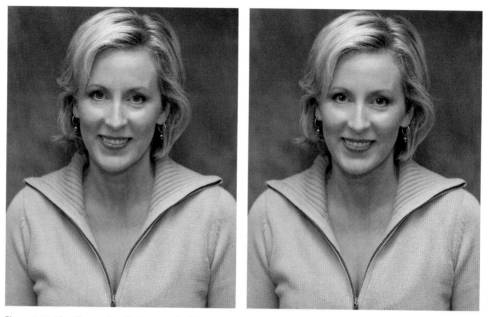

Figure 2.35 The effect produced by bouncing the light off a small reflector approaches the quality of beauty light.

Figure 2.36 Adding catch lights helps the overall effect.

Even the lighting from a tiny point-and-shoot camera with a built-in flash can be improved with a little tape and some facial tissue (Figure 2.37). This setup can help you get decent lighting for those happy snaps at parties (Figure 2.38). Although this type of lighting won't win any awards, you will still generate a more natural effect and spread the light around so it bounces off walls to give a little more natural fill. The tissue over the tiny flash will soak up some of the intensity, so you may have to use a little higher ISO setting to shoot at any distance from your subject.

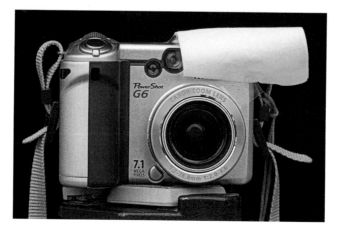

Figure 2.37
Bow the tissue over the flash rather than taping it right onto the flash window. This will make the light bigger and spread it out more to soften it.

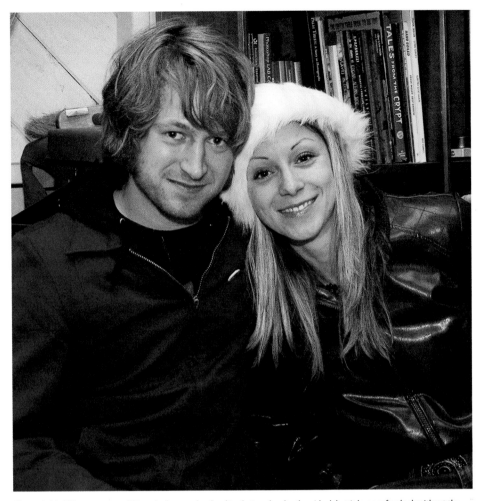

Figure 2.38 This party snap still has shadows under the chin that are harder than ideal, but it has a softer look without the typical glare that a tiny on-camera flash would normally have.

Breaking the Rules

So far we've been looking at the standard formulas for portrait lighting, but sometimes the best pictures break the rules. An unusual face deserves unusual lighting, as we can see in this portrait of Michel Karman (Figure 2.39), the master B+W printer responsible for most of Helmut Newton's prints, as well as many other famous photographers' prints. This image was captured in available light. The main light source is sunlight coming through an open doorway and bouncing off the floor just to the left of the subject (Figure 2.40). This low-light angle is sometimes referred to as *Boris Karloff lighting*, after the famous character actor who played Frankenstein's monster in the movies of the 1930s and 1940s. To fill the shadow side of his face, Michel held a white card just out of frame to the right. You can see the bright patch of light on the floor and the fill card reflected in his glasses.

Look for unusual lighting opportunities. A pocket mirror can do wonders. An unusual camera position can create an unusual lighting direction. Don't get stuck with the ordinary approaches. Remember that rules are meant to be broken.

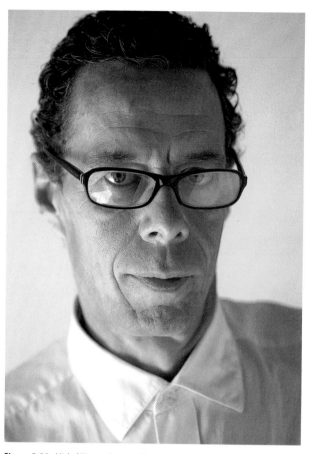

Figure 2.39 Michel Karman's strong features are well served by the unusual lighting angle.

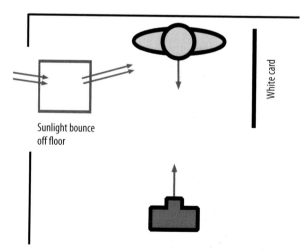

Figure 2.40 All the light for this image comes from sunlight bouncing off a polished wood floor.

Advanced Lighting Techniques

Once you've mastered the basics, it's time to start exploring alternatives. Photographers have a lot of fun creating complex artificial lighting effects, often using specialized equipment. Sometimes this requires lots of lights in different combinations of hardness and softness with different lighting directions. Sometimes, as you'll see, one simple light is all that is needed. Lighting for people photography is typically not as difficult as product or still life photography, but it can become surprisingly complex when you're trying to re-create an enhanced natural light effect.

Ring Light

One easy way to get a different look is to use a *ring light*. A true ring light, such as the one in Figure 2.6, has a unique look. Figure 2.41 (by Ken Chernus) and Figure 2.42 (by Aaron Rapoport) demonstrate the classic ring light effect. There is a distinctive halo shadow all around the figure when the background is not too distant. The light fills everything evenly, but the edges darken slightly as the light wraps to the rear, creating a subtle modeling or three-dimensional effect. As a result, there is no shadow under the chin, but the chin edge is still strongly defined.

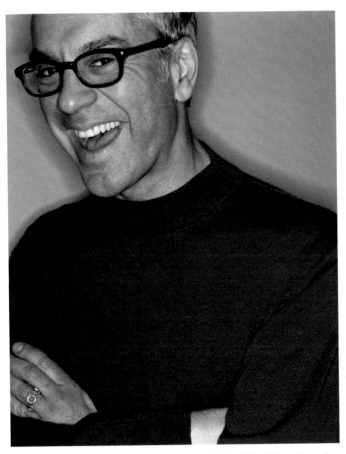

Figure 2.41 Strong contrast without shadows is typical of ring light. This man is wearing glasses without lenses to avoid the direct reflection that would normally occur with this type of light. (Photo by Ken Chernus)

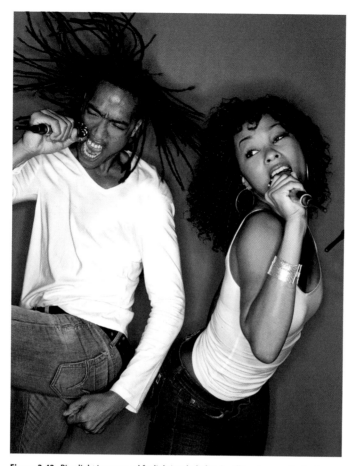

Figure 2.42 Ring light is very good for lighting dark skin. It will create a good reflection off moisture in the skin. This produces highlights on dark skin. They are the most noticeable on the man's forehead, but they also appear as a slight sheen on the woman's arm and face. (Photo by Aaron Rapoport)

Ring light lends itself to a high-contrast altered look, as you can see in the next shot by Aaron Rapoport (Figure 2.43). In this shot, Aaron deliberately overexposed and pushed the contrast to render the young woman's skin pure white. The edge-darkening effect of the ring light lends a kind of illustrated effect and enhances the *goth* look. A side effect is that the light carries nicely into the room behind her. The ring light is truly a one-light wonder.

In yet another application of the ring light, Aaron Rapoport photographed this somber group outdoors in broad daylight. By using a powerful source and a shorter shutter speed, he overpowered the daylight (Figure 2.44). The natural falloff of the light, as it reaches the figures in the back, creates the "group emerging from the darkness" effect seen here.

Many photographers feel like they are cheating when they use ring light because it's so easy to create something cool by using it. The examples shown here prove that ring light can be used in lots of different ways without looking too obvious.

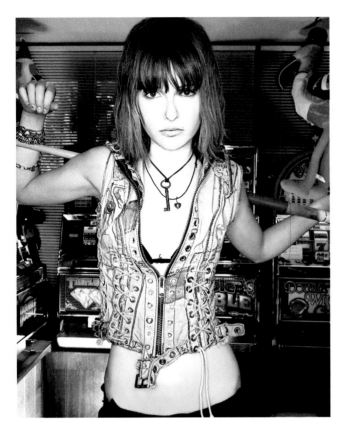

Figure 2.43
Pure white vampire skin enhances this goth-girl portrait. (Photo by Aaron Rapoport)

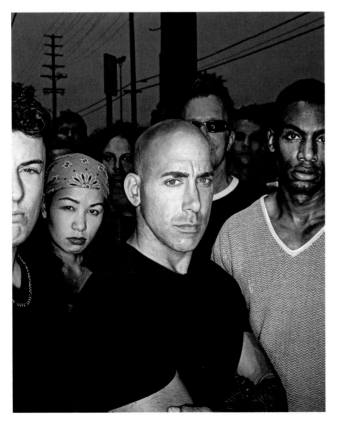

Figure 2.44
Strong catch lights are typical for the ring light. You can also see a reflected image of the ring itself in the sunglasses of the man standing behind the main figure. (Photo by Aaron Rapoport)

Note: The "flash overpowering daylight" effect works when you can sync the flash to a high shutter speed. Most digital camera systems don't use mechanical shutters but instead electronically time-capture the signal off a sensor, allowing for flash synchronization up to $^1/_{500}$ sec. The flash reaches full intensity in $^1/_{600}$ sec or less; therefore, short shutter speeds have no effect on the level of flash light. Daylight (as a continuous light source) is affected; therefore, shorter shutter speeds let in less light. The normal intention of daylight flash fill is to balance the flash so it acts as a fill for shadows in daylight. Reversing the ratio of flash intensity to daylight can create day-for-night effects or dramatic motion-stopping effects. Some digital cameras are capable of even shorter flash sync speeds—up to $^1/_{1000}$ sec or more. You might need to be careful not to use too high a speed to avoid reducing the intensity of the flash as well as the daylight.

Combination Lighting: Daylight Plus Flash

It has become very fashionable to combine daylight and flash light to create interesting altered effects rather than simply fill the shadows inherent with daylight lighting. This usually means that flash lighting will be the dominant source, with daylight acting as fill or accent. Figure 2.40 gave you a glimpse of this technique. Here is another more complex example by Aaron Rapoport (Figure 2.45). The wide-angle lens and stark arrangement of faces combine with multiple light sources and strong shadows to emphasize the tension in this scene. There is no attempt at realism here. Although the scene clearly takes place in daylight, the artificial flash lighting reflects the emotional state of the recruit in the center of the frame. Aaron utilized direct flash heads in small reflectors to create the high-contrast lighting (Figure 2.46).

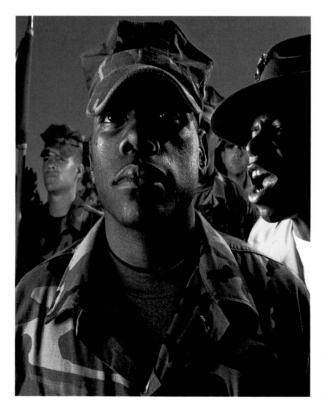

Figure 2.45
The strong contrast lighting transports us into the mind of this young recruit. (Photo by Aaron Rapoport)

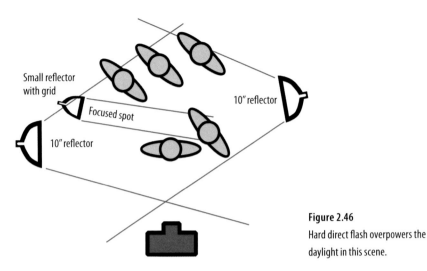

Figure 2.46
Hard direct flash overpowers the daylight in this scene.

The classic approach to combining flash with daylight is commonly called *flash fill lighting.* In this style of lighting, daylight is the dominant light source and flash is used to fill the shadows. Another image by Aaron Rapoport, this shot of a young soccer player uses flash fill lighting, but the key light is really the flash right above the lens (Figure 2.47). The very strong daylight is directly behind the subject. This would ordinarily place him completely in the shade and open sky light would be very soft with low contrast. By lighting the subject with a direct flash, Aaron has created much higher edge contrast and added catch light sparkle to the boy's eyes (Figure 2.48).

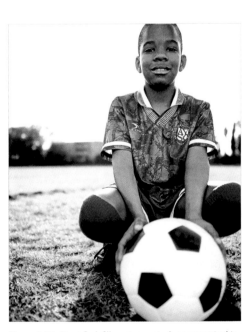

Figure 2.47 Direct flash fill creates great edge contrast in this shot by Aaron Rapoport.

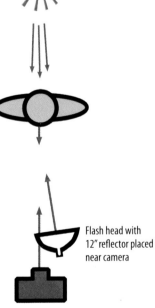

Figure 2.48 The two light sources are directly opposite each other.

This image combines fire and flash for an interesting public relations shot of Polynesian fire dancers (Figure 2.49). In this image, the fire is more of an accent because it doesn't really provide much illumination. Most of the lighting comes from flash heads bounced out of V-flats placed to the rear of the figures. A medium softbox directly over the lens fills from the front. The shutter speed was slowed enough to allow the swinging fire lantern to burn in the circle around the dancers (Figure 2.50). All other ambient light, including the flash modeling lights, were turned off so that they didn't affect the exposure during the long shutter.

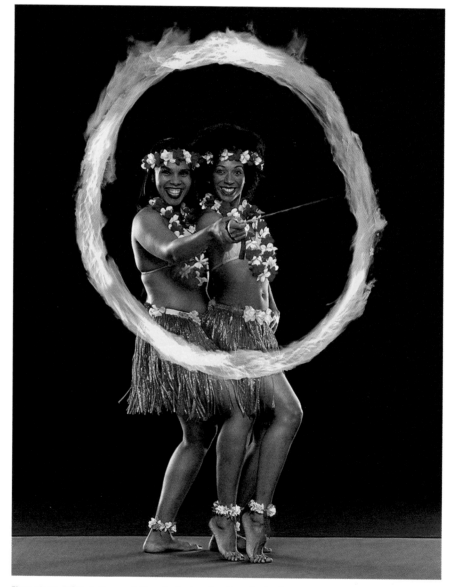

Figure 2.49 A slow shutter speed allows the fire to make a frame for the dancers.

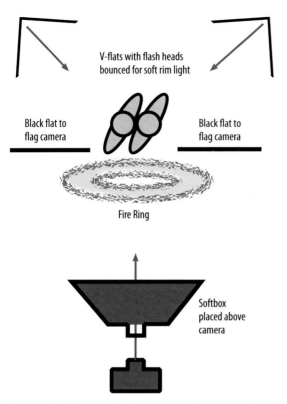

V-flats with flash heads bounced for soft rim light

Black flat to flag camera

Black flat to flag camera

Fire Ring

Softbox placed above camera

Figure 2.50 V-flats bounce light to create edge highlights on the figures.

Controlling Natural Light

Natural light can be the most beautiful light available, but it often poses many problems when you want a subject-flattering effect—especially if you are trying to preserve a natural look. There is always one light source with natural light: the sun. When you aren't trying to create a stylized, altered look, photos taken under natural light conditions should look as if there is only one light source. Any lighting should be invisible. Sometimes this is easily achieved, but sometimes it is not so easy.

One of Anthony Nex's specialties is photographing kids for advertising and stock. He typically utilizes broad, even illumination because kids don't stand still for very long, and he likes to make sure they have a large area to move around in and still be in the ideal light. In this adorable portrait of three little girls, the lighting is extremely simple (Figure 2.51). They are outdoors in a broad area of open shade looking up at the photographer. The open sky is directly behind the camera, and the only additional lighting is a large, white reflector board positioned just out of frame, camera left (Figure 2.52). This reflector is the brightest thing in the vicinity of the girls, so it actually acts more like a soft-light source, providing a gentle direction for the light as well as the bright catch lights in the girls' eyes.

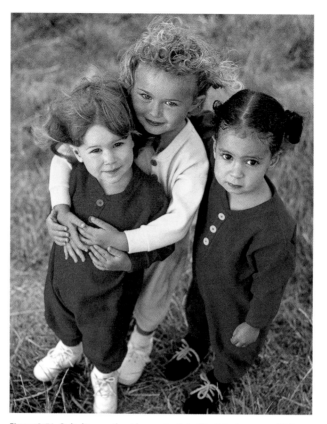

Figure 2.51 By looking up, the girls are actually looking into the source of light behind the camera. (Photo by Anthony Nex)

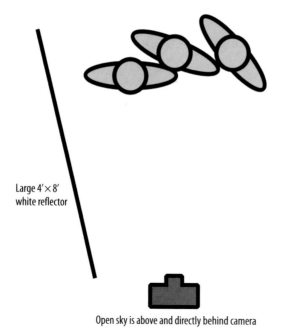

Large 4′ × 8′
white reflector

Open sky is above and directly behind camera

Figure 2.52 The reflector is the only addition to the natural skylight that illuminates this scene.

An assistant holds the reflector board. If the kids move, it is easy to follow them around because the overall sky lighting is so even from spot to spot. In these situations, Anthony shoots hand-held so he can move with the kids.

Ken Chernus is another master of natural light control. He shoots lifestyle stock imagery in various locations. Sometimes he can be very lucky. In this shot of the man at the beach (Figure 2.53), there is no additional lighting. This kind of luck has to be planned. In this case, timing was everything. Right after the sun dips below the horizon after sunset, light takes on a special quality photographers like to call magic light. This period of time after sunset is sometimes referred to as *the magic hour*. It can offer many opportunities, depending on the weather. This particular shot benefited from a soft haze that covered the area and provided a natural diffusion for the bright sky. The light sand was a natural source for bounce fill light. All Ken had to do was position the subject, point his camera, and shoot. All the elements of the scene were within the dynamic range capabilities of his Canon digital camera.

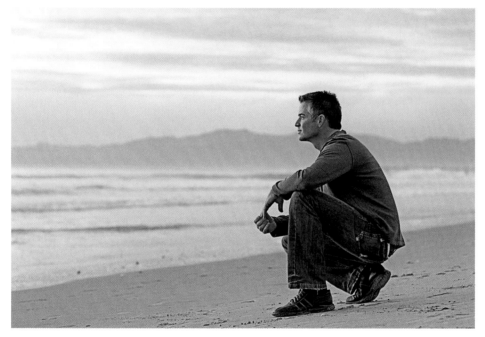

Figure 2.53 Weather, time of day, and location combined to create the ideal set of circumstances for this shot. (Photo by Ken Chernus)

For the next shot, Ken had to make his own luck (Figure 2.54). Shooting in the back yard in the middle of the day is a far cry from magic light. He created a soft backlight effect using a translucent silk *scrim* to diffuse the harsh sun.

Note: A *scrim* is a translucent panel often used in movie lighting to soften a direct light source. It is sometimes referred to as a silk, after the fabric commonly stretched over an aluminum frame to create the scrim. Spring frame panels, as mentioned earlier in this chapter, can also come in a translucent version used for the same purpose.

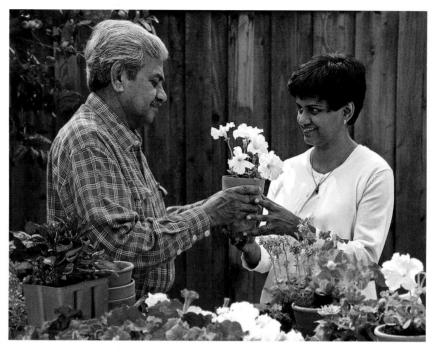

Figure 2.54 This father/daughter portrait was captured by diffusing the direct sunlight with a silk scrim.
(Photo by Ken Chernus)

The scrim doesn't completely cover the subjects; however, Ken pulled the silk away from the frame at the back edge to allow a small shaft of direct sun to hit the girl's right shoulder. This put a splash of hot white light right behind the flowers to provide a little contrast and create the effect of sunlight filtering through the leaves. A white card, just out of frame to the right, provided fill from the front. The overall effect is quite natural, but it took a bit of rigging to get the light to work (Figure 2.55).

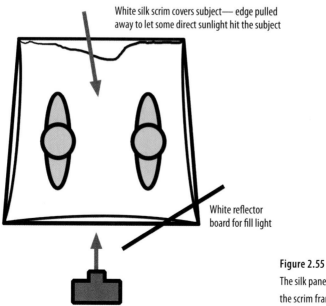

White silk scrim covers subject— edge pulled away to let some direct sunlight hit the subject

White reflector board for fill light

Figure 2.55
The silk panel was pulled away from the edge of the scrim frame to allow a little bit of direct light to hit the subject.

Available light can also be found inside, and the photographer has to be prepared to deal with whatever light is present at the scene. Mark Harmel's work often takes him into hospital settings where the available light is ubiquitous but not particularly dramatic. Mark often solves this problem with the use of small portable flash units that supplement the existing light. In this shot of a doctor examining an MRI (Figure 2.56), he placed a flash head low to the subject's right, shining through the transparent sheet of film (Figure 2.57). This brilliantly connects the doctor to the film he's looking at and dramatizes the intensity of the subject's expression.

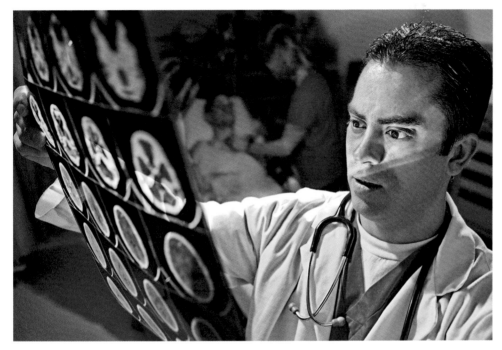

Figure 2.56 The unusual light hitting the subject's face is shaped by the MRI transparency he is holding.

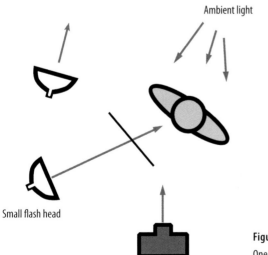

Ambient light

Small flash head

Figure 2.57
One small flash adds the key element to this dramatic image.

Shooting in direct sun is usually a recipe for harsh shadows. In this case, Ken Chernus carefully filled the shadows by using white reflector boards (Figure 2.58). The subject is facing the late afternoon sun. Ken placed a large white board on the ground in front of the guitar player and another white board behind him, just out of frame to the left (Figure 2.59). Situations such as this call for close attention to lighting ratios. The huge dynamic range of natural light can be completely tamed only through lighting control. Take a reading of the highlight and shadow in the subject and reduce the difference by filling the shadows so the two values are within four f-stops of each other. This image shows a highlight (Lab) L value of 85 on the man's forehead. The shadow side of his face shows an L value of 53, which is a difference of 32 or 3.2 EV. In the field, of course, you'll have to rely on a good light meter to get EV readings directly. Move reflector cards closer or farther away to get the desired ratios.

Well-placed reflectors are mandatory with direct sun, but they are sometimes also necessary with soft overcast lighting. This final shot from Ken Chernus was taken during the same magic hour light as Figure 2.53, but a small fill card was still needed to fill the subject's face (Figure 2.60). The majority of the soft skylight is coming from the woman's left rear. The position of her head causes her hair to block the light from her face. The fill card redirects the light back into her face to provide the even beauty-light look (Figure 2.61).

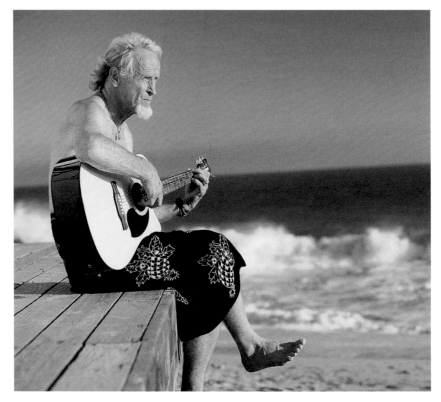

Figure 2.58 The harsh direct sun has been softened in this shot by Ken Chernus.

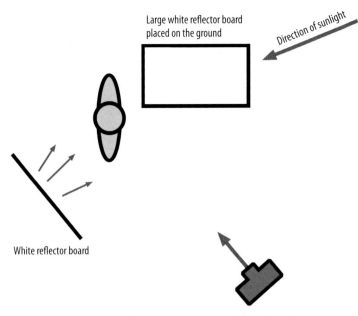

Large white reflector board
placed on the ground

Direction of sunlight

White reflector board

Figure 2.59 Reflectors are used to adjust the lighting ratios. Fill shadows to bring the ratio within four f-stops.

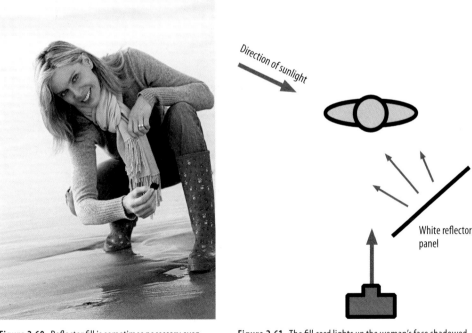

Figure 2.60 Reflector fill is sometimes necessary even with soft overcast lighting. (Photo by Ken Chernus)

Direction of sunlight

White reflector
panel

Figure 2.61 The fill card lights up the woman's face shadowed by her hair.

Action Stopping Lighting

People don't always stand still. Sometimes they move and often we have to capture them when they are moving quite fast! A very short flash duration is needed to obtain maximum action-stopping effects. Modern flash units can vary the intensity of the light by shortening the duration of the flash. Turn the flash intensity down all the way to get the shortest flash duration. The best strategy for action stopping is to use the intensity controls to shorten the flash duration and add multiple lights to build up the intensity to desired levels. Figure 2.62 shows this action-stopping effect. The woman jumping on a trampoline is stopped in midair by the short flash duration of multiple synchronized flash units.

The figure is wrapped in a soft rim light that comes from V-flats and soft-boxes positioned to the rear. A 40-inch umbrella provides the front fill lighting. Large 4-feet × 8-feet white foamcore boards act as front fill and shade the camera from the rear lights. In all cases, multiple lights are used at low power for all the sources—three lights in each V-flat, three lights in the rear softbox, and one light from the front (Figure 2.63).

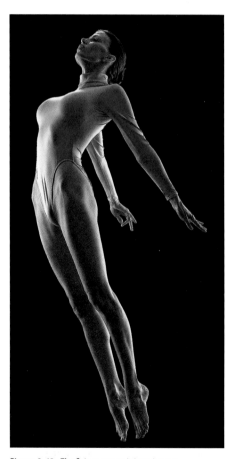

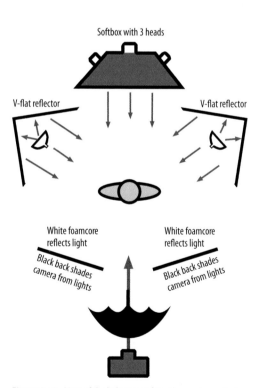

Figure 2.62 The flying woman is jumping on a trampoline.

Figure 2.63 Most of the light comes from the rear to create the soft wrap-around rim light. Action stopping comes from multiple lights at low intensity for shorter duration.

The same lighting scheme was used for the next shot. This time the flash lighting froze the water splashing off the figure as she emerged from the pool (Figure 2.64). The rigging for this setup was much more complicated because everything was done in the backyard of the photo shoot's art director.

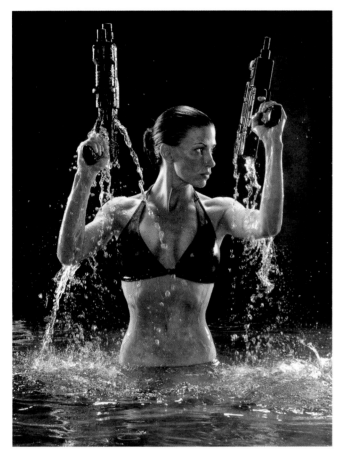

Figure 2.64
An action hero shot with maximum action stopping light

The following production stills show the elaborate rigging of softboxes, flags, and reflectors that went into the production of this shot:

- Three softboxes were positioned at the rear of one end of the pool, and black plastic was laid into the pool and held down with sand bags to create a black bottom (Figure 2.65).

- A black foamcore card was placed to shade the camera from the top softbox.

- To block the side softboxes from the camera, black cloth flags were cantilevered over the water on the ends of C-stand arms (Figures 3.66 and 3.67).

- My assistant, Kent Jones, took meter readings from the subject position to balance the light intensity (Figure 2.68).

The rigging took all day, but by nightfall we were ready to shoot. In Figure 2.69, you can see the 8-foot Octodome softbox directly behind the camera used for the front fill lighting. This large source helped to light up the water droplets even though most of the light came from the softboxes at the rear. The rear lights provided the soft rim effect on the figure that enhances the dramatic nighttime feeling (Figure 2.70).

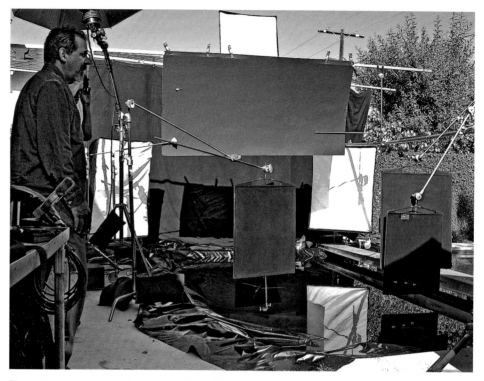

Figure 2.65 I survey the setup. You can see the three softboxes, black cards, and the black plastic laid into the pool.

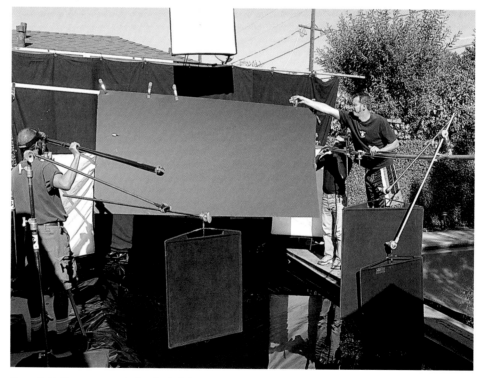

Figure 2.66 The crew sets up the flags for the lights.

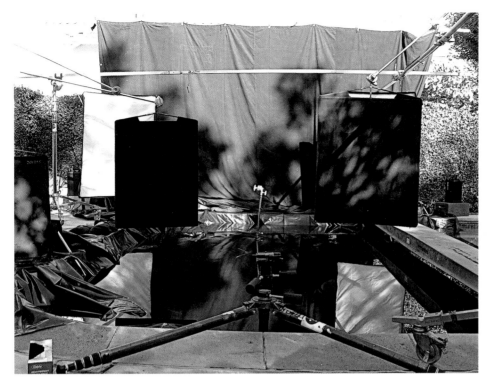

Figure 2.67 Here you can see how the flags were used to hide the rear lights from the camera position to prevent flare.

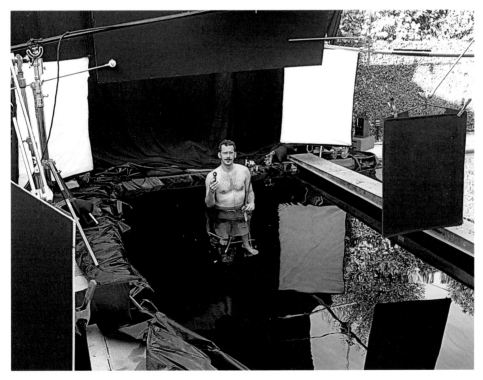

Figure 2.68 Kent Jones takes a meter reading.

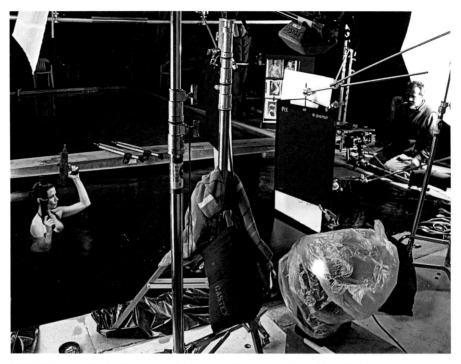

Figure 2.69 I am giving directions to the model; you can see the large Octodome softbox behind me. The camera is on a tripod that's halfway into the water. Plastic bags cover the flash units to protect against splashing water.

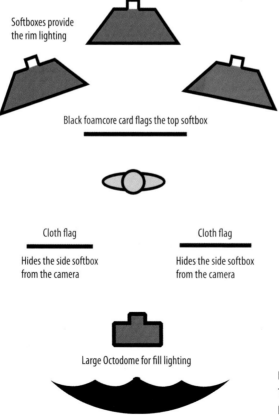

Softboxes provide the rim lighting

Black foamcore card flags the top softbox

Cloth flag

Hides the side softbox from the camera

Cloth flag

Hides the side softbox from the camera

Large Octodome for fill lighting

Figure 2.70
The lighting diagram shows the basic layout of lights and flags.

Experimenting with Light

Good lighting is often what separates the great photographers from the ordinary ones. Quality light is not something you can re-create inside Photoshop; it must exist in the shot as captured. You can enhance things that are already there, brighten shadows, correct color, and so forth, but the hardness or softness of the actual light and the direction of the actual light in a shot cannot be altered in any substantial way. It pays to get the light right when you capture. Pay attention to lighting ratios so you won't have to fix them later; you will always get better quality this way.

Playing with light is ultimately much more rewarding than playing with Photoshop filters. The immediate gratification with the instant review capabilities of digital capture make it easier than ever to experiment with light on the shoot. Try things and see what you can discover. Sometimes the best lighting is the kind that breaks all the rules. For example, Figure 2.71 has hard shadows and a splash of red color. Most of the image is in deep shadow with just the barest hint of white light revealing her features. As you can see, you don't always have to try for a "detail everywhere" technically correct rendering.

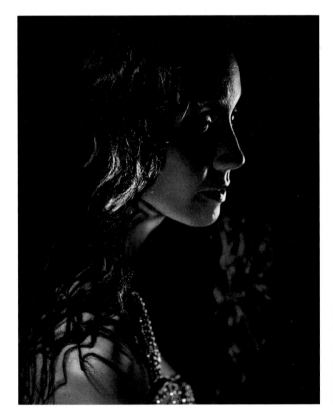

Figure 2.71
The odd direction and red color create a moody theatrical look in this shot by Aaron Rapoport. The thin but intense rim of white light barely lights the features.

You don't necessarily have to color balance to the light source. Shoot with a daylight default color temperature in tungsten light or choose tungsten color temperature for flash or daylight, as was done for the chapter opener image. When you are on an assignment, you'll need to get the expected shot to satisfy a client; however, if you have time, move the lights or turn off the extra lights and shoot the subject with one light. Make some time to play with light, so you can discover really cool effects (Figure 2.72) that go beyond the push button, CGI-filter stuff that is so popular today because it is so easy.

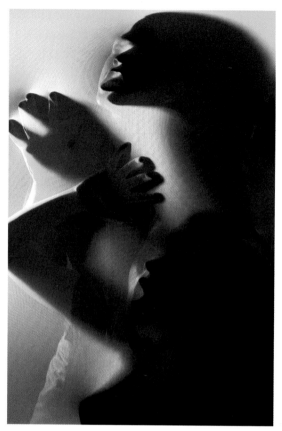

Figure 2.72
This complex horror light was created with only one flash head in a 10-inch reflector. A silk diffusion panel was placed in front of the subjects to catch the shadows and light coming from the left rear.

The latest digital cameras have incredible low light capabilities—you can often get great results at upward of ISO 3200. I took advantage of my Canon 5D mark II's high ISO to produce this Film Noir image (Figure 2.73). Here the key light comes from a match! The only other light on the man is coming from the top rear, a focused spot that provides the rim light on him and lights the table. All other lighting is balanced to the low-level intensity of the match. The image is actually a composite of two different shots to suggest the smokey interior of a night club.

Creative application of unusual light sources can often create spectacular lighting effects. One technique that I've been exploring uses a flashlight to "paint" light onto the subject by moving the light during a long exposure (Figure 2.74). To make this work, the subject must remain motionless. In this shot, the model is lying on a black cloth on the floor. The camera is clamped to a ladder high above her. The shot is the result of several different exposures blended together in Photoshop. It was actually fairly easy for the model to stay still, and slight movements were not an issue because the lighting was built up in isolated sections: the hair was done in one 8-second exposure, the face in another, and the arms took two other exposures. The overall effect is very illustrative. More information on this technique is available on the website: www.varis.com/skinbook.

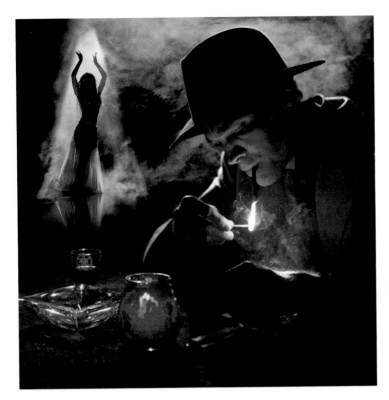

Figure 2.73
The match is the only light
illuminating the man's face.

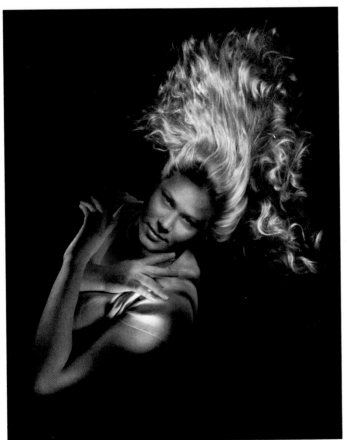

Figure 2.74
To create this haunting image,
a flashlight was waved over the
subject in multiple exposures,
which were later combined in
Photoshop.

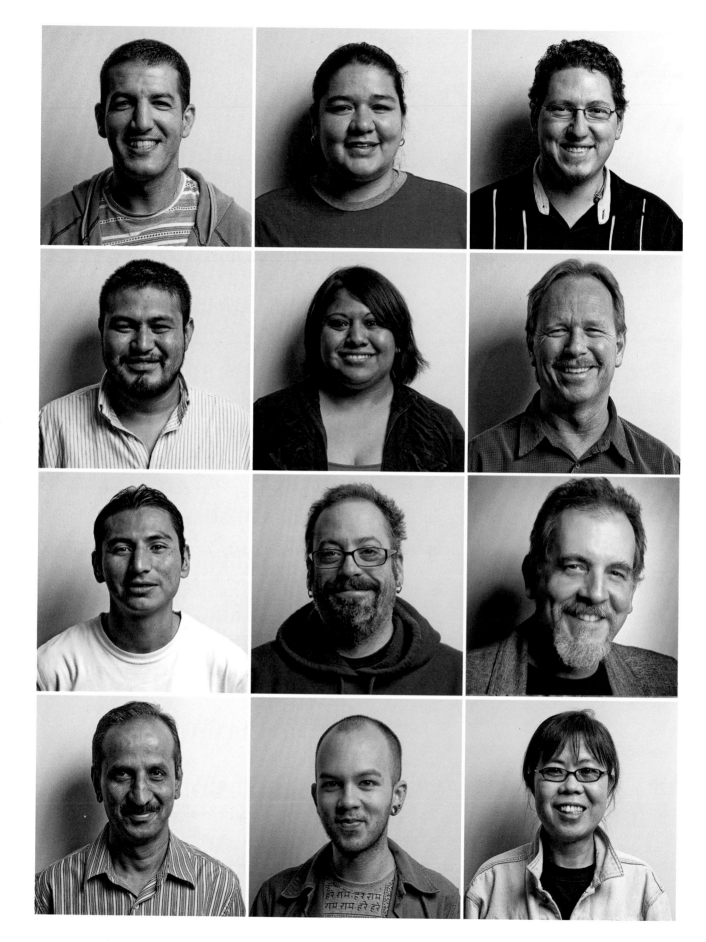

The Color of Skin

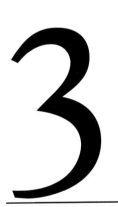

Most people will say they want "accurate" color, but what they prefer (and what clients buy) is "pretty" color—not wild surrealism, but usually some departure from reality. In reality, the color of skin is quite varied but viewers tend to accept a much narrower range of color as "natural" in reproduction. This is where color control becomes important.

You cannot fully explore color without first dealing with value—the lightness/darkness structure of an image. Establishing an appropriate value range from black to white is an important first step in any color correction process because without light and dark you don't really have a recognizable image.

Chapter Contents

White Points, Black Points, and Places In-Between
Zone System: Contrast and Tone
Neutral Color: Using Balanced Numbers
White/Black Point Correction
Adjusting the Numbers for the Color of Skin
The Family of Man: Cultural and Psychological Issues

White Points, Black Points, and Places In-Between

By far, the biggest problem that digital photographers face is getting the color right. If you've been photographing traditionally for any number of years, you've most likely learned how to expose images properly and you've assembled a collection of lighting tricks that have served you well. Before digital capture became practical though, you never really had to take much responsibility for your color rendering beyond choosing the right film emulsion for the color temperature of the light. If you shot negative film, you could leave everything up to the lab. Even if you shot transparencies, the lab was mostly responsible for delivering credible color based on what the film manufacturer created with a batch of film.

Nowadays, that's not quite the case. Even if you have all your printing done at a lab, you still must assume at least part of the responsibility for the exact rendering of the color in the digital file. Most photographers approach this as a problem in color calibration or color management. This is consistent with a traditional film testing approach—you get a new batch of emulsion and you test it by taking photos through different colored CC filters: 025Y, 5M, 81A, and so forth. The idea is to find the particular bias of a certain emulsion and compensate for it. The concept behind digital color management is similar, although it's a bit more complex. The problem is that, with film, the basic tonal/color rendering is fixed at manufacture. The photographer/lab has only minor influence on the color rendering. Digital, on the other hand, is much more malleable. Hue, saturation, and value rendering can be manipulated to extremes. This kind of control is scary for the traditional photographer because the safety valve of fixed rendering is no longer present. The color can be anything you want it to be... so what *do* you want it to be?

Many digital photographers attempt to replace that safety valve with a rigorous ColorSync color management system. By shooting targets of color patches and using software to build detailed color description *tags* for digital files, the idea is to create color that is accurate to the original scene. Debates about exactly how to do this are ongoing—we examined one method using Adobe Camera Raw (ACR) in Chapter 1, "Digital Imaging Basics, Workflow, and Calibration." There are many other methods for creating accurate color. For some commercial photographers, this "accurate color" may be all they need because all creative color decisions will be made later on in the post-production phase of a project.

ColorSync

ColorSync is the underpinning of all color transforms in Photoshop—you cannot escape it! An ICC or ICM profile is a component of the ColorSync system adopted by the International Color Consortium, a group that includes Microsoft, Apple, Adobe, and just about all manufacturers of color equipment, like X-Rite and Epson. Any time you use or build a profile, you are using ColorSync.

Unfortunately, accurate color is often boring color. For many people, as professional photographer Jeff Schewe likes to say, "Reality sucks." We are conditioned to expect an idealized Hollywood version of color in photos. This is not necessarily super-saturated Kodachrome-Velvia color, but usually it is a departure from strict accuracy.

Zone System: Contrast and Tone

Ansel Adams, one of the most famous photographers of all time, began publishing his technical treaty on photography in 1948. Until this time, technical information about photography—full of log scales and exposure tables—was useable only by engineers and chemists. Ansel simplified all of this into a system of identifying and controlling 10 discrete tones that he labeled using Roman numerals I through X—he called this the Zone System.

When you mention the Zone System, certain people break out in a sweat. Most old timers, like myself, associate the Zone System with tedious technical exercises and tests, and it's all so dry. Didn't we leave all that behind in high school science labs? Bear with me here. The following discussion is fairly technical, but I promise to relate this to color correction for people photography in a minute.

Photoshop has a wealth of tools for manipulating color; however, before you can begin to fix color problems, you should understand what we are trying to achieve in producing a two-dimensional representation of reality on a printed piece of paper. The real challenge in reproduction is how you compress the vast dynamic range of visual reality into the limited range of ink on white paper. If you simply map all the tones inward in a linear fashion, you will end up with an image that looks very gray. Typically, photographers try to compress tones at the highlights and shadows and separate tones in the midrange to create something that approximates how the human visual system treats local contrast in areas of interest.

The typical human observer can see approximately 100 to 150 tones, or steps of value change, simultaneously. This is one of the reasons that 256 steps of tone in an 8-bit grayscale image are more than enough to create the impression of continuous tone. Ansel Adams created the Zone System of 10 steps as a way to simplify the classification of observable tones for reproduction purposes, and we can use this system today with even more precision.

Table 3.1 gives the 8-bit values for zones of 10 percent value change in Adobe RGB color space. In this table, L is lightness (the L in Lab), 0 is black, and 100 is white. Figure 3.1 demonstrates these values visually.

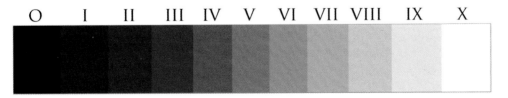

Figure 3.1 A Lab Zone System

Table 3.1 Zone System Values in Adobe RGB

Zone	RGB value	Lab value
Zone 0	0, 0, 0	L=0
Zone I	33, 33,33	L=10
Zone II	51, 51, 51	L=20
Zone III	72, 72, 72	L=30
Zone IV	94, 94, 94	L=40
Zone V	118, 118, 118	L=50
Zone VI	143, 143, 143	L=60
Zone VII	169, 169, 169	L=70
Zone VIII	197, 197, 197	L=80
Zone IX	225, 225, 225	L=90
Zone X	255, 255, 255	L=100

You can see that there are actually 11 zones in this digital zone scale. This is necessary in order to place Zone V at the midpoint (L=50 in Lab) mathematically. The traditional Zone System uses Zone I as black but the basic idea is the same.

Differentiating Values in Print

It is extremely difficult to predict exactly how well values will differentiate in print. The accompanying graphic shows a series of step wedges that divide a gray ramp from black to white into progressively smaller "steps." The red arrow identifies the midpoint. The wider-spaced tick marks show divisions for the 11 steps of the digital Zone System. The 20 steps of gray above that are one-half zone steps. The narrow-spaced tick marks show the division points of the 40 gray steps directly below the marks. Beneath the 40 steps, there is a smooth ramp from black to white, and beneath that there is a 60-step ramp.

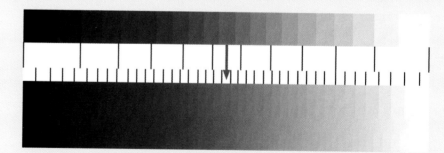

Can you see the "steps" in the 60-step ramp? These steps are represented by a change of five levels in RGB. Chances are that you will be able to see finer steps in values lighter than middle gray, and you will have a hard time seeing steps below Zone II in even the 40-step ramp. This same file printed on an Epson R2400 with Enhanced Matte paper shows clear value changes in the 60-step ramp down through Zone I.

With little effort, most people can clearly see a difference in one-half zone of value change in shadow values, Zone 0 through Zone II (roughly 15 RGB levels between values) if tones are right next to each other. It becomes harder to see finer differences in shadow values darker than Zone I. This impacts how you might approach contrast and brightness correction in an image. This has to do with the way the human visual system focuses on changes in value at the midrange over either extreme. Visually, the change from Zone V to Zone VI seems more noticeable than the change from Zone I to Zone II.

Neutral Color: Using Balanced Numbers

Being able to see differences in five levels between steps of tone near neutral does not mean that humans are particularly good judges of neutrality. This poses certain problems when we try to adjust colors visually. The human visual system adjusts dynamically to the color temperature of a given light source. This gives us the ability to evaluate colors independently from the color of the light illuminating those colors. This is called color constancy. Basically, it means that white looks white even if it's illuminated by yellow tungsten lighting.

The downside of this phenomenon is that the longer we look at something that is close to neutral, the more neutral it starts to look—we tend to compensate for color casts. Sometimes we can see that there is some kind of color cast, but we may not know precisely what to do to correct for it if we must rely only on our visual system.

This is where numbers come to the rescue. The Info panel and the Eyedropper tool can help tremendously when you are evaluating and correcting colors. If you can neutralize highlights, shadows, and midtones that should be neutral, all other colors will fall into place. In an RGB image, a neutral gray color is always represented by equal RGB values (R=G=B).

Look at Figure 3.2. Medium gray, white, and black squares are stacked into each other. This image has maximum local contrast and maximum neutrality... or does it?

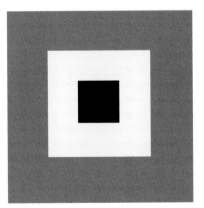

Figure 3.2
This image appears to have neutral tonality through black and white.

Now turn the page and check out this image again, in Figure 3.3.

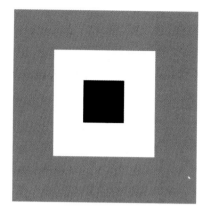

Figure 3.3
These values are actually neutral. Compare them to the version in Figure 3.2.

You may, or may not, have noticed that the squares have shifted somewhat and that now they are, in fact, more neutral (or at least a slightly different hue). Did you notice that the white square is brighter? How about the black square? Without something to compare them to, the previous squares looked neutral. Yet, if you measure the numbers for the gray, white, and black squares, you could clearly evaluate the color cast in the previous image, as the numbers for Figure 3.2 (listed in Table 3.2) show.

Table 3.2 RGB Values for Figure 3.2

Gray =		White =		Black =	
	R: 120		R: 245		R: 0
	G: 125		G: 245		G: 10
	B: 132		B: 250		B: 15

The lesson here is to avoid placing too much trust in your eyes when you're making critical color judgments. You should keep the Info panel visible and get in the habit of checking the numbers.

The discolored band running through the middle of the squares in Figure 3.4 shows the tones of the original squares next to the neutral values of the current image. When the tones are next to each other, you can easily see how far from white and neutral gray they are. In order to have maximum range in your prints, you must be careful to set white and black points appropriately. In a more complicated image, the white and black points might not be so obvious. Always check the numbers and adjust so that neutral values are all equal in the RGB channels.

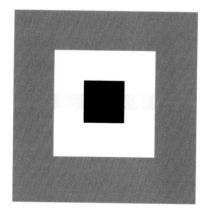

Figure 3.4
A discolored band contrasts with the neutral gray and white.

When choosing values for white and black points in an image, be aware of the textural limits you may want to enforce. The traditional Zone System sets Zone III as the darkest value that will show texture and Zone VIII as the lightest textured value. The digital Zone System places those limits in Adobe RGB at a level of 51 for dark and 197 for white. Absolute black should still be placed at 0, and spectral highlights should still come to 255. These rules are not iron clad, and stretching the range from a dark value of 15 to a light value of 245 could be more appropriate in many cases. Many of Ansel Adams' early prints look rather dark and somber because of a rather rigid insistence on textured high values of Zone VIII. Later in his career, he let tones go all the way to Zone X or paper white, and these prints have a lot more life in them.

Color images have other challenges besides setting white and black points; however, it is interesting to note that as a tone approaches black or white, it gets more neutral numerically (R=G=B). A very dark shadow in a region of green will always measure more neutral as it gets darker. By neutralizing shadows and highlights, you frequently can eliminate color casts automatically. I'll show you a practical application of setting white and black points in color correction in the following pages.

Curves: The Basic Color and Tone Tool

The primary tool for color and tone manipulation in Photoshop is the Curves adjustment. You open the Curves dialog by choosing Image > Adjustments > Curves. You can apply the adjustment directly to the image, but it is almost always better to use an adjustment layer. This allows for nondestructive changes and more flexibility during the editing process. To create a Curves adjustment layer, click the Curves icon in the Adjustments panel or click the Adjustment Layer icon at the bottom of the Layers panel and select Curves from the resulting menu (Figure 3.5).

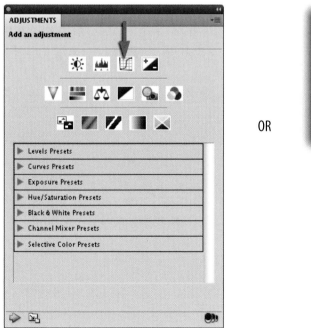

OR

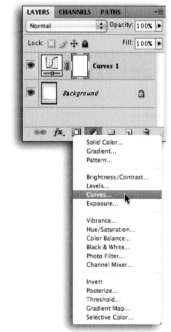

Figure 3.5 Creating a Curves adjustment

The Curves adjustment (Figure 3.6) is an *xy* plot of input to output values—input values plot along the bottom and output values plot along the left edge. The diagonal line represents the relationship between input and output. This perfect diagonal means that there is no change (that is, *x* equals *y*), and output values are the same as input values. The gradient along the bottom and the left edge indicates the progression of values from light to dark as they are mapped to the line.

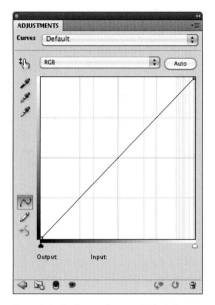

Figure 3.6 The Curves adjustment in the Adjustments panel

The default arrangement of this gradient for RGB files represents "light" values progressing from black (no light) at the left to white (maximum light) at the right. CMYK files default to the opposite with white (representing paper) at the left and black (representing maximum ink density) at the right. This can be changed by selecting Curves Display Options from the Adjustments panel options flyaway at the upper right of the panel. We will use the RGB default arrangement (black at the left) in this book.

You can choose a finer grid by Option/Alt+clicking the grid to toggle between fine and coarse views. The input and output values for any point that the cursor is over will be shown below the curve.

The Channel drop-down at the top of the panel allows you to affect all channels or individual channels depending on what you select. I will confine myself here to examining the contrast and tonal effects of the curve so I will only look at the composite (RGB) channel.

Contrast Control: The Basic Curve Shapes

In the next few figures, several different curves are applied to a black-and-white image, and a 10-step zone scale is placed at the bottom of the curve in each to help you visualize the different effects of various curve shapes. The straight diagonal line in Figure 3.7 provides an undistorted linear gray zone scale—there is no change in tone or contrast.

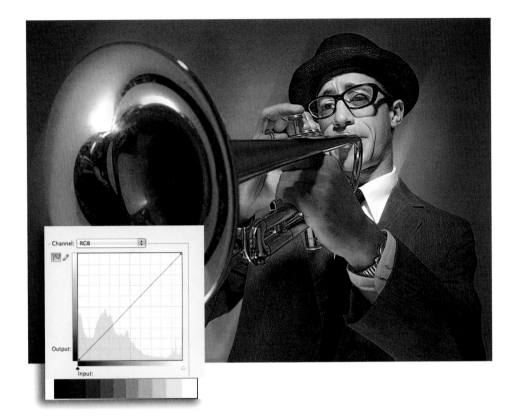

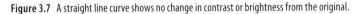

Figure 3.7 A straight line curve shows no change in contrast or brightness from the original.

Click and drag the endpoints inward along the edge of the grid and you will *clip* the light and dark ends of the scale. This results in more contrast—the change from black to white happens more rapidly (Figure 3.8). You can see the Zone IX value has merged with the Zone X value. The same thing has happened at the other end of the scale. The midtone values have more *separation*, a more obvious change from one value to the next. The more vertical the line, the more contrast you will have. When your image has no tones below Zone III or above Zone VIII, you can greatly expand the range by forcing the Zone III value to Zone I and the Zone VIII value to Zone X, mapping the darkest point in the image to black and the lightest point to white.

To achieve the opposite effect, click and drag the endpoints in the other direction, down and up along the right and left edges of the grid. White and black are suppressed to light gray and dark gray. The whole scale becomes grayer with less noticeable change from one tone to the next. Here you can see that the more horizontal the line is, the less contrast there will be (Figure 3.9). This is one reason images with less contrast are called *flat*. This compression or expansion of tone is how we manipulate the color and contrast of our images.

So far, we've only looked at straight line "shapes" for the curve. Things get more interesting when you place extra points on the curve.

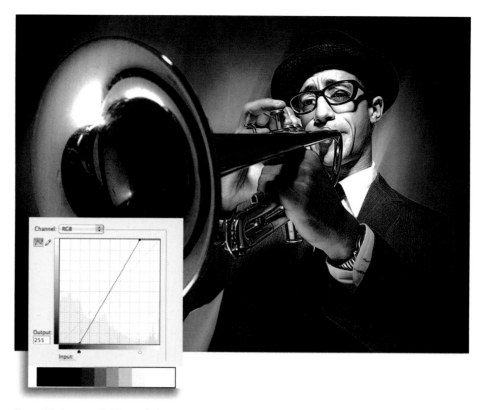

Figure 3.8   A more vertical line results in more contrast.

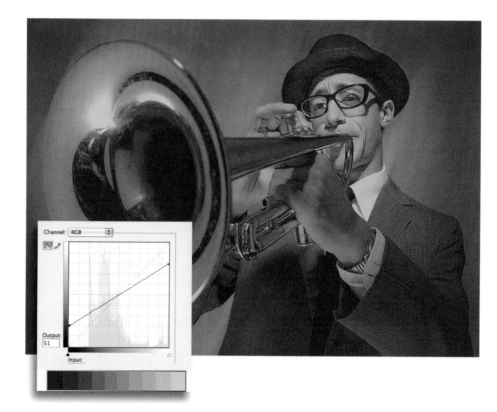

Figure 3.9   A more horizontal line results in less contrast.

Figure 3.10 shows the classic S-curve that is considered a contrast enhancing shape. By leaving the endpoints alone and placing two additional points on the curve, you can twist the center portion of the line (highlighted in pink) into a steeper incline and increase the contrast in the midtones. You can see this effect quite prominently in the zone scale at the bottom.

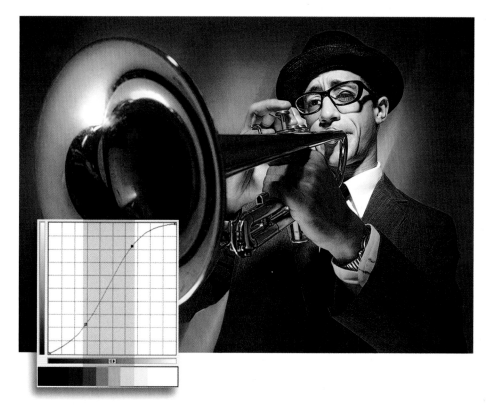

Figure 3.10 The classic S-curve has more contrast in the midtones but less at either extreme.

We've avoided clipping the highlights and shadows, but by adding contrast to the middle, we've reduced contrast at the ends. It is important to note that this shape can have a deleterious effect on detail in the shadows and highlights. In other words, there is no free lunch! If you increase contrast somewhere, you will decrease it somewhere else.

Most of the time we are more concerned with detail in the midtones, but not always.

The curve shape in Figure 3.11 shows a lower contrast in the midtones but more contrast and separation of tones in the highlights and shadows. Very often, we have to adjust curves to steepen the line at areas where we want more tonal variation and allow other areas with little inherent detail to compress.

The curve shape in Figure 3.12 is characteristic of a brightness-enhancing move. All of the points, save the endpoints, have moved up. The upper half of the tonal scale has compressed, and the lower half has been expanded. The line is steeper in the low end and flatter at the high end. Typically, images that are too dark need to have more details brought out in the shadows. The high end of a dark image may be relatively unpopulated with tones, so the compression of high values won't be noticed.

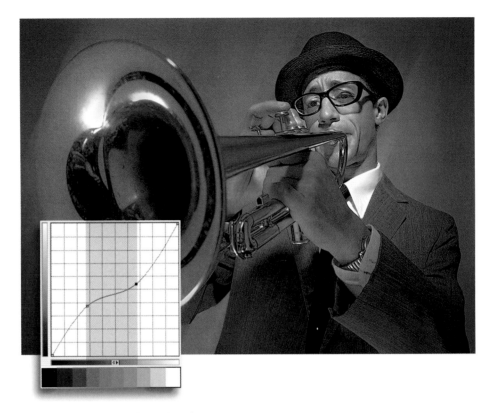

Figure 3.11 A reverse S-curve flattens the midtones.

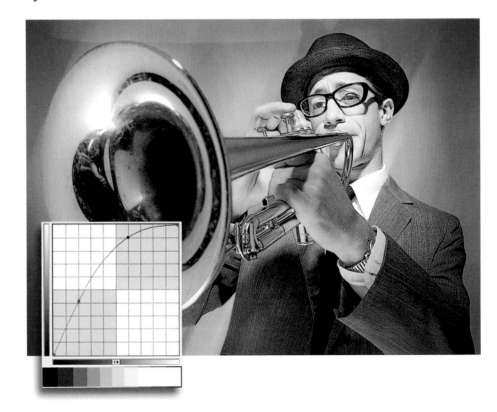

Figure 3.12 A tall bulge pushes values up, resulting in a lighter image

The exact opposite would be true of a light image. If you could get more detail and contrast in the high values, you wouldn't care if the few dark tones compressed together. If Figure 3.12 were reversed and all the points were lowered, you would have a very flat section at the lower part of the line and a steeper section at the top.

The real power of curves is that you can place points of interest and position them precisely to hit desired values and the rest of the values in the image move smoothly to accommodate the new values. Keep these curve shapes in mind as you work the values in your images. Try to work more steepness into areas where you need contrast.

Keep Saturation in Mind

So far, we've been looking at monochrome images because we've been concentrating on tone and contrast. When we start including color, we have to be careful with contrast-enhancing curves because they almost always increase saturation as well. If you need to increase contrast without increasing saturation, you can use RGB curves in an adjustment layer and change the layer blending mode to Luminosity.

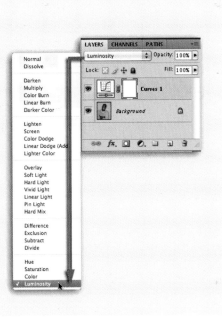

Info Panel: Reading Basic Numbers

Now you need to set up so that you can read numbers properly. Select the Eyedropper and set the options in the Tool Options bar to a Sample Size of 11 by 11 Average (Figure 3.13). This means the reading given in the Info panel will be the average of an 11 by 11 pixel area under the cursor, minimizing the effect of random noise on the reading. You can use the RGB and CMYK numbers as guides to help you evaluate color more consistently. You will learn more about *specific* color numbers later—for now we're just concerned with white, black, and neutral values.

Before going any further, you need to look at the Info panel. Make sure the Info panel is open (by choosing Window > Info), and then select Panel Options from the drop-down menu (accessed from the triangle in the upper right of the panel, as in Figure 3.13). Set the options as shown, with First Color Readout set to Actual Color and Second Color Readout set to CMYK. When you move the cursor into the image, the Info panel will display the numerical values for the color under the cursor.

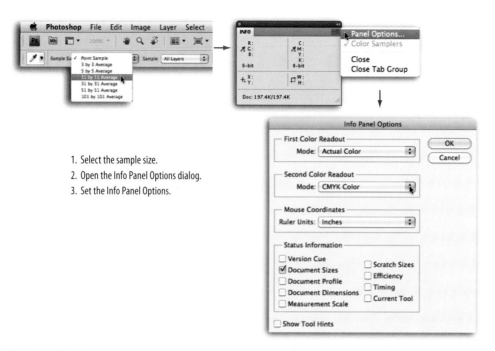

1. Select the sample size.
2. Open the Info Panel Options dialog.
3. Set the Info Panel Options.

Figure 3.13 The Info panel and panel options

White/Black Point Correction

Now that you have a basic understanding of numbers, tonal values, and curve shapes, you can start to develop strategies for dealing with color correction. The first approach you need to master is identifying color values that need to be neutral (R=G=B). You can use points on a curve correction to force these values to be neutral. Once you've established the neutral values, any color cast in the image will usually be eliminated. Then you can concentrate on the actual color values for skin. The remainder of this chapter will deal with color correction of skin tones starting with a simple step-by-step tutorial in which black point and white point neutrals are identified and then ideal skin tone values are forced by using a Curves correction.

I'm going to work with a photo of my kids, Aaron and Erika (Figure 3.14). At first glance, it doesn't seem like there is a huge problem with this image, but let's check the white and black points to be sure. Make sure that the Info panel is open before you do anything else. You can place multiple sample points in the image using the Color Sampler tool (find it under the Eyedropper tool). When you do, it will be easy to watch the numbers change in more than one point as you modify the color using adjustment layers. You can make a good guess at the darkest point in the image—it has to be a shadow area—perhaps between the Erika's cheek and Aaron's chest. The white point is a bit different. When you pick a white point, you have to look for something other than a specular highlight or a reflection. Therefore, the hot glint off the cabinets behind the kids will not work. Most people would guess that the next lightest thing would be the white T-shirt showing at Erika's neck. Actually, this is wrong, too—it's not the lightest area and it's not even white! Let me show you a little trick to help you locate the lightest and darkest points in this image.

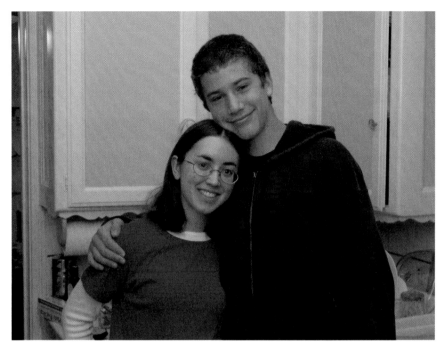

Figure 3.14 Aaron and Erika

You can use a temporary Threshold adjustment to locate the lightest and darkest points in the image. With the Color Sampler tool still selected, make a new Threshold adjustment layer by clicking the Threshold Adjustment icon panel in the Adjustments panel (Figure 3.15). Move the slider in the Threshold panel to the right to set the break point between black and white at a high value—that will locate the lightest points in the image by turning everything else black, as shown in Figure 3.16.

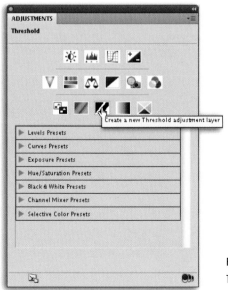

Figure 3.15
The Threshold layer

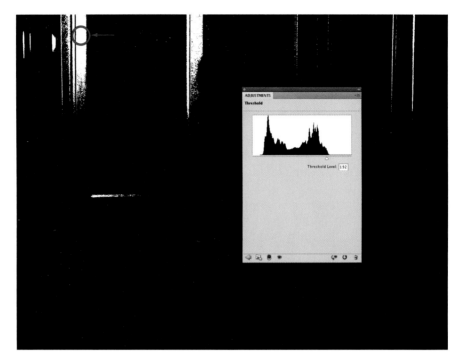

Figure 3.16 Identifying the lightest point (red circle)

Select the Color Sampler tool and click in the white area that represents the light part of the cabinets (shown circled in red in Figure 3.16). Do the same for the black point. Return to the Threshold Adjustments panel and move the slider to the left until only the small black shadows are visible. (Figure 3.17) Now, click with the Color Sampler tool to place a second sampler for the black point.

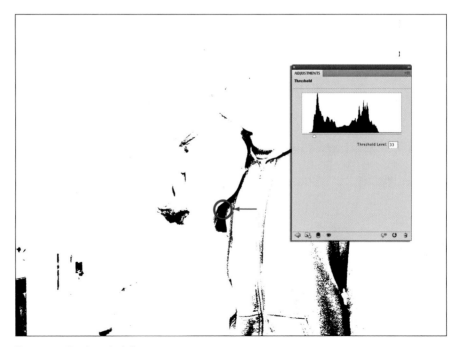

Figure 3.17 Identifying the darkest point

Now that you've identified and placed samplers for the white and black points in the image, you can discard the Threshold adjustment layer and begin color correcting. Drag the Threshold Adjustment thumbnail to the Trash icon at the bottom of the Layers panel or click the Trash icon in the Adjustments panel to discard it. The Color Samplers remain ready for use—their values appear at the bottom of the Info panel and are labeled #1 and #2. When you start making your corrections, there will be two columns of numbers for each Color Sampler, as shown in Figure 3.21. The column on the left represents the starting values. The column on the right represents the new values. Adjust for a black point value of 15-R, 15-G, 15-B and a white value of 245-R, 245-G, 245-B.

Notice the value for the white T-shirt, right now it is 190-R, 171-G, 170-B. The cabinet highlight is lighter at 211-R, 188-G, 186-B; this is obvious when you place the colors next to each other (Figure 3.18). The white T-shirt looks whiter because it is next to much darker colors. This is an important observation. Humans evaluate colors in the context in which they are presented. Optical illusions depend on this phenomenon, and one should always be on guard for misread color cues. The Threshold adjustment technique for locating black and white points should be a standard procedure for your color correction routine.

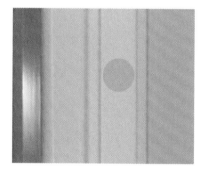

Figure 3.18 The darker "dot" is the color of the white T-shirt.

Now that you've found the cabinet to be lighter than the T-shirt and you know that the T-shirt should be white, you can assume that the cabinets are white as well. Start your color correction by making the cabinets white! Create a Curves adjustment layer by clicking the Adjustment Layer icon at the bottom of the Layers panel and selecting from the resulting menu. Your strategy for correcting this image will be to set black and white points in each channel and make sure that they are neutral. Then, sample various points for the skin tone and wiggle the curves for each channel so that you hit a good recipe of RGB/CMYK numbers for skin tone.

Adjusting the Numbers for the Color of Skin

You'll need the secondary color readout set to CMYK to properly evaluate the color of the skin tone. You get only one readout for the numbered Color Sampler points, and it is much harder to evaluate skin color with RGB numbers. (In CMYK, the relationship of CMY will be fairly consistent—but more about that later.) Make sure your Info panel has CMYK specified for the secondary color readout. A good skin tone value for a Caucasian will have the highest values almost equal in magenta and yellow, with yellow a little bit higher (more on this later). Cyan will be one-fourth to one-third of the high value for yellow. The dark and light point numbers will be near neutral in images that do not have a color cast even if they are part of a colored subject. Once you start making your corrections, there will be two columns of numbers for each Color Sampler, as shown in Figure 3.21. The column on the left represents the starting values. The column on the right represents the new values.

Start correcting by moving the endpoints in the curve for each channel—aim for a black of 15,15,15 and white of 245,245,245 (Figure 3.19). Set black first and then move to white. You may have to tweak the black endpoints after you work with the white—keep an eye on the Info panel. Do not be tempted to move the black point all the way to zero because there is no texture in the dark shadow. Anything darker than 15 will collapse into black when the image prints. Keep the dark point high enough that dark values that should be lighter than black will actually print that way. This will help to preserve shape in the black sweatshirt. The white cabinets should go to 245 but not higher to leave room for the specular highlight to the left—it will go all the way to 255 or paper white, and it should appear brighter.

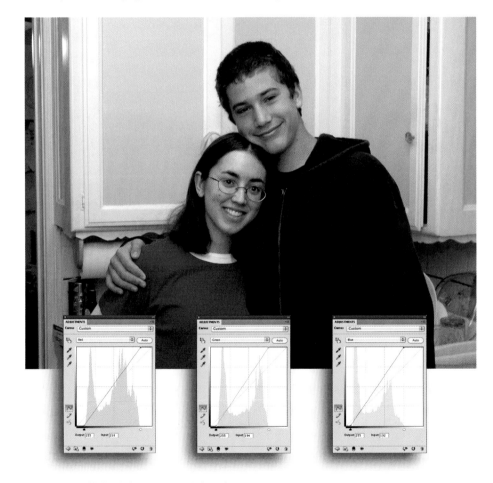

Figure 3.19 Set black and white points in each channel.

Note: These black and white point numbers serve only a general guide for RGB images that will be printed on desktop inkjet printers. Values for CMYK offset lithography might need to be even more conservative, depending on the image and the artistic intent. You can push values lower and higher if there is no texture or detail that you want to preserve in the shadows or highlights.

By setting white and black points, you expanded the range and put some contrast into the midtones; however, you still need to address the color of the skin. Here we are looking for CMYK numbers like those in Figure 3.20; these are within the range for medium skin tone for a Caucasian.

INFO		
R: 180/ 185	C: 25/ 17%	
G: 151/ 152	M: 41/ 40%	
B: 128/ 125	Y: 49/ 50%	
	K: 1/ 1%	
8-bit	8-bit	
X: 2.585	W:	
Y: 1.625	H:	
#1 R: 17/ 15	#2 R: 244/ 245	
G: 15/ 15	G: 244/ 245	
B: 15/ 15	B: 246/ 245	

Figure 3.20 These CMYK numbers are in a good range for Caucasian skin color.

You'll remember I told you that it is much harder to evaluate skin color with RGB numbers. Here's why. In CMYK, the relationship of CMY will be fairly consistent: Magenta and Yellow should be roughly equal, with Yellow usually a few points higher but typically, not more than 10 to 15 units higher. Cyan should be about one-fourth to one-third of the value for Magenta or Yellow; if it is too much higher, the skin will look too gray. Of course, there are all types of skin tone and even a considerable variety of correct numbers within the same subject. Highlight values will be smaller, and shadows will have more cyan relative to medium skin values. Different ethnicities also vary somewhat from these standards (more on this later). Use the CMY numbers as guides to indicate how you need to move the curve to correct the color.

Right now, the skin reads a little high in yellow (15 to 30 units higher than magenta in most areas of skin)—thus, the slight greenish cast. Select the Blue channel, click the finger icon in the Curves Adjustments panel, and click on Aaron's forehead to place a point on the curve in the *Blue* channel. Keep your cursor on his forehead while you use the arrow keys to adjust the channel. Start by moving the point *up* in the Blue channel. You can keep an eye on the RGB and CMYK values while you move the point with the arrow keys (Figure 3.21).

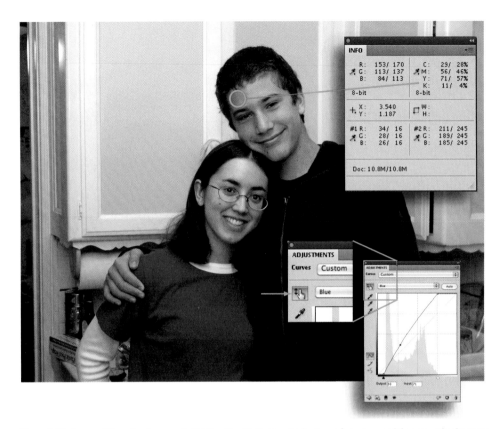

Figure 3.21 To correct the yellow/green cast, click the skin with the Target Adjustment finger icon, and then move the skin point up in the Blue channel with the arrow keys.

Remember that once you start making your corrections, there will be two columns of numbers for each Color Sampler, as shown in Figure 3.21. The column on the left represents the starting values. The column on the right represents the new values. The RGB and CMYK numbers at the top of the panel are at the location of the cursor. The #1 and #2 numbers represent the white and black point samplers.

Use the same strategy for the other channels: raise the values for red and blue and lower the values for green until you arrive at the desired values in the Info panel. Try to keep your neutrals (white and black) within a three-point spread. The CMYK values for the skin tone should put yellow within 10 to 15 points of Magenta with Cyan approximately one-fourth to one-third of the value for Yellow. Remember that to reduce cyan, you add red. To reduce yellow, add blue. To add magenta, reduce green. Try to keep your cursor in the image and use the arrow keys to move your points on the curve. Figure 3.22 shows the final color balance.

Once you get the values for skin to where you want them, you will probably have to reedit the values for the black and white points. Feel free to place additional points, by clicking on the curve near the endpoints to tweak the low and high values into shape without pushing the skin values around too far. If you go by the numbers, you will have a much easier time of zeroing in on the color you want. This image required extra points in the Blue channel and Red channel to neutralize the black sweatshirt without pushing the skintone out of range.

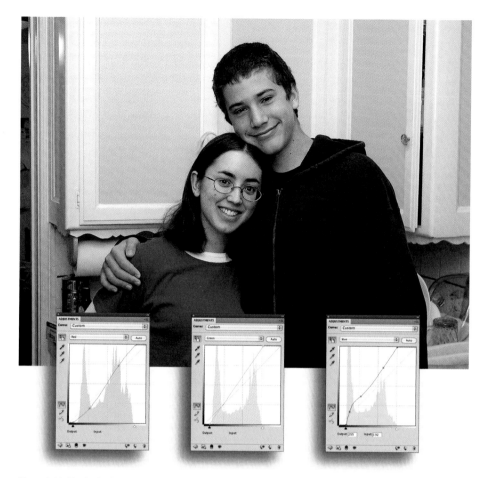

Figure 3.22 The final color balance

Opponent Colors

When working skin color in digital photography, you'll end up editing RGB numbers but looking at CMYK numbers. For many photographers, this is a bigger hurdle than it needs to be. RGB numbers work in "opposition" to CMYK values. To reduce cyan, you add red. To reduce yellow, you add blue. To add magenta, you reduce green. The Info panel contains a hint to help you determine opponent colors, as shown next.

If you read across the top, you will see that R is opposite C, G is opposite M, and B is opposite Y. You can see to the right that increasing red has reduced cyan and increasing blue has reduced yellow. The slight increase in green has served to keep magenta where it was even though the image got brighter overall.

INFO					
R:	184/ 218		C:	21/	9%
G:	140/ 187		M:	48/	27%
B:	115/ 156		Y:	56/	38%
			K:	1/	0%
8-bit			8-bit		
X:	3.747		W:		
Y:	1.147		H:		
#1 R:	35/ 15		#2 R:	210/ 245	
G:	27/ 16		G:	188/ 245	
B:	25/ 15		B:	185/ 245	

The image of Aaron and Erika represents a fairly easy correction. The image was originally a well-exposed camera JPEG. The color bias most likely was due to a standard color temperature setting in the camera, probably Daylight – 5000 K, used with a mix of indoor tungsten "warm" light. Warm colored walls, out of frame, might also have contributed to the overall yellow bias in the skin color. Many possible lighting scenarios can result in "off color" shots. Many times, even the best-calibrated color management systems can fail to deliver anything close to the ideal color for a particular image. (For more on calibration, take another look at Chapter 1.) The ideal color may not be the actual color of the original subject either.

Photoshop offers knowledgeable photographers a wealth of tools to shape the tones and colors of their photography in any way imaginable. Using the Info panel numbers as a guideline, you can fine-tune color and tone very quickly to get the best reproductions possible. Color correction can become a labor-intensive chore of trial and error when you don't understand basic color "numbers." Most of the time, you won't know if the color is the best it can be without at least referencing the color numbers as a point of departure.

However, color numbers are only a guide. Even when you use them, you still have to use your own eyes and judgment to arrive at the right color appearance for your needs. These guide numbers are the result of years of printing images and developing a cultural consensus for what constitutes good skin tone. Before departing from that consensus, you should know how to truly control the color to get what you want. If you know how to hit the numbers, you will know how to hit any color interpretation you want.

The Family of Man: Cultural and Psychological Issues

The subject of skin color is a fairly complicated one that you can only begin to comprehend here. The following images are presented with their corresponding Info panel numbers to illustrate some of the varieties of photographically acceptable skin tones in various cultures. It is interesting to note that in print the acceptable skin colors of different ethnicities are more similar in their CMY ratios than not.

The mother and daughter portrait in Figure 3.23 illustrates typical Anglo-Caucasian skin color values—magenta and yellow close with yellow slightly higher, and cyan at one-fourth to one-third the value of magenta/yellow. Children's skin tones are typically lighter and pinker (more magenta) than adults'. Still, you'll want to avoid having magenta be equal or higher than yellow except in cheeks and lips. Take several readings from the forehead, chin, shoulders, etc., to get a general idea of the color ratios rather than relying on a single point.

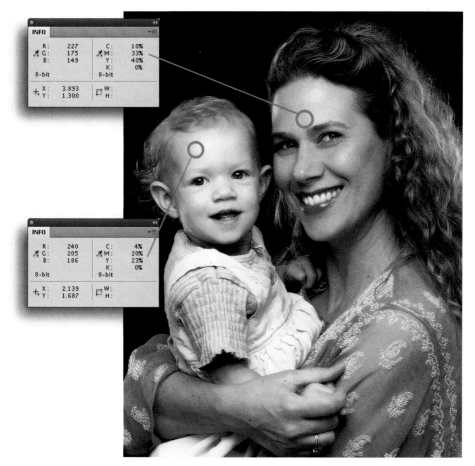

INFO	
R: 227	C: 10%
G: 175	M: 33%
B: 149	Y: 40%
	K: 0%
8-bit	8-bit
X: 3.893	W:
Y: 1.300	H:

INFO	
R: 240	C: 4%
G: 205	M: 20%
B: 186	Y: 23%
	K: 0%
8-bit	8-bit
X: 2.139	W:
Y: 1.687	H:

Figure 3.23 A mother and child with Caucasian skin: slightly higher Y and lower C

African American skin values usually look better with a little more magenta than you might use for Caucasian skin—especially if the skin tone is very dark. In Figure 3.24, the magenta is equal to yellow. This is about as much magenta as I would tolerate. In reality, skin values are all over the place, and it's common to find black skin that has a very yellow bias. While this is real, it usually is not desirable in print because it makes the skin look green. Darker skin will have a higher percentage of cyan—this is what adds weight and shape to the skin tone. As the skin gets darker, I tend to raise the level of magenta in the ratios to balance out the yellow-cyan "greenness." To raise the magenta values (you guessed it), subtract green. Really dark charcoal-colored skin can have an almost blue cast—but again, this is undesirable in print most of the time.

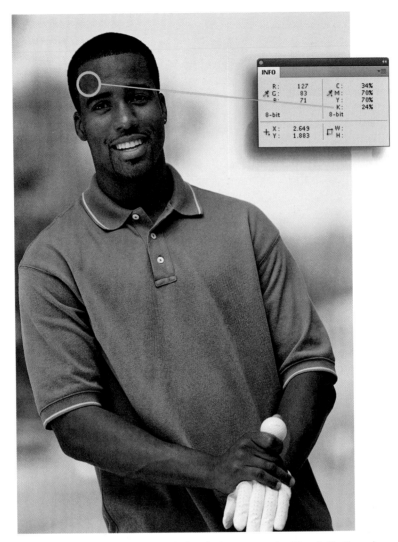

Figure 3.24 This African American man's skin has a higher magenta value. (Photo by Ken Chernus)

Asian skin is more yellow; the trick is to not let it get too yellow. In Figure 3.25, the arm reads just slightly more yellow than average. For the most part, you are better off keeping the skin values close to the normal Caucasian color.

Whenever a subject is very close to grass, you'll need to be careful of an overly yellow bias in the skin color. You can see that quite prominently in Figure 3.26. Both the highlight and shadow values of the face show over 30 units more yellow than magenta. The bias is also polluting the red hair color. The corrected version (Figure 3.27) shows that by paying attention to appropriate numbers for the peaches-and-cream complexion of this cute little girl, you can clean up the color considerably.

Overly red skin tone is a common problem with digital capture, especially where the skin tone is a little on the red side anyway. As a result, the baby on the left in Figure 3.28 appears to be beet red. Everywhere in the skin, the values with magenta are noticeably higher than yellow. If you want a baby that doesn't look sunburned, you will have to reverse that.

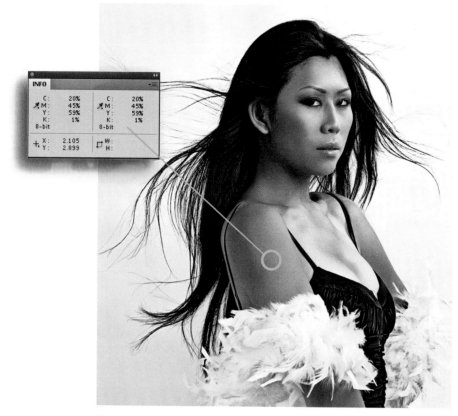

Figure 3.25 Asian skin color should not be allowed to go too yellow. (Photo by Paul Blieden)

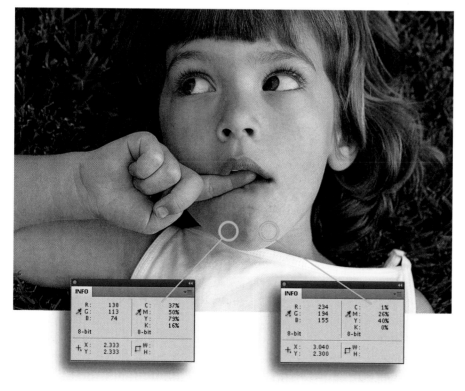

Figure 3.26 The original image, by Erin Manning, has a decided yellow bias.

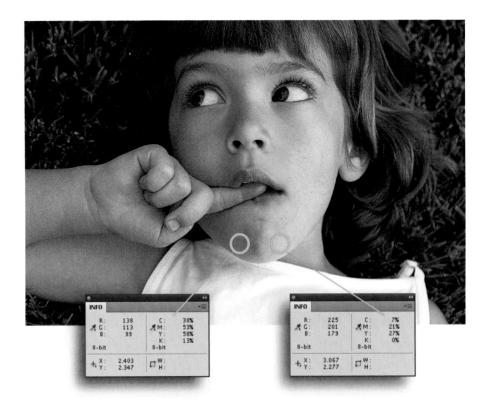

Figure 3.27 The corrected version has truer colors in the skin and hair.

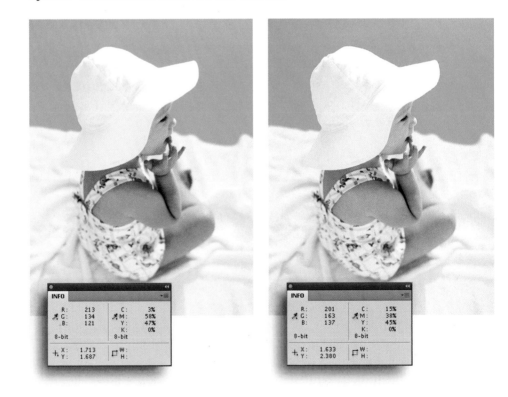

Figure 3.28 Correct the baby's overly red skin tone by balancing the white numbers. (Photo by Anthony Nex)

In the image on the left, the baby's skin is very red. The shadow areas in the hand near the face are practically glowing. Note that the Info panel shows too much Magenta. Balancing the white numbers to neutral in the hat helps reduce the red everywhere else, resulting in more natural skin tones. A few more points on the curve to add more green in the shadow values of the skin produces the image on the right in Figure 3.28.

Cultural and Personal Color Bias

In reality, there is no ideal skin tone—skin color is all over the place. There is considerable variation in different ethnicities, ages, and skin conditions—not to mention makeup! While all this variation exists in the real world, we tend to tolerate much less variety in print for various reasons. One reason is cultural norms, and this can get you into trouble if you're not aware of it. I can illustrate this with a couple of stories that actually happened to me.

It happened when I was working on a catalog that was going to be printed in Hong Kong. There were numerous shots of models interacting with the product, and we were shooting digital. This was in the early days of digital production photography. Printers were just trying to get up to speed with the whole process, and clients were not completely comfortable with things yet. Our particular client decided to use a printer in Hong Kong to save money. The client had done a few packaging projects with them but never a full catalog and never with human subjects.

Well… we tested, calibrated, and color managed the heck out of that shoot. We supplied inkjet cross-rendered press simulations for the SWOP standard separations (even though the printer was in Hong Kong, they assured us that they printed to SWOP, a standard for U.S. web presses). The client loved it and signed off on everything. We sent everything off to China.

The Chinese printing representative called back and said there were a lot of problems with the color—they had to color correct all the people. The client agreed to pay for additional color correction and was mad at me (it somehow always ends up being the photographer's fault). Finally, the matchprints/press proofs started coming back and they were horrible—all the people shots were pale, washed out, and kind of yellow. Hmmm…

The client convinced the printing rep to come to the United States for a meeting. We showed her our nice, healthy, saturated skin-toned proof prints, whereupon she said, "See… skin look dead!"

Apparently, in China, when skin is rendered in a way most Americans would consider healthy, it means the opposite. The Chinese preference is for pale, ivory-colored skin tones. Any red in the skin color is considered bad. If you look in Chinese magazines, you can see this preference in operation. There are regional preferences and different cultural preferences (Peking Opera posters can have very light pink makeup for certain characters). In the end, it was almost impossible to explain that American clients usually preferred a "California tan" look in the skin tone.

My second story concerns a job I did in this country for the Belly Dance Twins, Neena and Veena. I did some promotional photography for these two gorgeous Indian dancers—several of the shots were taken with traditional Indian costumes that were quite colorful. My first prints looked like the image on the top-left of Figure 3.29.

The Twins were not happy—they thought the skin tone was too dark. To me it looked authentically Indian, which I thought was the whole point. I was not aware of the cultural issue here: Dark skin is associated with the lower caste—pale skin color is more desirable. (In Hindu religious iconography, the color of the various female Devas is almost always very pale—in some cases, blue-white.) Everything I did for them had to be revised with a lighter color.

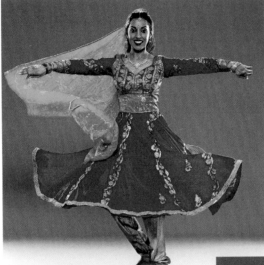

This image of the Indian dancer was fairly true to life, but that wasn't what she wanted.

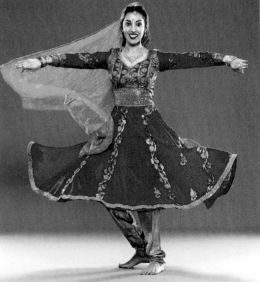

In Hindu religious iconography, the color of the various female Devas is almost always very pale—in some cases, blue-white.

Figure 3.29 You have to be prepared to edit the color to satisfy the cultural, personal, or psychological needs of your clients.

In conclusion, getting the right skin color is far from trivial. Simply calibrating your capture system is not going to guarantee that you will get an ideal skin tone. You have to be prepared to edit the color to satisfy the cultural, personal, or psychological needs of your clients or yourself. There are many creative departures possible as well. You need to develop the color "chops" necessary to get the color you want consistently, and a thorough grounding in Photoshop color editing is an absolute must.

Remember that the color of skin that is acceptable in reproduction is most often a departure from reality. The numbers supplied here are good guidelines, but they are only *guidelines*. Don't forget that you might need to deviate from these values.

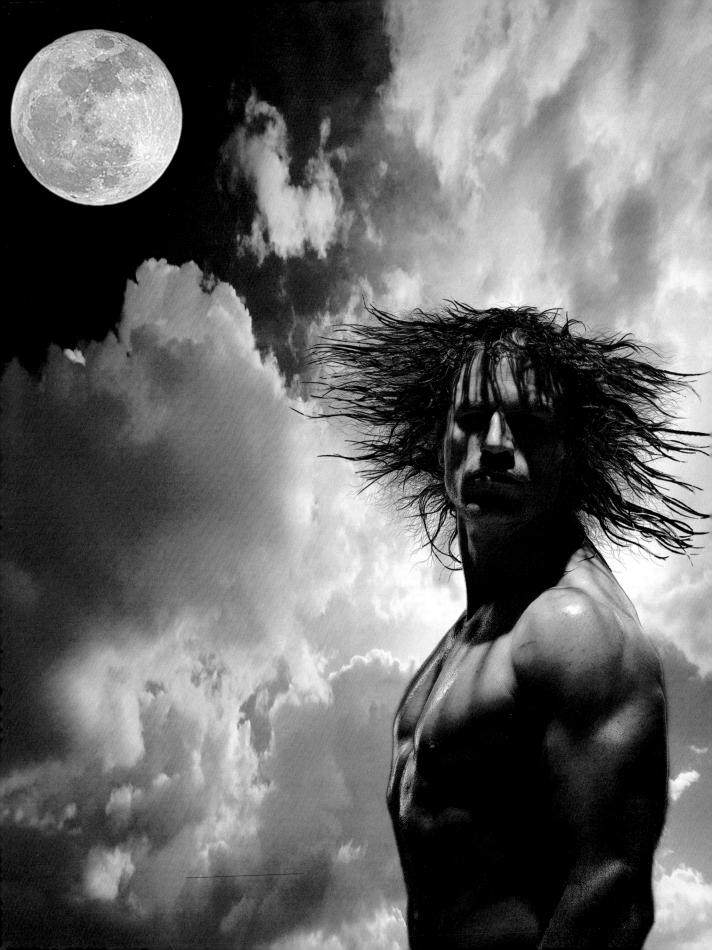

Tone and Contrast: Color and B+W

The B+W aesthetic is familiar and often desirable for photographing people. Unfortunately, with digital photographs, the process of converting from color to B+W is often treated as a trivial mode change followed with contrast-enhancing curves. Photoshop provides many different methods for creating monochrome images. After you learn the types of controls available, a whole new creative frontier opens for you to explore. Photoshop can truly become the ultimate B+W darkroom, allowing the digital photographer to go well beyond the Ansel Adams Zone System.

We are going to examine a wide range of B+W options and also see how to apply B+W tonality to color images.

4

Chapter Contents
Converting to B+W
Split Channels: Layer Blending
Luminosity Blending
Hue/Saturation Toning Effects
The Power of B+W

Converting to B+W

Using the image shown in Figure 4.1, let's explore the process of converting to black and white. Let's start by examining some different approaches to creating a black-and-white (B+W) rendition of this RGB color image.

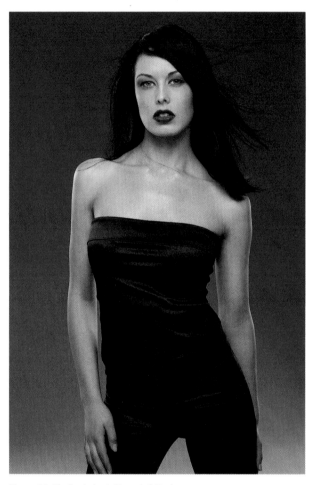

Figure 4.1 The lovely Jamie Bjorge in full color

The first and obvious approach is to choose Image > Mode > Grayscale and use the default conversion to arrive at a grayscale version. Although this is certainly not a horrible approach, it doesn't really offer much control over the way colors are rendered into gray values. To start to understand what's happening, you need to realize that RGB image files are made up of three different grayscale images—one for each color channel. When these three grayscale versions are combined in RGB, the final image contains the full range of color as defined by the additive color space of the particular variety of RGB—be it sRGB, Adobe RGB, ColorMatch, or whatever.

Examining the channels individually and noting their differences in this image can be especially instructive. To do so, go to the Channels panel and click the Eye icon for each of the channels (Figure 4.2).

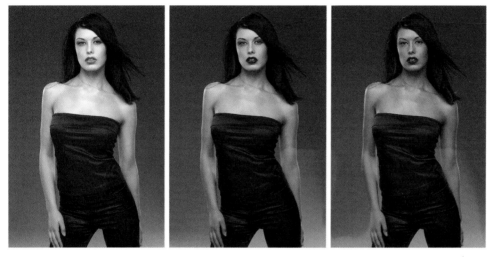

Red channel   Green channel   Blue channel

Figure 4.2 Note the differences among the channel images.

The Channel Mixer

The default grayscale conversion utilizes a formula for blending the different gray-scale channels into a single composite version. A convenient method for controlling this process is to use the Channel Mixer to create the grayscale blend. Go to the Adjustments panel and click the Channel Mixer icon (Figure 4.3). Once the Channel Mixer is open, select Black & White With Orange Filter from the Presets drop-down. The Output Channel menu at the top of the dialog will change to gray, and you'll see a B+W version that represents 50 percent of the Red and 50 percent of the Green channels of the image. Move the sliders so you can see that the default conversion (Image > Mode > Grayscale) is basically identical to a channel mix of 30 Red, 60 Green, and 10 Blue (Figure 4.4), resulting in a "standard" gray rendering.

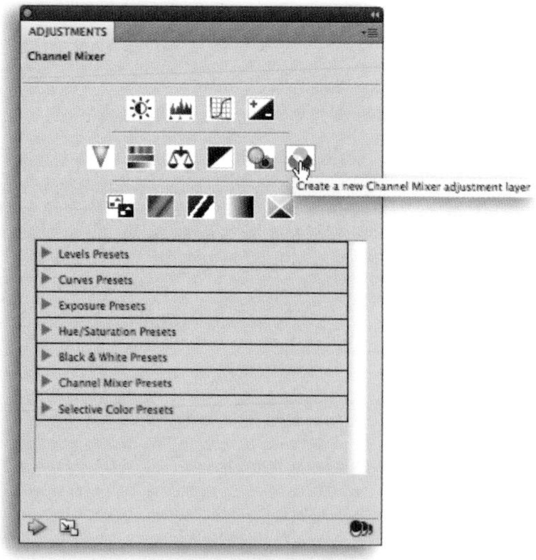

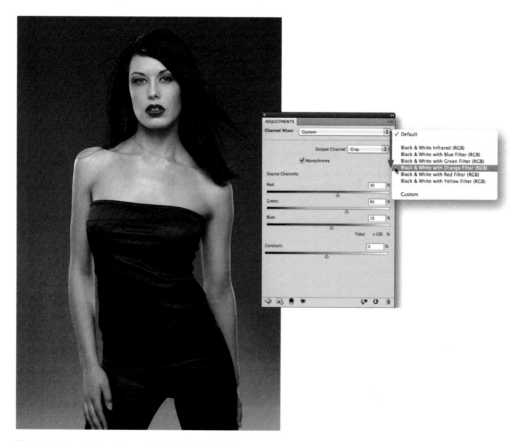

Figure 4.3 Make a Channel Mixer adjustment layer
by clicking the Channel Mixer icon in the Adjustments panel.

Figure 4.4 These slider positions mimic the look of Plus-X film.

The different percentages in the sliders add up to 100; this preserves the overall luminosity of the image. You can try other percentage mixes, and as long as you maintain the 100 percent total, you should arrive at a fairly reasonable rendition.

> **Note:** You can think of the different combinations of channel percentages as somewhat equivalent to traditional B+W film shot with colored filters. As you've seen, a 50 percent Red/50 percent Green mix would be similar to using an orange filter, and a 100 percent Red mix would be similar to using a red filter.

You might prefer the version in Figure 4.5 (a 70/30 blend between red and green) because it has a slightly lighter skin tone that some find more attractive for a woman.

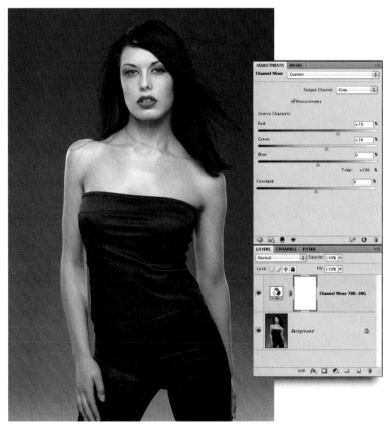

Figure 4.5 A higher percentage of Red will result in a lighter skin value.

If, on the other hand, you are not looking for reasonable but instead want dramatic, you might want to deviate from the normal approach (with positive values that add up to 100) and do something similar to Figure 4.6.

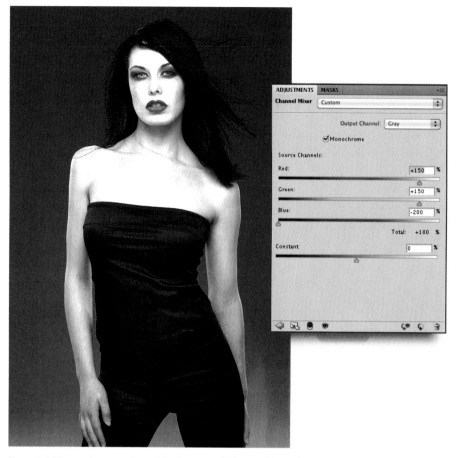

Figure 4.6 These settings cause the model to have very pale "vampire" skin and dramatic eyes.

Yes, you can subtract channels in the Channel Mixer. Obviously, this approach will yield much different results than using color filters with B+W film.

Why stop there? Now that you realize all rules are to made to be broken, let's really try to "break" this image (Figure 4.7). You can easily see that the Channel Mixer gives you the same control (and then some) that traditional B+W photographers have when using color filters and specialty films.

Note: The Channel Mixer method works on RGB images by duplicating the "mix" into all the channels; when you flatten the image, you will end up with a monochrome RGB file. If you need an actual single-channel grayscale document, you must convert to grayscale using the Image menu (Image > Mode > Grayscale).

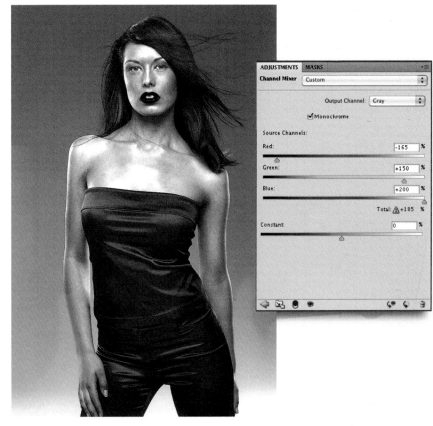

Figure 4.7 In this version, the skin has an almost metallic sheen.

Split Channels: Layer Blending

There is another method of blending channels that offers additional controls. Starting with the RGB original, go to the Channels panel, click the Options triangle in the upper-right corner to get the drop-down menu, and select Split Channels (Figure 4.8).

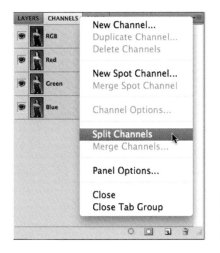

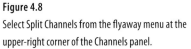

Figure 4.8

Select Split Channels from the flyaway menu at the upper-right corner of the Channels panel.

This will "split" the RGB file into three separate grayscale files and name them according to the channels from which they originated. You can drag one file on top of the other to create a layer stack that you can use to blend the channels (Figure 4.9). You can re-create the 70/30 Channel Mixer version by dragging the green document on top of the red document using the Move tool—click and drag from inside the one document window to the other while holding down the Shift key to maintain layer registration.

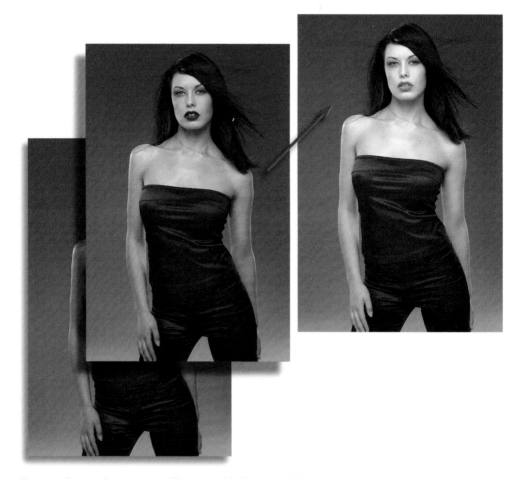

Figure 4.9 To ensure that two images will be registered, hold down the Shift key when dragging one document onto another.

Note: If you have your windows arranged as Tabs in the Photoshop interface, you need to drag from inside the document window to the tab for the other document. Remember to hold down the Shift key while you do this to ensure that the "layers" are registered.

Change the Layer Opacity to 30 percent. You can duplicate any Channel Mixer blending effect that uses positive slider values (that add up to 100) by stacking the channels in layers and adjusting the relative opacities. Place all three channel documents into a layer stack and work your way up from the bottom. Adjust the opacity of the first layer first by temporarily turning off the visibility of the top layer (click the Eye icon to the left of the thumbnail). Once the first layer is adjusted, turn on the visibility of the top layer and adjust the opacity against the other two. You'll need to experiment with the layer order to arrive at the best combination. This makes it less convenient than the Channel Mixer method for simple blends.

To really appreciate the power of stacked layers, you need to take advantage of the additional controls available in the form of layer masks and blending options. You can start by making a layer mask for the Green layer. Make sure visibility for the top Blue layer is turned off. Now, press and hold the Option/Alt key and then click the Layer Mask icon at the bottom of the Layers panel; this will create a Black layer mask and hide the Green layer. Now, you should see only the bottom Red *background* layer (Figure 4.10). Immediately after the layer mask is created, the mask is selected. A double outline should appear around the black mask thumbnail. Check to make sure it's there. Now when you paint the mask with white, you will reveal the contents of the Green layer. By doing this, you can selectively paint parts of the Green channel on top of the Red channel.

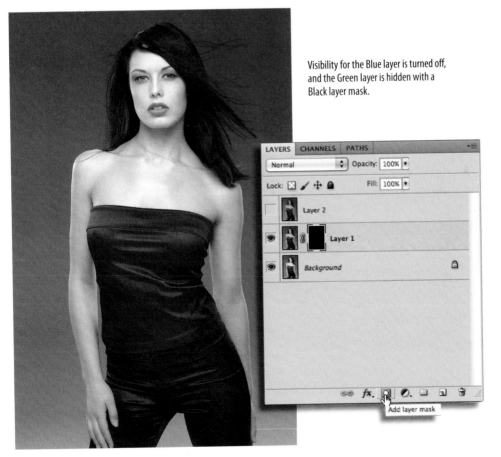

Visibility for the Blue layer is turned off, and the Green layer is hidden with a Black layer mask.

Figure 4.10 Only the Red background layer is visible.

The final stacked version (Figure 4.11) uses the Red channel as the base primarily for the lighter skin. The eyes were painted in the Green layer, creating the darker eye shadow and lightening the pupils (the model had green eyes). The Blue layer was used to create subtle shading on her arms, shoulders, and cheeks. The darker skin color was painted over the edges of the figure. (To do this, use a lower opacity for the brush and build up your strokes slowly.) The darker lips of the Blue layer were also painted. The result is dramatic but very natural. The image can be further refined with Curves if necessary; however, simply combining the best parts of each channel frequently will do the job. Save the layered version so you can revise it later if needed. When you are done, you can flatten the file by going to the Layers menu and selecting Flatten Image or by selecting Flatten Image from the Layers flyaway menu. You will then have a single layer grayscale document.

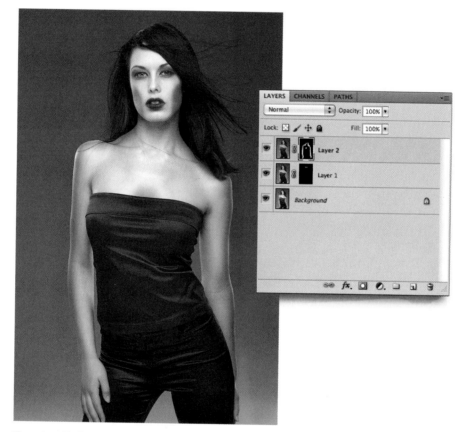

Figure 4.11 The final B+W with enhanced tones

Figure 4.12 is another good example of classic B+W. I originally shot this image of my daughter in color using a Canon EOS-1DS Mark II. I converted it to B+W using the methods just described. To create the feel of an old Hollywood studio portrait, I enhanced the lighting quality with additional contrast from Blue and Green channel documents layered on top of the Red channel document as was shown in the previous image.

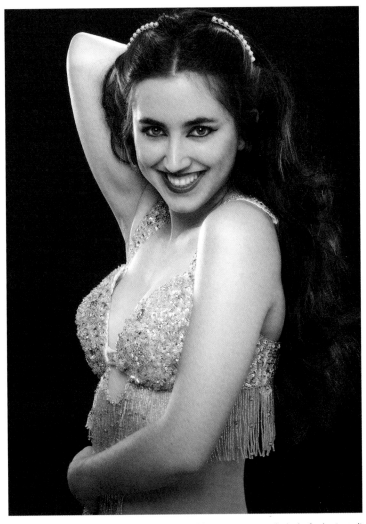

Figure 4.12 The quality of the lighting plus channel layering re-creates the look of a classic studio portrait from a bygone era.

Luminosity Blending

Something very interesting will happen when you drag the new B+W version (the one shown in Figure 4.11) on top of the original color version (Figure 4.1) and change the Layer Blending mode to Luminosity. (Remember to hold down the Shift key when you do this.) You should get the results shown in Figure 4.13. The Luminosity mode will take the value structure from the B+W version and the color from the underlying layer to render a new version of the color image. The result has more contrast and contouring in areas of skin, lighter garments, and more tonal separation in the hair and pants. It would be much harder to achieve a similar effect using Curves alone.

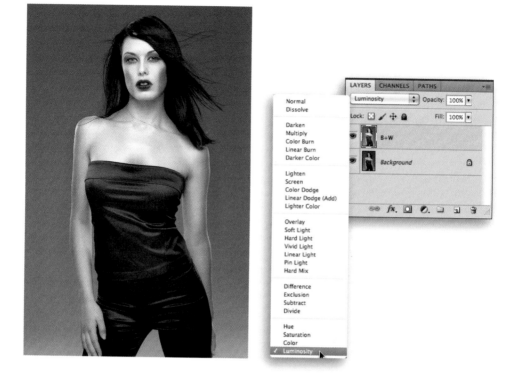

Figure 4.13 The color image has the contrast and tonal structure of the B+W version.

One of the most compelling things about good B+W imagery is the way the tonal structure of the image is simplified by eliminating the influence of color. Light and shadow often provide most of the visual impact in a photograph, even an extremely colorful one. Viewers can tolerate color deviations quite well; however, if an image lacks tonal interest, they will complain bitterly. Differences in value are easier to visualize and, therefore, control in B+W. This is perhaps one of the reasons Ansel Adams was never that fond of color photography: those darn colors kept getting in the way.

The key problem in color-correcting photographic imagery is maintaining control over tonal shape—the value structure underlying the colors in the image. Color and contrast seem to be inextricably mixed in an image, and normal contrast-enhancing moves tend to seriously impact hue and saturation. Color correction will be easier if you can separate the color from the tonal values and deal with them separately. The luminosity blending approach offers a powerful method of doing this.

Instant Tan

Before we return to monochrome imagery, let's examine how luminosity blending can be used to solve some vexing problems.

Figure 4.14 is a portrait of Nathan, a martial arts instructor in Southern California. Unfortunately, the soft lighting has given the skin a pale, pasty look that is less than ideal. The problem is one of tone or value, not color. Darkening the skin without also darkening the already dark clothing will be difficult.

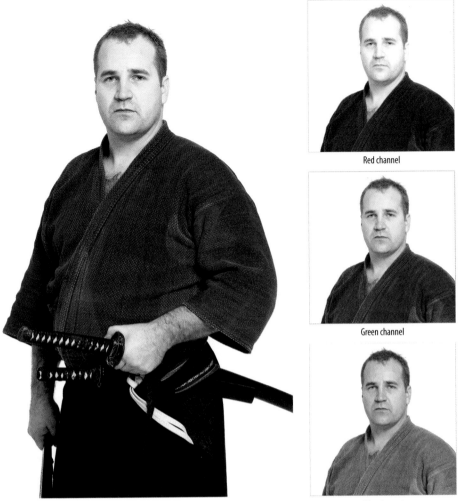

Red channel

Green channel

Blue channel

Original pasty image

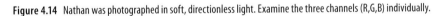

Figure 4.14 Nathan was photographed in soft, directionless light. Examine the three channels (R,G,B) individually.

Before you make any adjustments, examine the three channels individually so that you can get a feel for the B+W value structure of the image.

You can see that the skin in the Red channel is almost completely white, and this is contributing to the pasty look. Usually, the Green channel is the best overall; however, in this case, the darker tones in the Blue channel should work to your advantage in a luminosity blend. Start by creating a Channel Mixer adjustment layer: select Channel Mixer from the Adjustment Layer menu at the bottom of the Layers panel. Select Black & White With Blue Filter (RGB) from the presets drop-down menu. You should have a B+W version that is 100 percent of the Blue channel (Figure 4.15).

Now the magic starts. Change the Blending mode to Luminosity (Figure 4.16). (Now, that's a tan.) His face has some tone; however, his beard shadow hasn't darkened, so it is minimized somewhat. The blue clothing and his blue eyes have gotten lighter.

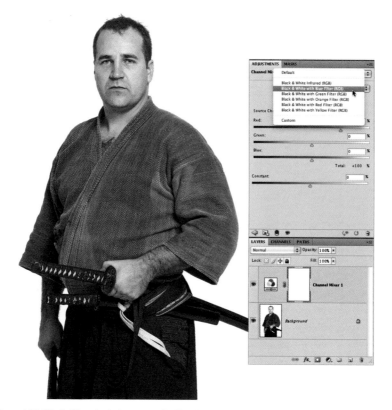

Figure 4.15 This B+W version is the same as the Blue channel of the color version.

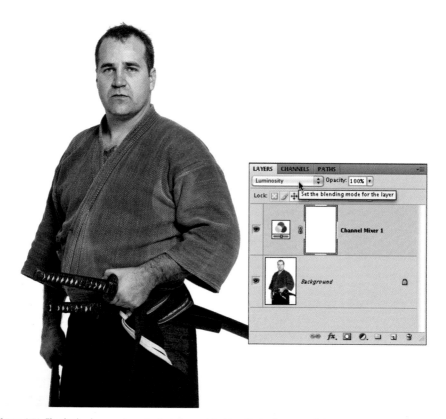

Figure 4.16 The skin has become dramatically darker, and the blue gi jacket has gotten lighter.

You might not like the light blue rendition of the gi jacket even if you prefer the lighter and more detailed gi pants. If not, you can hide the effect of the Luminosity layer by painting the adjustment layer's mask with black (Figure 4.17). This Blue channel luminosity blend is great for generating that swarthy look for men. Although you might still prefer more dramatic lighting, the subject does have more tone and a sense of texture, which were created without using Curves.

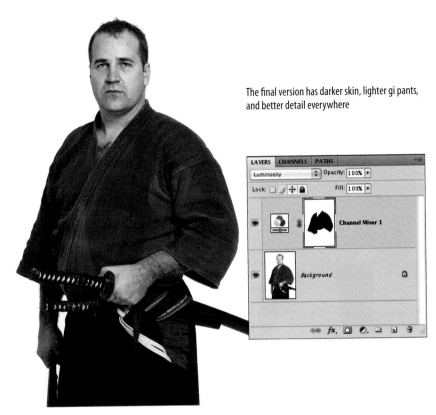

The final version has darker skin, lighter gi pants, and better detail everywhere

Figure 4.17 All the enhancements were made without using any Curves adjustments.

When Color Overwhelms: Look for the Good Channel

The next example has a unique problem (Figure 4.18). The dancer has been captured behind the sheer veil, but I'd like to be able to see more of her face. The red veil is very saturated, but the face behind it has very little contrast. It would be impossible to apply a Curve adjustment steep enough to bring out the desired detail. This problem is something photographers see all the time when they are dealing with highly saturated colors. Everyone says they want bright, saturated colors, but they often come with a price.

The solution is to forget about the color, for a moment, and concentrate on B+W. To begin, look at the grayscale channels that make up the full-color image (Figure 4.19). You are looking for an ideal candidate for a B+W conversion of this image. When you look at the individual channels, you can see that Red is obviously where the biggest problem appears. There is no face in that channel at all; Red is so highly saturated in this image that most detail has clipped to white in the Red channel. Blue is better. However, most of the detail resides in the Green channel.

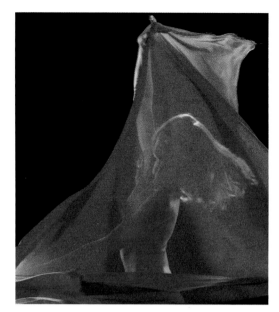

Figure 4.18
The dancer's face is obscured by the red veil.

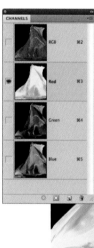

The Red channel has no detail.

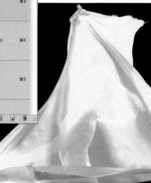

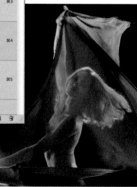

The Green channel has the best contrast in the face.

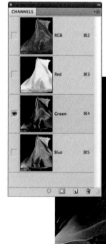

The Blue channel has tone but little contrast.

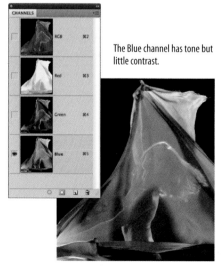

Figure 4.19
The solution is to forget about the color and concentrate on B+W.

The detail and contrast is clearly in the Green channel, even though the image is a little dark. You can use this information to create a monochrome Channel Mixer adjustment layer and push the Green slider past 100 percent (Figure 4.20).

Next, change the Blending mode to Luminosity (Figure 4.21,). You can see the face more clearly, but the veil now has harsh black shadows and a slightly posterized look.

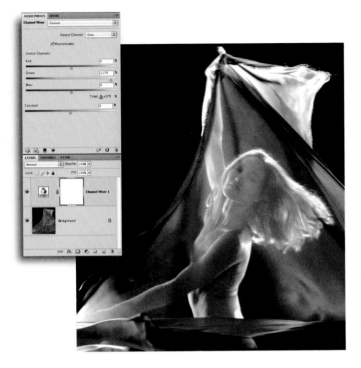

Figure 4.20
Pushing the Green slider past 100 percent lightens the values and increases the contrast.

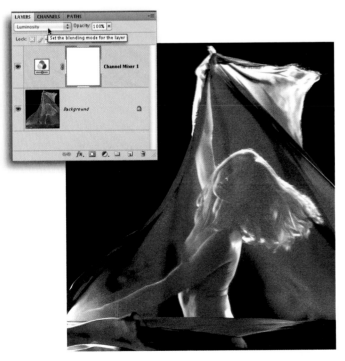

Figure 4.21
The face is visible, but now there are harsh, unattractive shadows in the veil.

To solve this problem, you can use a little-known Photoshop trick: advanced Blending Options. Select Blending Options from the Layer options flyaway menu at the upper right of the Layers panel (Figure 4.22).

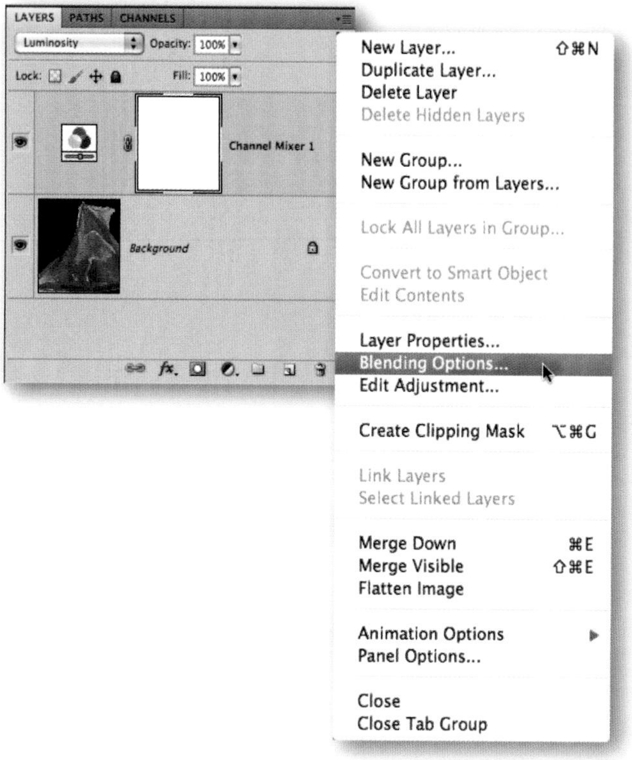

Figure 4.22 The Blending Options menu

The Layer Style dialog box will appear. You can use the Blend If sliders to control where the Green channel luminance blends back into the original image in the underlying layer. The idea here is to bring back the tone and color of the original image in the areas that turned black after the luminosity was applied. Because you are using the Green channel luminosity in this layer, you will use that channel in the Blend If area of the dialog. To select the Green channel, change the Blend If drop-down to Green. Drag the black triangle on the This Layer slider to the right until the black parts of the image regain their original tone. You can feather the transition by holding down the Option/Alt key and splitting the triangle into two halves; drag the right half to the right until the tones are smooth (Figure 4.23).

Note: The Blend If sliders are extremely powerful tools for seamlessly blending layers based on the channel luminosity in each layer. By combining different channel slider positions in the top and bottom sliders, you can achieve very complex blends.

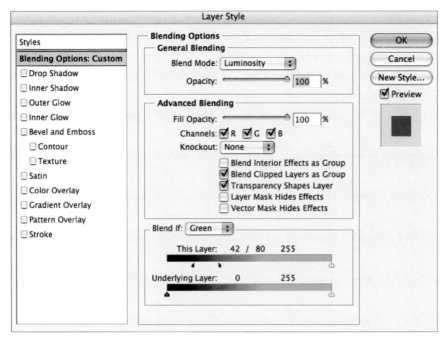

Figure 4.23 Split the Blend slider to feather the transition between the upper layer and the background.

In Figure 4.24, the image has been further adjusted by masking off sections of the figure that had better contrast in the original background layer.

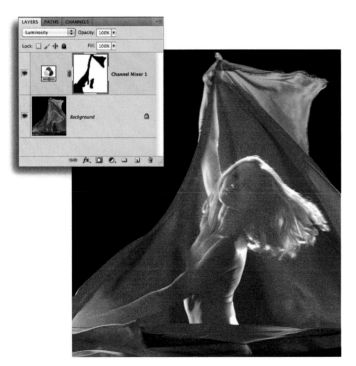

Figure 4.24 To retrieve better areas from the original background layer, paint with black into the mask.

This example clearly shows the advantage of using grayscale information to affect the tone and contrast of color images. Very often, even good color images can be enhanced in unexpected ways by applying B+W tonality to the color values.

Another very common use for Luminosity blending is with darker-skinned subjects. A direct reflection on the skin (shine) helped to lighten the dark skin in the portrait by Ken Chernus shown in Figure 4.25. This is a great dramatic shot, but it is still too dark for certain types of reproduction.

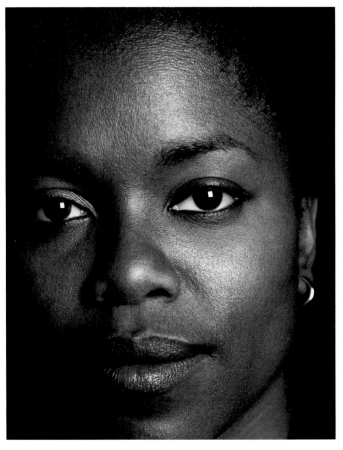

Figure 4.25 This dramatic portrait could still be too dark for some print conditions.

Make a monochrome Channel Mixer adjustment layer using 100 percent of the Red channel, change the Blending mode to Luminosity, reduce the opacity of the layer a bit, and you'll get Figure 4.26.

The Red channel is lighter in all shots of people. By applying the Red channel Luminosity to the color image, you can lighten dark skin color. In this example, the skin highlights are lightened too. You can reduce the highlight intensity and minimize the skin texture by blending back into the original highlights using Blending Options. Flatten and place the lighter version in a layer above the original. Figure 4.27 is the result of blending into the highlights of the original image in an underlying layer using the slider positions shown.

I could write a whole book about applying B+W luminosity in color images. I hope these few examples have opened some frontiers for you to explore.

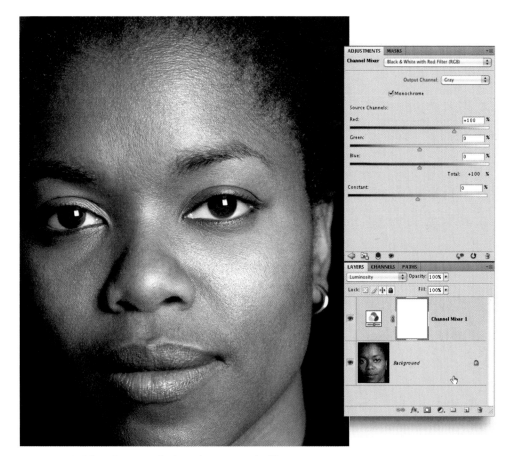

Figure 4.26 Red channel Luminosity brightens the image considerably.

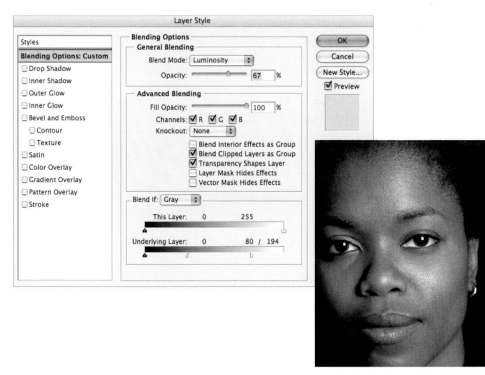

Figure 4.27 By blending into the darker highlights of the original, you can minimize the skin texture for a smoother effect.

Hue/Saturation Toning Effects

Let's return to monochrome images to explore working in the opposite direction—
applying color to B+W. Monochromatic images don't have to be neutral gray. The
creative use of color in B+W imagery has a long tradition. Silver bromide prints were
often *toned* using various chemicals to impart color to otherwise colorless images.
Sepia, selenium, gold, and blue toners were used sometimes with a "split-tone" effect.
All of these effects and more are possible with digital techniques that offer far more
control (and much less odor). Let's start with this B+W image of an African drummer
(Figure 4.28).

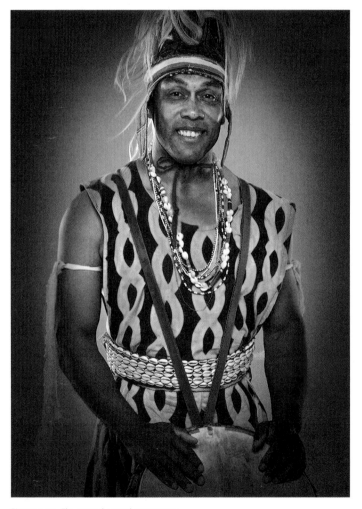

Figure 4.28 The original neutral gray version

Before you can colorize a grayscale image, you must convert it to RGB. Select Image > Mode > RGB to set the grayscale image to your default RGB workspace. After you do that, you can *colorize* the image using Hue/Saturation.

Create a Hue/Saturation adjustment layer and check the Colorize check box when the dialog appears (Figure 4.29).

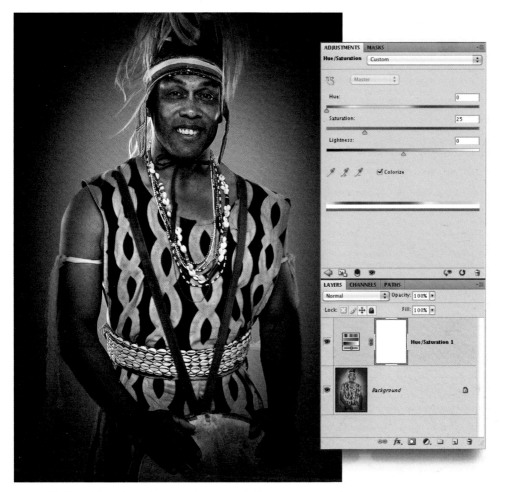

Figure 4.29 Hue and Saturation settings for a selenium-toned look

The default color effect here is a fairly rich reddish brown. If you move the Saturation slider down to about 10, you'll end up with a fairly convincing imitation of selenium toning. Shift the hue toward yellow (set the Hue slider to about 30), and you'll be in sepia territory. An infinite variety of color-toning effects are possible with this approach. The Hue/Saturation adjustment layer is very interactive, making it easy to see the color change as you move the sliders.

Ken Chernus used an almost olive brown tone to simulate the look of old-fashioned, warm-toned Chlorobromide photographic paper in Figure 4.30 and Figure 4.31, which were taken for a series on Baptist churches.

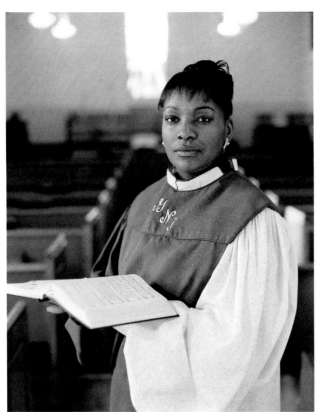

Figure 4.30
The olive color simulates the look of old, warm-toned Chlorobromide paper. (Photo by Ken Chernus)

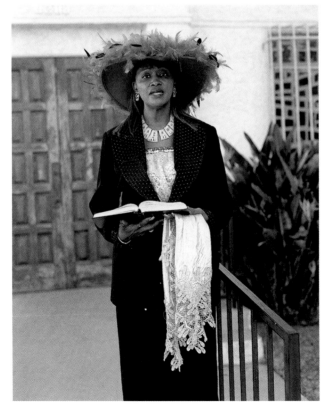

Figure 4.31
The warm tone enhances the nostalgic feeling of the photograph. (Photo by Ken Chernus)

Split-Toning

Split-toning is a classic toning effect. This effect is traditionally achieved using selenium toner warmed up to about 80° F. The print is pulled from the toner tray when the shadow values just start taking the color, and then it is rapidly immersed in cold water to stop the process. High values remain untoned; cooler or more neutral and shadow values develop the rich, purple-brown look of selenium toner. This process is very "hit or miss," difficult to control, and very toxic. Fortunately, *digital* split-toning does not suffer from these disadvantages.

To perform split-toning, make another Hue/Saturation adjustment layer above the first one. Check Colorize and shift the hue to a different color, as in Figure 4.32.

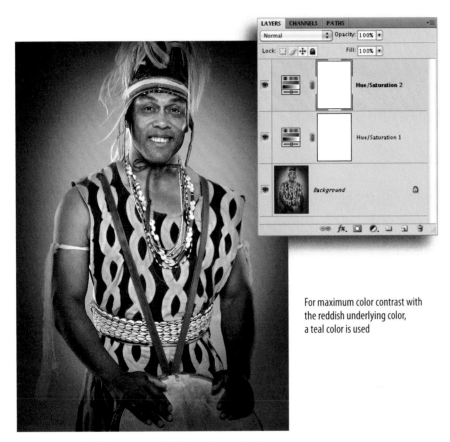

For maximum color contrast with the reddish underlying color, a teal color is used

Figure 4.32 You should experiment with different color combinations.

Now for the magic trick: choose Blending Options from the Layer Options flyaway menu at the upper right of the Layers panel. When the Layer Style dialog appears, go to the Blend If area and move the black triangle slider (either layer will work—here we're using This Layer, which is the top layer) to the right until the brown, dark values from the underlying layer show through (Figure 4.33).

The tones are now split. To soften the transition between the two toning colors, hold down the Option/Alt key and split the slider into two halves, moving them apart until the desired look is achieved (Figure 4.34).

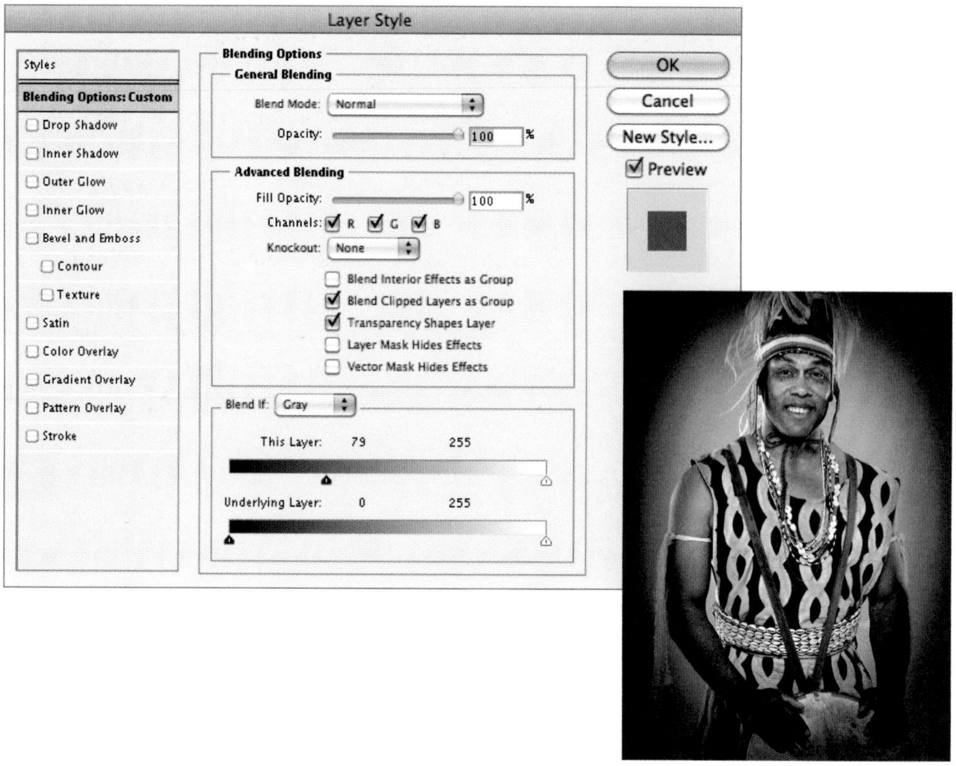

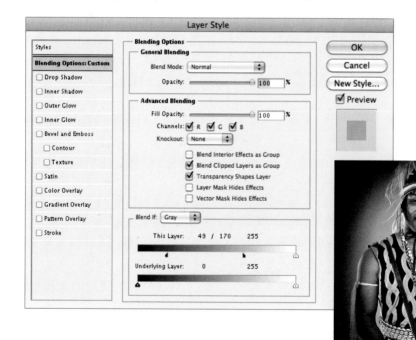

Figure 4.33 The color split is a fairly hard transition, which creates an almost posterized look.

Figure 4.34 This version has a softer transition between the different color tones.

Fairly strong colors were used for the example so that the "split" is easier to see. You can create a more subtle effect by reducing the opacity of the Hue/Saturation layers. First, group the layers by selecting them in the Layers panel (Shift+click the thumbnails), and then select New Group From Layers from the Layers panel menu. Now you can reduce the opacity of the Group to desaturate the effect (Figure 4.35).

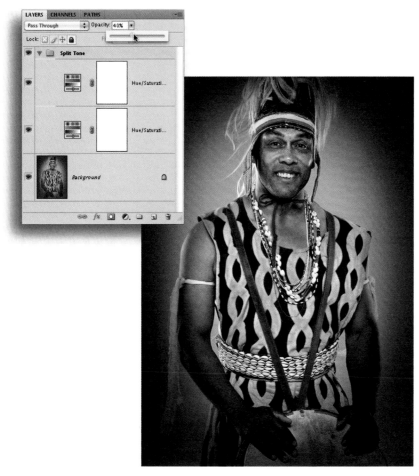

Figure 4.35 This more desaturated split-tone can be used to suggest more dimensions in the monochrome image through subtle hue shifts.

The beauty of having the toning effects in a Hue/Saturation layer is that the colors can be edited after you've established the basic effect. It's very easy to generate variations by double-clicking the adjustment layer to activate the Hue/Saturation dialog again and change the Hue or Saturation sliders (Figure 4.36).

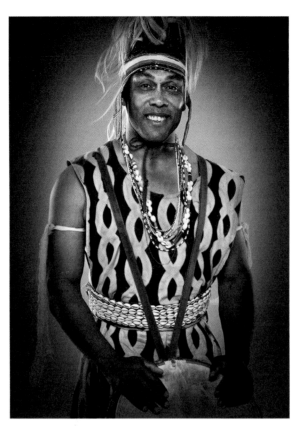

Figure 4.36
This version puts a warm color in
the highlights and a cool color in the
shadows.

Figure 4.37 is a slightly more subtle example of a simple, cool shadows/warm highlights "split."

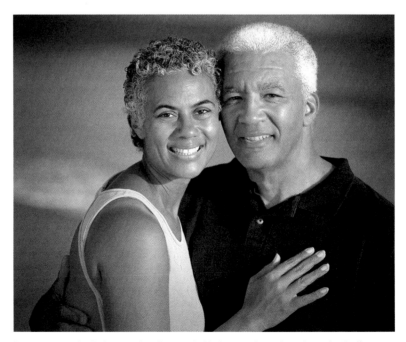

Figure 4.37 Cooler shadows recede and warmer highlights come forward to enhance the 3D effect.
(Photo by Ken Chernus)

You don't have to stop at two colors. When you add another Hue/Saturation adjustment layer, you can split the color tones into highlight, midtone, and shadow values. If you use colors that synchronize with the value structure of the image—deep colors for low values, medium colors for midtones, and light colors for highlights—you can create the illusion of extended dynamic range. This can give your monochromatic images a more three-dimensional look (Figure 4.38).

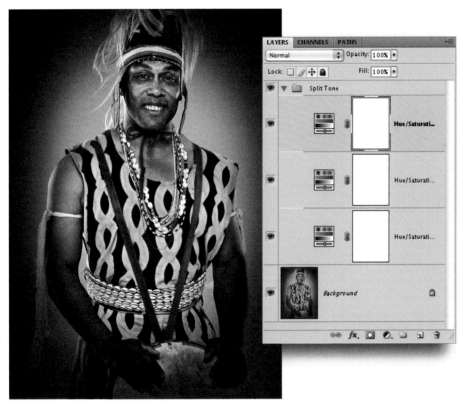

Figure 4.38 By moving from deep purple through reddish brown to pale cyan-blue, you can enhance the grayscale contrast with color contrast that seems to extend the dynamic range.

Gradient Map Colorizing

More complex colorizing effects can best be achieved using the Gradient Map adjustment layer. Starting with the original grayscale image, select Gradient Map from the Adjustment Layer menu, which is accessed by clicking the New Adjustment Layer icon at the bottom of the Layers panel (Figure 4.39).

1. Click the triangle to the right of the gradient in the Gradient Map dialog.

2. Select the Blue, Red, Yellow gradient in the resulting Gradient Picker. Click inside the gradient to bring up the Gradient Editor (Figure 4.40).

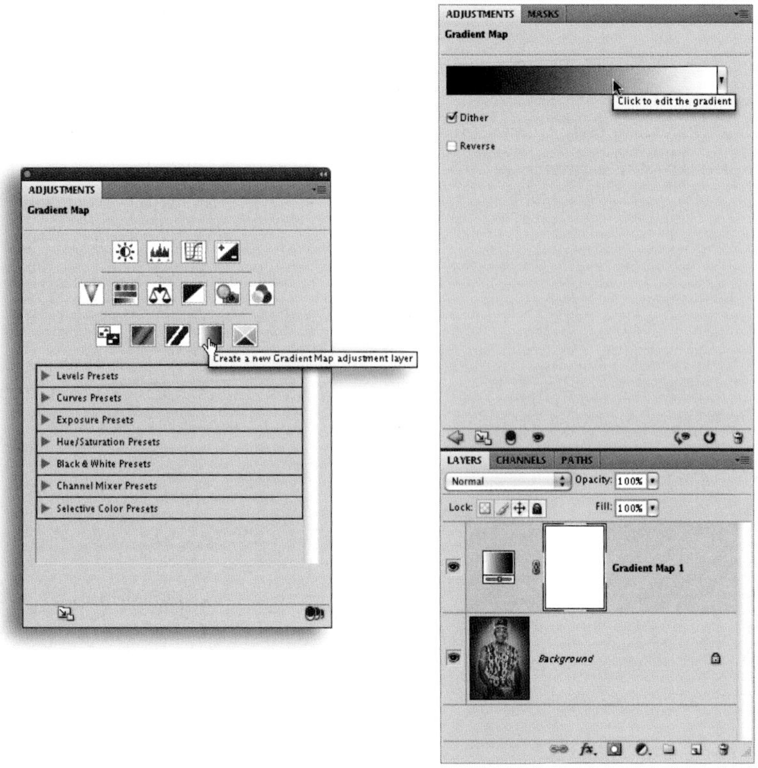

146

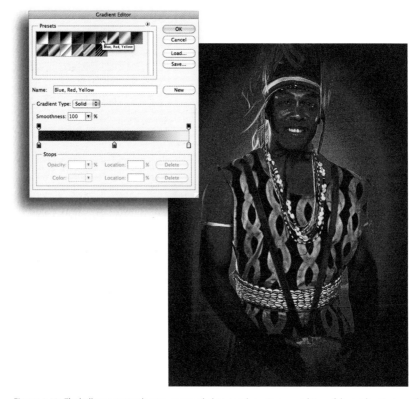

Figure 4.39 Gradient Map is a special adjustment layer accessed from the Layers panel.

Figure 4.40 The brilliant saturated tones are overwhelming and require some editing of the gradient to tame the image.

3. Use the Editor to customize the gradient. The pointers along the top control the opacity of the gradient—leave them alone. The bottom pointers determine the colors in the gradient. By clicking anywhere along the bottom edge of the gradient, you can add a new color "stop" to the gradient. You can drag these new color pointers (while you preview the effect in your document) and also adjust the blend between colors by dragging the small diamonds between the stops. Click the Color patch in the Stops area to bring up a Color Picker that allows you to select a new color. When you have finished designing a new gradient, you can enter a name and click the New button to add it to your gradient presets. Click OK to return to the Gradient Map dialog and click OK again to apply the effect. In this example, I created a very wild saturated-color crossover effect that progresses from black through purple, red, orange, and yellow to white (Figure 4.41).

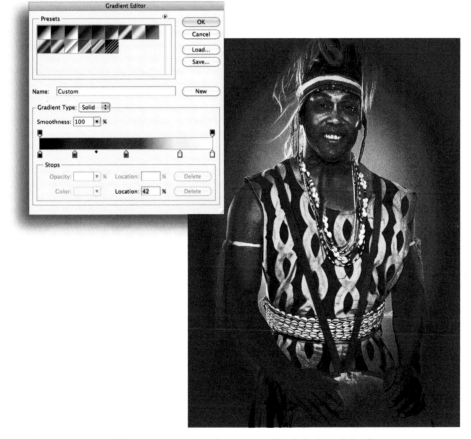

Figure 4.41 It is usually best to design a gradient that progresses from dark colors to light colors.

You can simply change the opacity of the Gradient Map layer in the Layers panel to create a whole range of more subtle effects (Figure 4.42). The big advantage of using gradient maps is that you can build multicolor split-tones with just one layer. The disadvantage is that it is a bit more difficult to control the interaction of color tone and crossover points using the Gradient Editor.

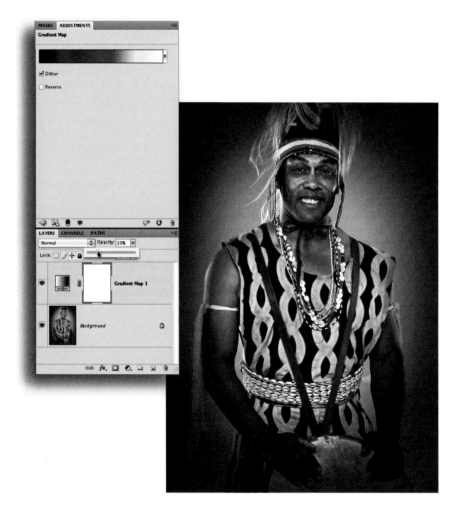

Figure 4.42 Change the opacity to create a subtle colorized effect.

Figure 4.43 shows another example of Gradient Map color toning. This lovely fine art portrait by Erin Manning has an interesting "faded color" effect created through a subtle application of a multicolor gradient map.

Besides Peter Max coloring, you can also achieve super "solarized" and other psychedelic effects by using more radical gradients. Experimenting is great fun!

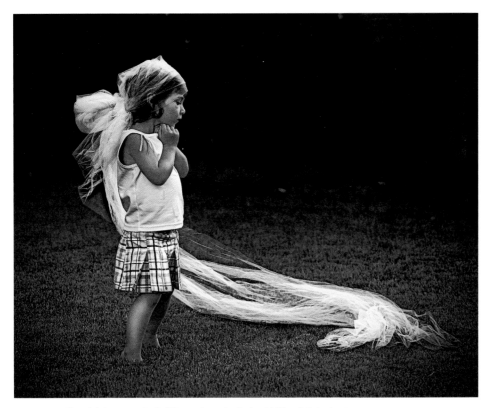

Figure 4.43 The subtle hues turn this B+W image into what looks a bit like a faded color photo.

The Power of B+W

Learning how to create outstanding black-and-white images can have more than just the obvious benefits. Converting color into B+W can be done for its own sake, or it can be utilized to control tonal structure in color photography. Good B+W can also serve as a springboard for creative color explorations through various toning techniques. The examples in this chapter are by no means exhaustive. Think of this introduction as the tip of the iceberg. The same principles used in layer blending and masking can be applied in many different ways to generate special effects or subtle corrections in color and B+W imagery.

A good basic image development strategy is

1. Begin with the lighting and exposure of your photograph—optimize them first.
2. Process the files into your RGB workspace. For most people photography, you will use Adobe RGB.
3. Perform basic color editing and corrective measures (retouching, etc.).

4. Examine the individual channels for grayscale information. Is a great black-and-white image lurking there? Can you utilize grayscale tonal structure in the channels separately or in combination to enhance contrast or detail in the color image?

5. Create a B+W version to test contrast and value.

6. Apply the B+W version to the color image; decide whether you can improve the image this way.

7. Fine-tune the color with curves.

In some cases, the color image will be just fine after you've made some basic edits. In many cases, the color image can be improved by the application of idealized grayscale information. The effects can be dramatic or subtle, and they are almost always worth exploring.

Let's put this strategy to use in this final image by Anthony Nex (Figure 4.44). The original shot is a great example of Anthony's high-energy style of kid photography. A great expression captured in the studio with motion-stopping flash lighting, the shot was processed into Adobe RGB.

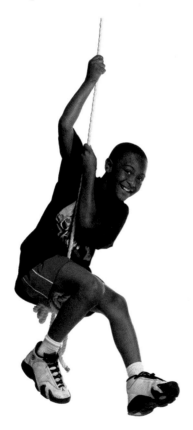

Figure 4.44
A great shot, but the boy's skin is a little too dark
for some print conditions. (Photo by Anthony Nex)

The biggest problem is that this handsome African American kid will likely reproduce too dark in the average magazine or book, so we need to look for a way to brighten up the skin. The solution is an application of Red channel luminosity using a Channel Mixer adjustment layer. Set the Red slider at +100 (Black & White With Red Filter preset) to further brighten the highlights, check the Monochrome check box, and change the Mode to Luminosity in the Layers panel (Figure 4.45).

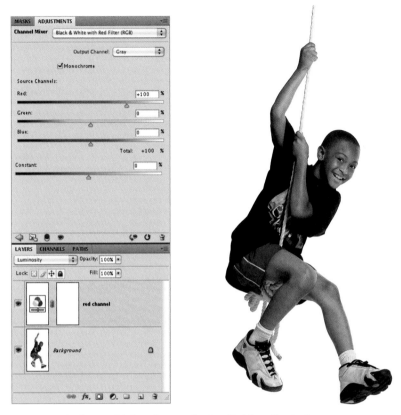

Figure 4.45 The skin is much lighter after an application of Red channel luminosity.

With the biggest problem solved, we now turn our attention to the skin color. The skin is too magenta and lacking in saturation. A Curves adjustment subtracts blue and adds red and green to boost the saturation and bring the yellow back into balance with magenta (Figure 5.46).

The finishing touch is a special "High Pass" sharpening technique to enhance the highlights on the skin even further (Figure 4.47). We will go over this technique in more detail in Chapter 7.

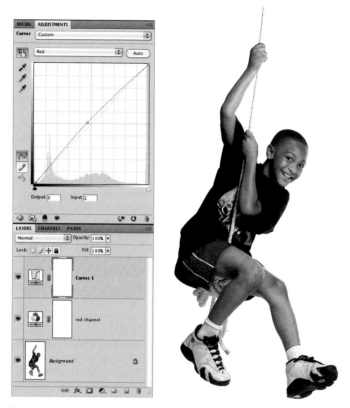

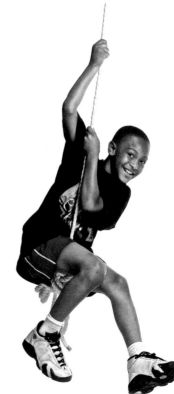

Figure 4.46 Curves adjustments add saturation and yellow to the skin tone.

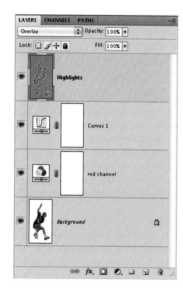

Figure 4.47 The highlights are enhanced with a High-Pass Overlay layer.

What about the Black & White Adjustment Layer?

First introduced in CS3, the Black & White adjustment layer modifies values by isolating color ranges. I don't like it much. It can cause posterizing and banding that becomes more noticeable when applied to color images in Luminosity mode. While CS5's Black & White adjustment layer is easy to understand from a novice user's perspective, I get better results with the techniques I've shown here.

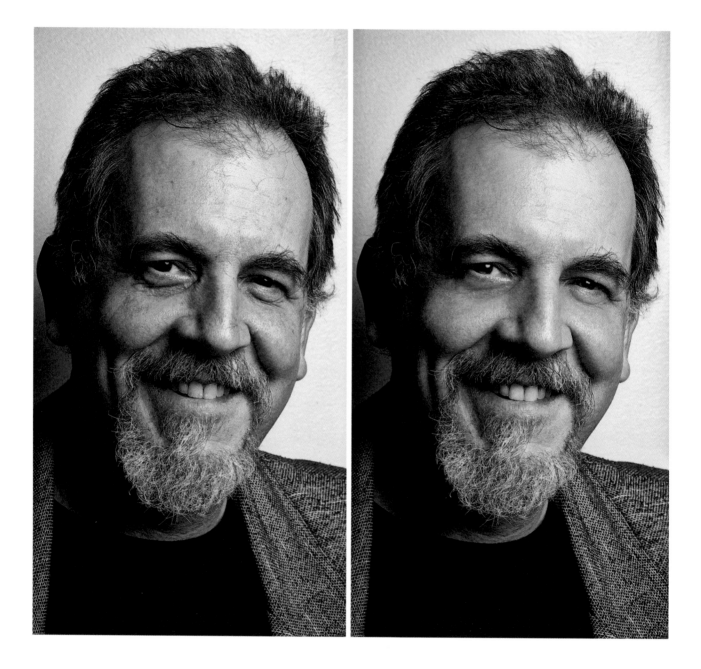

Retouching

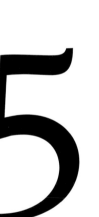

The days of airbrushing, dye transfers, spotting, and etching are long gone, but the need to clean up or enhance photographs has never been greater. Every professional photographer is expected to know enough to do basic digital retouching. Of course, what is considered basic today would have been beyond the capabilities of all but the most-advanced retouchers of the celluloid era. These days clients demand even more because the general public has unlimited expectations. The phrase "We can Photoshop it" is clear to just about everyone.

People photography has always required a certain amount of retouching to flatter the subject, and this chapter will cover some of the basic (and not-so-basic) techniques.

Chapter Contents
Basic Image Repair
Hue/Saturation Color Repair
Beauty Retouching
Subtle Retouching
Figure-Thinning Techniques

Basic Image Repair

Digital photography frequently requires only some basic cleanup—remove a mole, take out a stray hair, or remove a spot on the background. Photoshop includes a wealth of sophisticated tools for these kinds of remedial image repairs. The photo of me at the beginning of this chapter is an example of the normal, non-heroic retouching that is simply intended to show the subject in the best light. This retouch represents a combination of techniques:

- Hue/saturation color repair
- Healing, spotting, and patching
- Overlay/softlight dodging and burning
- Skin smoothing

You can examine each of these techniques individually in the following examples, starting with another photo of me taken by Jeff Boxer (Figure 5.1 left).

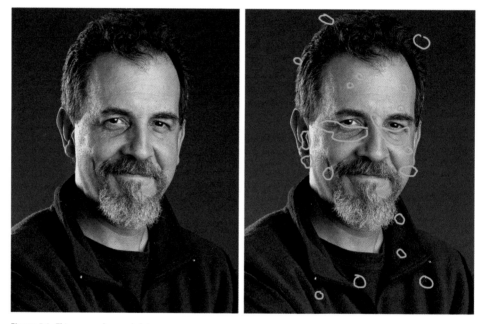

Figure 5.1 This guy needs some help!

Sometimes, I like to start with a markup to indicate the areas I'd like to fix. You may find this technique especially important when working with clients, so you can communicate what will be fixed before work begins. In Photoshop, create a new empty layer and then draw into this layer with a contrasting color to mimic a grease pencil on a print (Figure 5.1 right). You can leave this layer in the document and turn it off and on to double-check your progress.

Note: There are many different applications and techniques you can use for retouching, and we cannot cover everything in just one chapter. The methods outlined here should serve as a starting point for further exploration in your own work.

Once you've decided what to do, you can start your repairs. Photoshop has a wealth of specialized tools that make detailed retouching easy. Before you do anything else, make a new empty layer. Whenever possible put all the retouching into a separate layer so you can retrieve the original image at some later time if necessary (Figure 5.2).

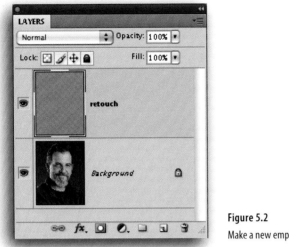

Figure 5.2
Make a new empty layer to hold your retouching.

Photoshop CS4 and Photoshop CS5 have a retouching tool above the venerable Clone Stamp tool in the Tool panel; click and hold it to see and select the different variations. The Spot Healing Brush (Figure 5.3) is the first choice in CS5. Most of the time, you can leave the tool options set to the defaults with Proximity Match checked. Make sure Sample All Layers is checked.

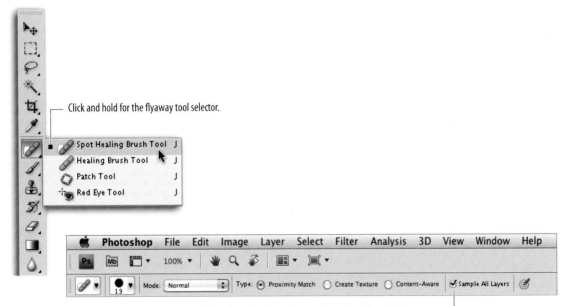

Figure 5.3 Select the Spot Healing Brush and turn on Sample All Layers.

This tool works like a Magic Spotting Brush; it fills in small dark or light spots with color and texture from the surrounding area. Size your brush so that it's big enough to cover the spot. The size of your stroke is pressure sensitive—more pressure, bigger stroke. However, the size of surrounding area from which you sample depends on the diameter of the brush. If you use a brush that is too small, you won't sample from enough clean skin to get a good color over the spot. A brush that is too large might sample an area that pulls in color from some nearby defect. Dab the brush over the spots you want to remove (Figure 5.4).

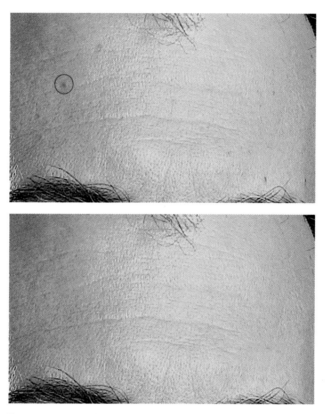

Figure 5.4 Paint over the spots you want to remove with the Spot Healing Brush.

Occasionally, when you work the Spot Healing Brush near an edge with a contrasting color and texture, the tool will pull some of that area into the brush area, as you can see near the hair in Figure 5.5. To avoid copying the wrong area, use a smaller brush and don't place the outer boundary of the brush circle into the other area. Larger brushes use larger sample areas. Sometimes this color pollution is unavoidable—in these cases you should switch to the Clone Stamp tool and clone from a corresponding area.

Note: When you are working over larger areas of skin, it is a good practice to work slowly, sampling and resampling many times to avoid obvious repeating patterns. It's OK to go back over a healed area to make sure a texture doesn't repeat.

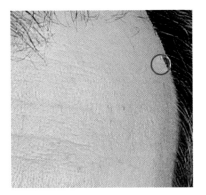

Figure 5.5 The hair from an adjacent area is pulled into the brush.

Spots are easy to get rid of; however, larger more-complex areas, such as the bags under my eyes, used to be more difficult to retouch than they are now. The next tool, first introduced in Photoshop CS, is the Healing Brush; this magic cloning tool makes short work of problem areas. Select the Healing Brush tool (Figure 5.6). Make sure your tool options are set to Sample: Current & Below and verify that Aligned is On. This allows you to retouch under a color correction layer without having the correction affect the newly "healed" area. For simplicity, I still recommend that you do any retouching before you do any color correction or, at least, turn off any color correction layers before you begin retouching. Option/Alt+click to sample an area of good skin (such as the top of my cheeks), and use a larger brush to completely cover the bags under the eyes (Figure 5.7).

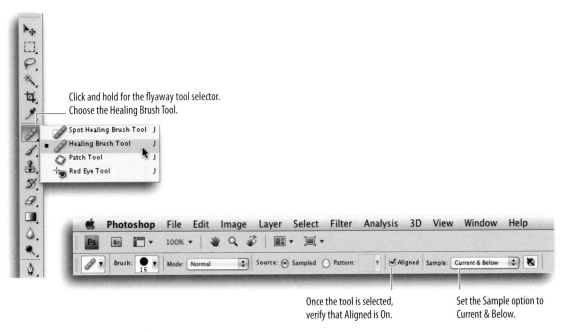

Figure 5.6 Select the Spot Healing Brush and turn on Sample Current & Below.

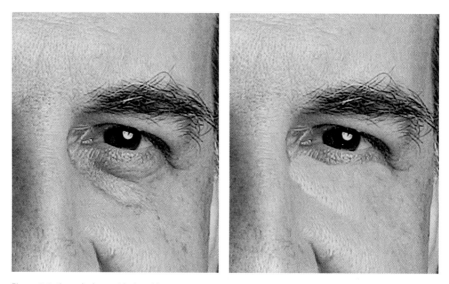

Figure 5.7 Cover the bags with clear skin.

The lighter skin contrasts with the surrounding area, and it looks horrible. However, as soon as you release the brush, the area magically blends in, replacing the original texture but keeping most of the underlying tone of the original (Figure 5.8). The retouching now blends seamlessly; however, as you can see, the newly retouched eye looks a little weird—like the eyes of an alien from outer space. The fix is simple if you did all this retouching in the new empty layer.

Change the layer opacity by dragging the slider to the left, revealing a little bit of the original underlying image. The bags are now soft folds, which are much more natural looking without being unattractive.

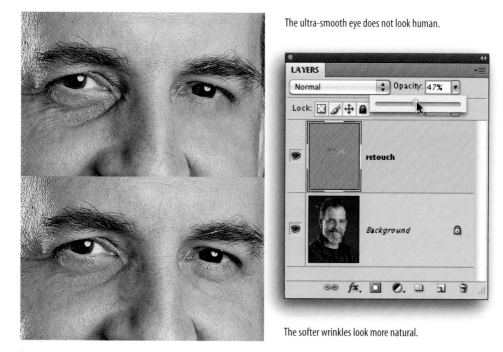

The ultra-smooth eye does not look human.

The softer wrinkles look more natural.

Figure 5.8 Lower the opacity to reveal more of the original underlying image.

You might be inclined to stop here, but there are still a few wrinkles that can be minimized a bit. Using another technique, you can do that without destroying the skin texture. First, hold down the Option/Alt key and click the New Layer icon at the bottom of the Layers panel. This will bring up the New Layer dialog (Figure 5.9).

New Layer	
Name: dodge-burn	OK
☐ Use Previous Layer to Create Clipping Mask	Cancel
Color: ☐ None	
Mode: Soft Light Opacity: 100 ▸ %	
☑ Fill with Soft-Light-neutral color (50% gray)	

Figure 5.9 The New Layer dialog allows you to change the mode and fill the layer with 50 percent gray in one step.

You need to make a special layer to *dodge and burn* (selectively lighten and darken). The trick is to change the mode to Soft Light and then check Fill With Soft-Light-Neutral Color. This will fill the new layer with 50 percent gray. In a Soft Light or Overlay layer, 50 percent gray has no effect on the underlying image; but when you use the Dodge tool to lighten the Gray layer, it will lighten the underlying image without affecting the color or texture. The Soft Light mode has a more gentle effect than Overlay, and it doesn't tend to increase the saturation as much. Select the Dodge tool in the Tool panel and brush over the wrinkles using a low opacity to gradually lighten them (Figure 5.10 and Figure 5.11).

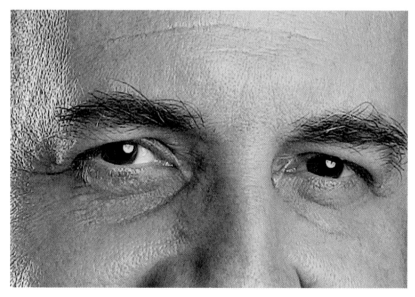

Figure 5.10 The wrinkles before dodging

If you temporarily change the Layer mode back to Normal, you can see the dodge marks clearly in the Gray layer. Just reduce the opacity to see where they line up on the face (Figure 5.12).

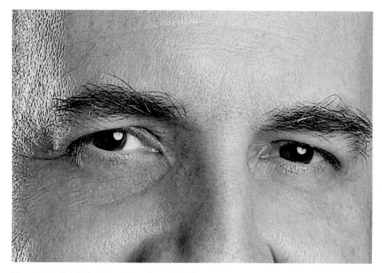

Figure 5.11 Subtle dodging softens the wrinkles but preserves the skin texture.

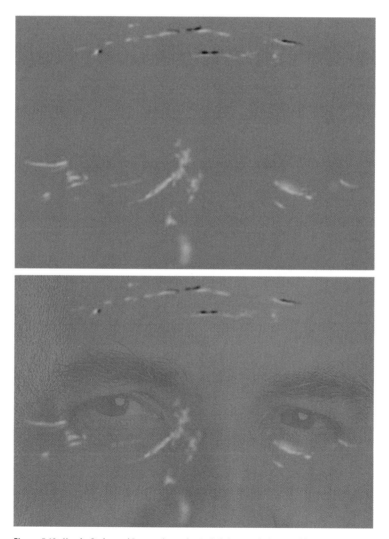

Figure 5.12 Use the Dodge and Burn tools to selectively lighten or darken wrinkles.

If you go too far, you can repair the effect by brushing back into the Soft Light layer with 50 percent gray at low opacity. If you need a stronger lightening or darkening effect, you can duplicate the layer by dragging the Layer thumbnail onto the New Layer icon at the bottom of the Layers panel. The final retouching softens and fills in wrinkles and pores without completely eliminating them (Figure 5.13). Wow, I look 10 years younger! (OK, maybe 15 years but who's counting?) Compare this with the original shown in Figure 5.1.

The Patch tool is found under the Bandage icon in the Tool panel (Figure 5.14). It is very useful for removing defects in a plain background. Leave the tool options set to Patch: Source. We will use it on the CCD dirt spots just to the right of the face.

To use the tool, select it and draw a selection outline around the spot (Figure 5.15). Simply drag the selection to an area that is free of spots. The area inside of the selection outline changes to the area to which you dragged. You can clean up lots of spots very quickly.

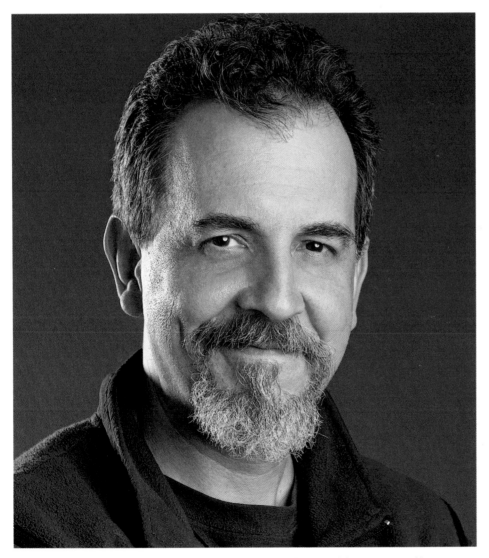

Figure 5.13 The final retouching should look natural and preserve as much of the original skin texture as possible.

The Clone Stamp

You may have noticed that we haven't really touched the classic retouching tool—the Clone Stamp tool that has been in Photoshop since the beginning. The Clone Stamp tool (sometimes called the *rubber stamp* because of the Tool icon in the Tool panel) still has its uses, but the newer tools are easier to use for this type of retouching. One of the biggest problems with the Clone Stamp tool is the tendency to smooth overworked areas. This happens when the soft edges of the Clone Stamp overlap, and multiple strokes tend to smooth out noise and texture.

Prior to Photoshop CS, most experts used really small brush sizes to retouch pore by pore. The new tools make this work much less tedious. The Clone Stamp is very useful, however, for duplicating areas or moving features.

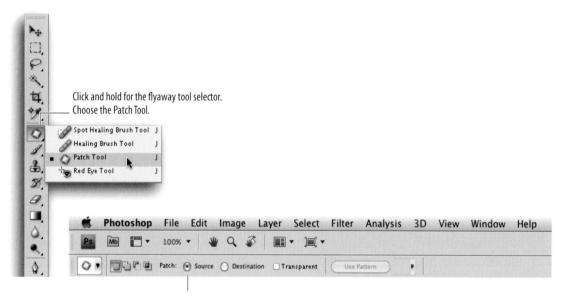

Figure 5.14 Select the Patch tool and leave the Patch option set to Source.

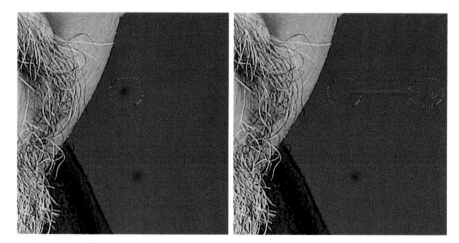

Figure 5.15 Use the Patch tool the same way you would use the Lasso and draw a selection around the spot you want to remove. Then drag the selection to an area that is clean.

Hue/Saturation Color Repair

The retouching I just did on my photo was relatively straightforward because the skin color was mostly uniform. What can I do with this image from Ken Chernus (Figure 5.16)?

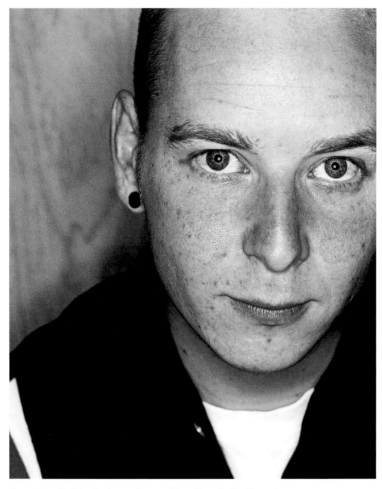

Figure 5.16 Red blotchy skin is a classic problem. (Photo by Ken Chernus)

Red blotchy skin can look worse in digital capture because of the tendency for Bayer pattern imaging systems to overemphasize the red component in skin color. Pimples and red blotches tend to go nuclear. Fortunately, there is a relatively simple fix that utilizes a Hue/Saturation adjustment layer. To perform this fix, call up the Adjustments panel by clicking and selecting from the Adjustments Layer icon at the bottom of the Layers panel. Once the panel is up, change the Edit drop-down menu to Reds (Figure 5.17). Select the Minus Eyedropper (toward the bottom of the panel). Move the cursor (the Eyedropper sampler) into the image and click the brightest red pimple. The selected range (at the bottom of the panel in the rainbow gradient) will move slightly to center over the selected color. Select the right Minus Eyedropper tool and click an area of good skin color. The sample region will shrink somewhat to indicate the more constrained sample area.

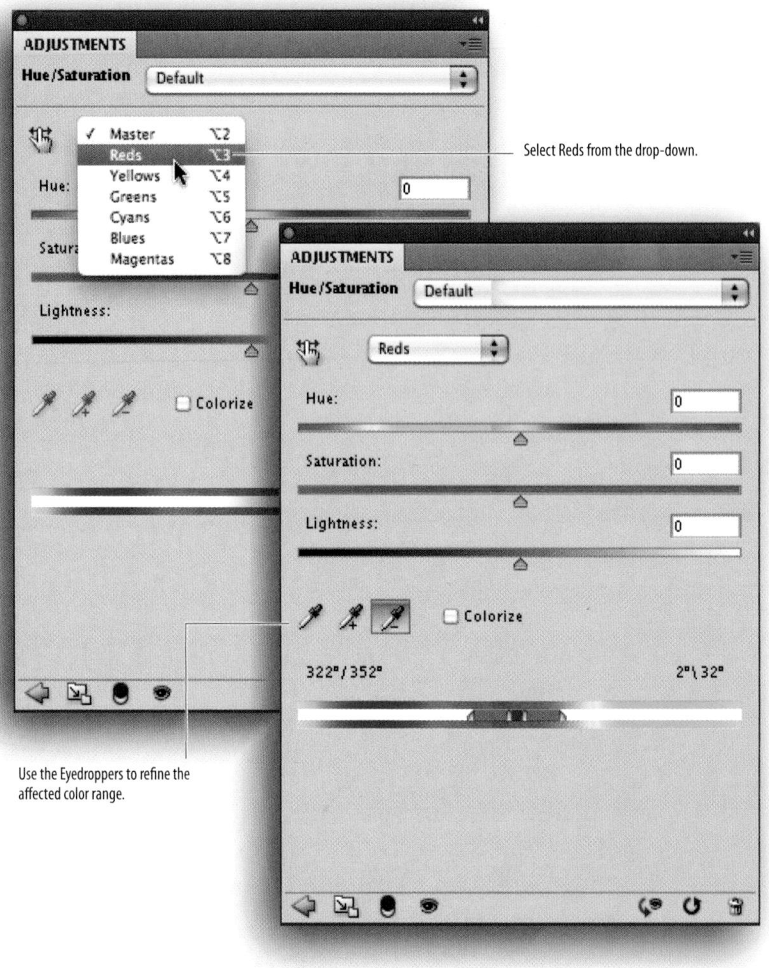

Select Reds from the drop-down.

Use the Eyedroppers to refine the
affected color range.

Figure 5.17 Select Reds and then use the Eyedroppers to refine the affected color range by clicking in the image.

This part is the trick: you can temporarily apply a radical hue shift to help visualize the selected region. Push the Hue slider all the way to the left; the selected reds in the face will turn bright cyan blue. Now you just need to drag the right gray-triangle slider to the left to trim the selected region in the rainbow gradient to limit the effect to those areas that are too red and blotchy (Figure 5.18).

After you have identified the region that will be affected, you can employ a more attractive color shift. Drag the Hue slider to the right, past zero and move the color toward yellow. Stop when you've killed the red curse. Use the Info panel numbers to determine if the skin values in the pimple regions are in the correct range (move the cursor into the image to get a reading). (Refer to Chapter 4, "Tone and Contrast: Color and B&W," if you need help with determining the correct range.)

Because pimples are also darker than normal skin, push the Lightness slider to the right until you get better tonal uniformity (Figure 5.19). Don't go too far with this; it will reduce the saturation of the skin tone and ultimately look unnatural.

Some areas of the face might be too yellow. You can adjust these areas in a similar fashion. Change the Edit drop-down to Yellows, use the Eyedropper tool to select the too-yellow region, subtract the red pimple areas with the Minus Eyedropper tool (these are now already shifted), apply the radical hue shift to trim the area further, and push the slider slightly to the left to make the yellow regions more red (Figure 5.20). The Edit drop-down, which did indicate Yellows, might change to Reds-2 to indicate that you are editing another red region. The Hue/Saturation adjustment has hidden most of the pimples and given the skin a much healthier look (Figure 5.21).

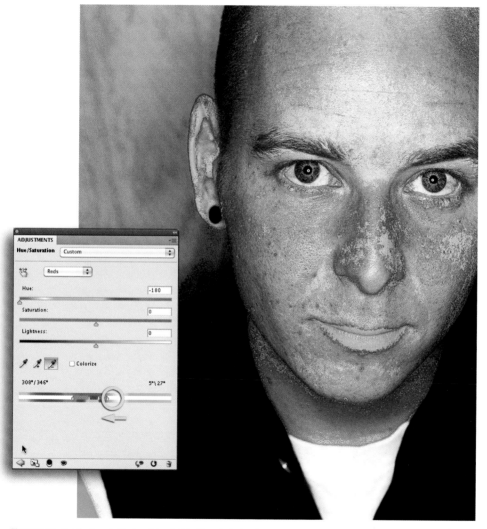

Figure 5.18 Use the Sample Region sliders to trim the selected region.

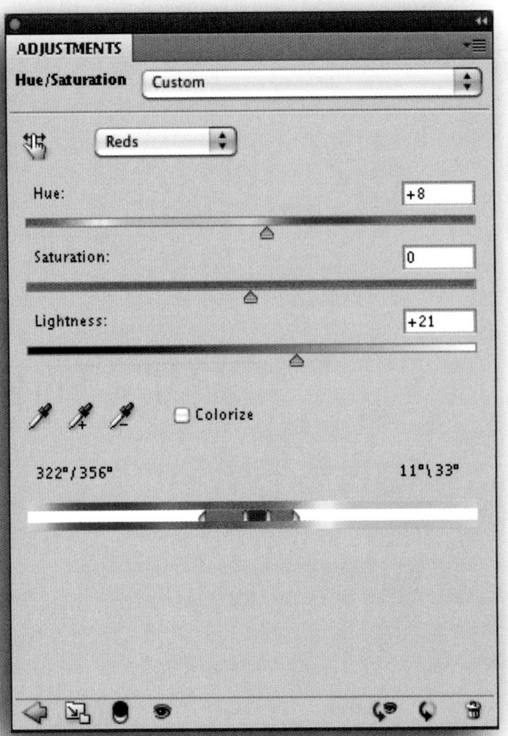

Figure 5.19
Adjust the sliders to bring the red regions into the same color and tonal range as the rest of the face.

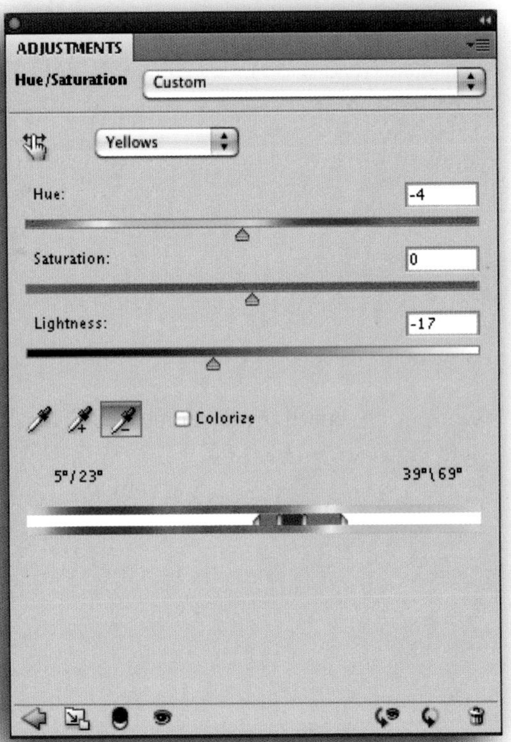

Figure 5.20
Edit additional regions as needed to create a more uniform skin tone.

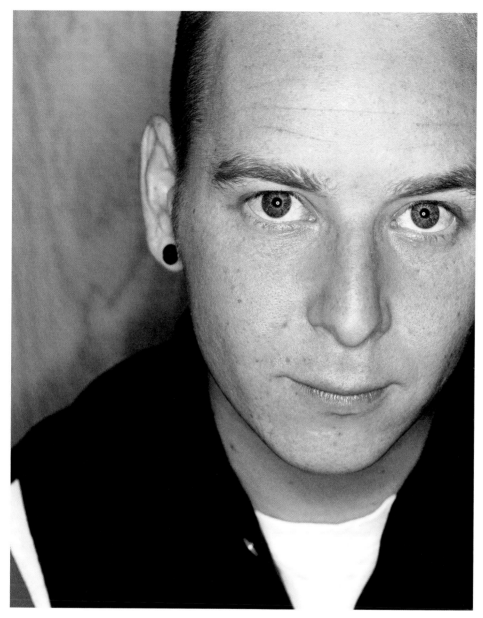

Figure 5.21 The skin appears to be much healthier, and we haven't touched a retouching tool.

To finish, you can use the Soft Light dodge-and-burn-layer trick to lighten the few remaining darker pimples. You might want to mask off the red to reduce the effect of the Hue/Saturation adjustment from the lips—especially with women. Just paint into the Hue/Saturation adjustment layer with black over the lips. In this image, I also brushed a little blue color into the eyes to relieve some of the monochromatic nature of the shot. In the end, all of the pimples have become soft freckles, and we have not corrupted the skin texture (Figure 5.22).

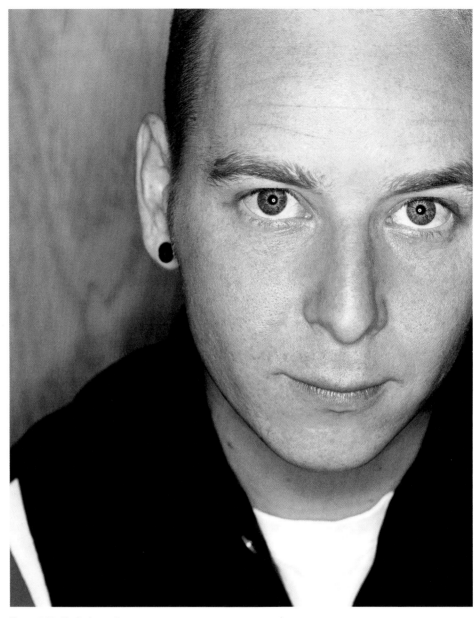

Figure 5.22 The final retouch

Skin Smoothing

Another skin repair technique was used for this shot of Dr. Doug (Figure 5.23). Doug is an acupuncturist, author, and longevity researcher. I would like him to look as healthy as he truly is. The digital camera emphasized the red tones in his skin, so you can use the Hue/Saturation adjustment techniques to equalize the skin tone. Next, I'd like to soften the wrinkles. Doug is an outdoor-sports enthusiast, and he has some unavoidable wrinkles and freckles due to sun exposure. I don't want to eliminate them, just soften them slightly. Let me show you a new technique to apply a global softening effect.

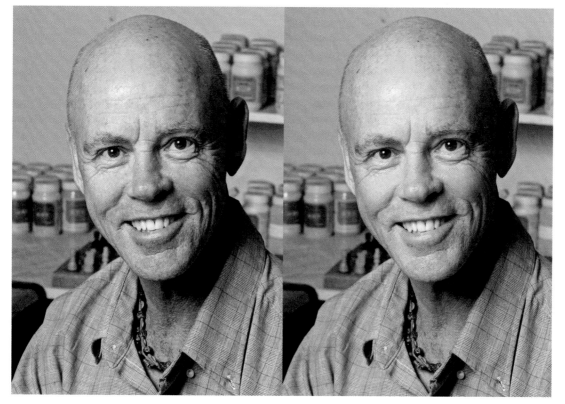

Figure 5.23 The original shot of Dr. Doug shows the typical overly red skin from a digital camera file (left), which can be corrected using the Hue/Saturation technique (right).

First, flatten the image (applying the Hue/Saturation adjustment layer in the process) by selecting Flatten Image from the Layers Panel Options menu (Figure 5.24). Duplicate the background by dragging the thumbnail to the New Layer icon at the bottom of the Layers panel (Figure 5.25). Now, run the Surface Blur filter (Filter > Blur > Surface Blur; see Figure 5.26), using a large Radius and Threshold to blur all the skin texture (Figure 5.27). Make a Black layer mask that hides this Blur layer by holding down the Option/Alt key and clicking on the Layer Mask icon at the bottom of the Layers panel (Figure 5.28). Paint into the layer mask with white over all the areas of skin except for the eyes, lips, and teeth (Figure 5.29).

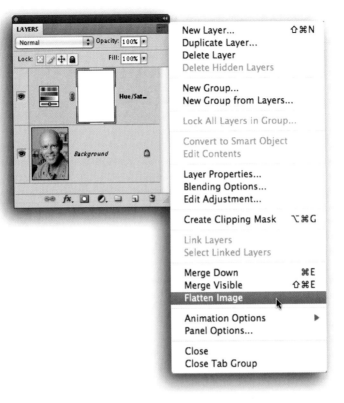

Figure 5.24 Flatten the image.

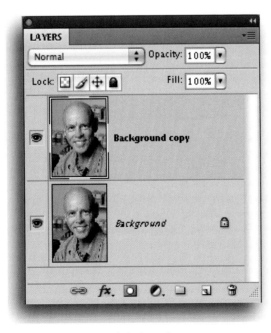

Figure 5.25 Duplicate the background.

| Layer | Select | **Filter** | Analysis | 3D | View | Window | Help |

Unsharp Mask	⌘F
Convert for Smart Filters	
Filter Gallery...	
Liquify...	⇧⌘X
Vanishing Point...	⌥⌘V
Artistic	▶
Blur	▶
Brush Strokes	▶
Distort	▶
Noise	▶
Pixelate	▶
Render	▶
Sharpen	▶
Sketch	▶
Stylize	▶
Texture	▶
Video	▶
Other	▶
Alien Skin Bokeh	▶
Digimarc	▶
George DeWolfe	▶
Nik Software	▶
Browse Filters Online...	

Blur submenu:
Average
Blur
Blur More
Box Blur...
Gaussian Blur...
Lens Blur...
Motion Blur...
Radial Blur...
Shape Blur...
Smart Blur...
Surface Blur...

Figure 5.26 Run the Surface Blur filter.

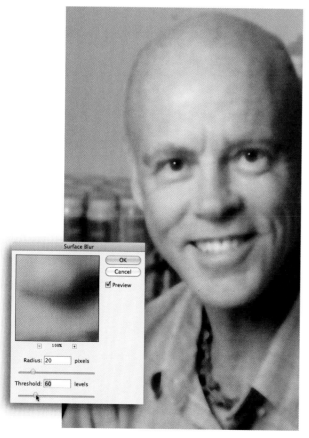

Figure 5.27 Blur all the skin texture.

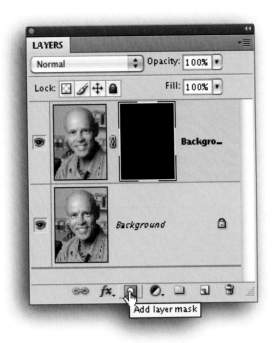

Figure 5.28 Hide the Blur layer with a Black layer mask.

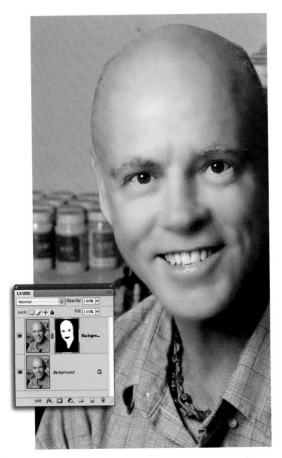

Figure 5.29 Paint into the layer mask to reveal the blur everywhere except the eyes, lips, and hair.

Now, duplicate the Blur layer so that you have two identical Blur layers. You are going to use one layer to darken and the other layer to lighten the wrinkles in the original, background image. Turn off the visibility of the top Blur layer (click the Eye icon in the Layers panel), and rename it to Blur-dark; then select the first Blur layer, rename it to Blur-light, and change the mode to Lighten (Figure 5.30).

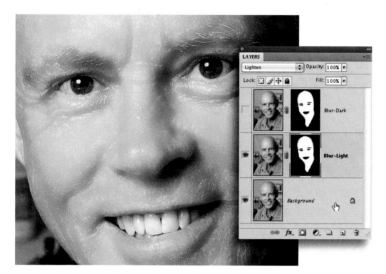

Figure 5.30 Two Blur layers, the first one in Lighten mode

Lighten mode applies the layer only where it can make the underlying image lighter. Because you applied blurred shadows into highlights, the highlights in the Lighten Blur layer are not as bright, so you can see the light lines from the original. The blur covers only the darker parts of the image. Now, you'll want to lighten the Blur Light layer so that it hides more of the light wrinkles. Bring up a levels adjustment (Image > Adjustments > Levels) for this Blur layer (Figure 5.31). Push the middle slider to the left a little bit, so that more (but not all) of the light wrinkles are hidden.

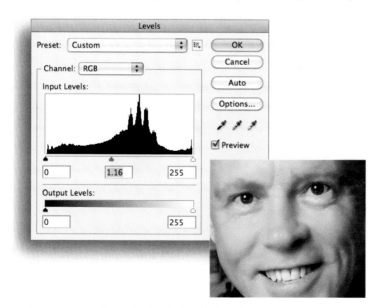

Figure 5.31 Move the Gray Levels slider slightly left to lighten the Blur layer and hide more of the lighter wrinkles.

Now, we will reverse things for the other Blur layer. Turn off the visibility for the first Blur layer. Turn on and select the top Blur layer. Change the mode to Darken (Figure 5.32).

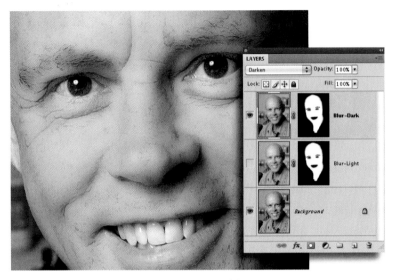

Figure 5.32 The Darken Blur layer covers the lighter parts of the image.

We need to do something similar to darken the Blur Dark layer to hide more of the dark wrinkles. As before, select Image > Adjustments > Levels (Figure 5.33). This time, push the middle slider to the right to darken the layer slightly and cover up more of the dark wrinkles.

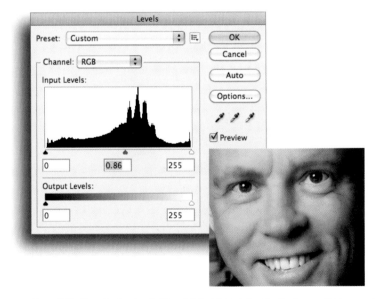

Figure 5.33 Move the Gray Levels slider slightly right to darken the Blur layer and hide more of the darker wrinkles.

When the two Blur layers are set up, you can adjust the opacity of Lighten and Darken blurs independently to get the desired skin-smoothing effect. The final version uses an opacity of 45 percent for the Lighten Blur and 30 percent for the Darken Blur layers. The overall skin texture is lightened slightly, and the wrinkles are smoothed without being removed. No cloning or healing was done. If you are ambitious enough, you can record all the steps to generate this effect as an action. Compare the new version with the unsmoothed version to see just how far we've taken the photo (Figure 5.34).

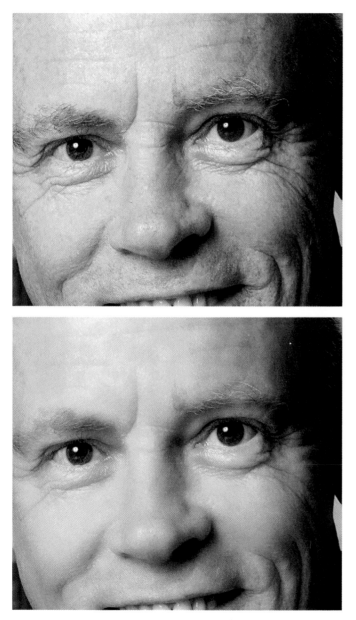

Figure 5.34 The unsmoothed version (top) shows a lot of skin texture hidden with skin-smoothing (bottom).

The final retouched version (Figure 5.35) achieves a skin-smoothing effect without obliterating the actual skin texture. This effect makes no attempt to remove wrinkles, but instead focuses on smoothing the texture of the skin in a subtle way; every detail is still there, just slightly less intense.

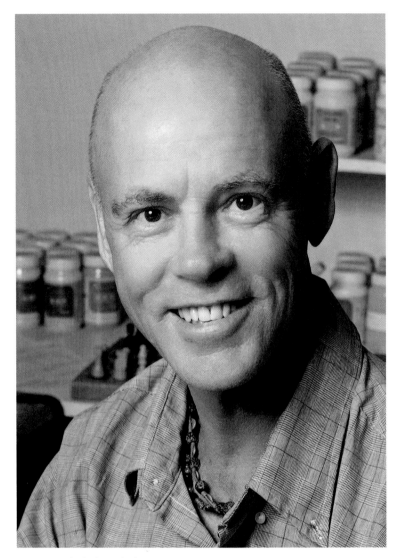

Figure 5.35 The final retouched version

Beauty Retouching

When you mention retouching, people often think about the impossibly flawless high-fashion models and cover girls they see in magazines. In this type of photography, there is no real attempt to be realistic. Instead, photographers try to create a believable impossibility. Flawless skin is expected; but at the same time, the skin shouldn't look like plastic. Often, the challenge is to create this effect with subjects that are not even close to ideal raw material. You'll need to know how to completely reconstruct the skin if an assignment calls for it. Of course, nothing is impossible nowadays.

In this example, we will work with the shot of an attractive woman in her fifties (Figure 5.36).

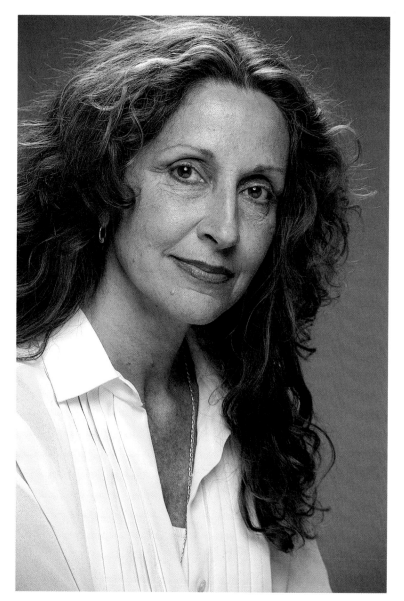

Figure 5.36 This woman is quite beautiful. She is, however, no longer 20 years old.

In our youth-obsessed culture, it is not surprising that photographers are asked to take 30 years off the faces of various authors, musicians, actors, and actresses. Its much harder to see skin details on television and motion pictures in general, not just because the resolution is lower, but things are moving so people are often unaware just how old some of their favorite idols are. With this in mind, we are going to completely rebuild this woman's skin.

Much as we did in the previous example, we'll start by making a new layer. In this case, we are going to duplicate the background image by dragging the thumbnail in the Layers panel to the New Layer icon. The strategy here is to blur this copy as the basis for the new skin, so let's rename the layer (by double-clicking the Background Copy name next to the new thumbnail) and call it Surface Blur (Figure 5.37).

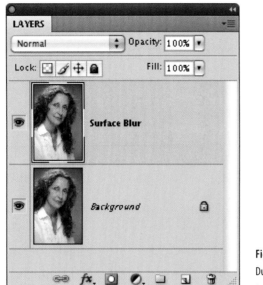

Figure 5.37
Duplicate the background to a new layer by dragging to the New Layer icon.

Choose Filter > Blur > Surface Blur (Figure 5.38). Surface Blur is a filter (new in Photoshop CS2) that is especially useful in this application. This blur maintains the major edge transitions, but it also manages to create a very smooth blur. The Radius slider controls the intensity of the blur, and the Threshold slider controls how much of the image stays sharp. Higher Threshold settings have a greater blurring effect. You'll want to adjust the sliders so that you can completely smooth the wrinkles and skin texture while leaving major features intact (Figure 5.39).

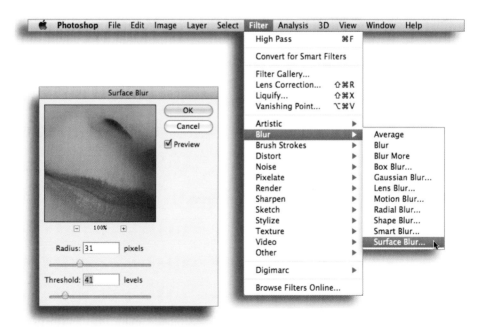

Figure 5.38 The Surface Blur filter is perfect for smoothing skin.

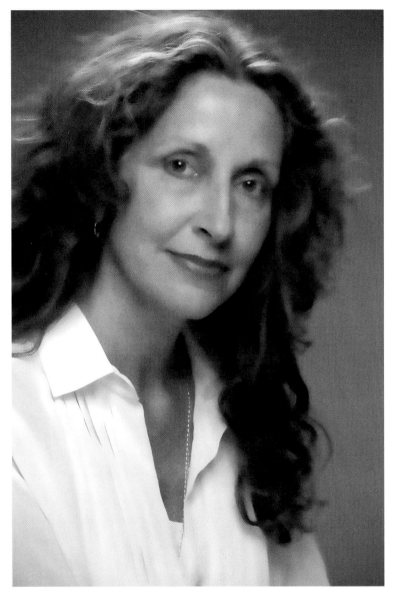

Figure 5.39 Skin and other textures are completely smoothed with the application of Surface Blur.

We will hide this Blur layer with a layer mask. Hold down the Option/Alt key and click the Layer Mask icon at the bottom of the Layers panel (Figure 5.40). This action creates a Black layer mask and hides the Blur layer while revealing the original image.

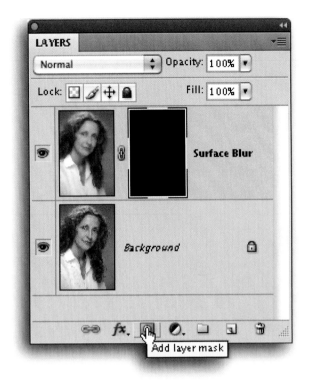

Figure 5.40 Option/Alt+click the Layer Mask icon to create a Black layer mask.

Now simply paint into the layer mask with white to cover the areas of skin that you want to smooth (Figure 5.41). The area you are working on can be difficult to see if you've covered everything. You can toggle off the visibility of the Background layer to see if there are any *holes*. To do so, click the Eye icon next to the Background thumbnail in the Layer panel (Figure 5.42).

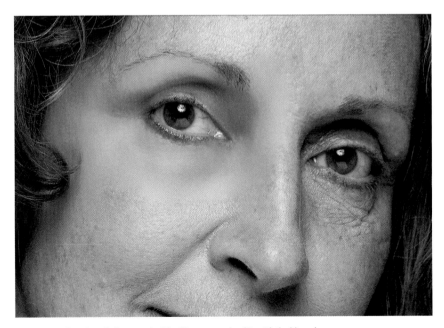

Figure 5.41 Paint into the layer mask with white to cover the skin with the blurred copy.

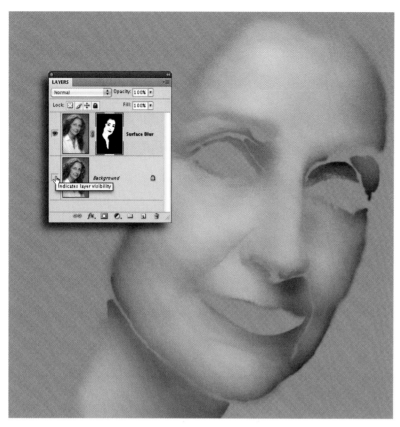

Figure 5.42 To check for holes, toggle the visibility of the Background layer.

Carefully paint around all the areas you need to keep—the eyes, lips, etc.—until you've covered up all the "bad" skin. At this point, you should have something that looks like Figure 5.43.

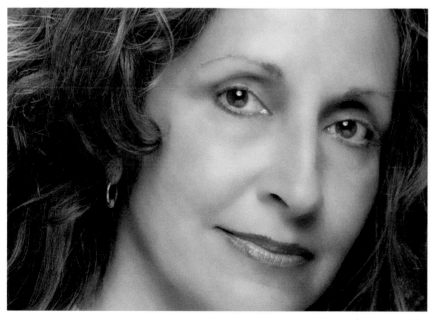

Figure 5.43 Work carefully so that you smooth the wrinkled skin, but keep other features sharp.

The skin will be smooth, but the colors and tone might be a little blotchy looking. To fix this, make a new layer, but Option/Alt+click the New Layer icon to bring up the New Layer Options dialog. Check the Use Previous Layer To Create Clipping Mask box (Figure 5.44). This will allow the mask in the underlying layer to control the new Paint layer.

New Layer	
Name: Paint smoothing	OK
☑ Use Previous Layer to Create Clipping Mask	Cancel
Color: ☐None	
Mode: Normal Opacity: 100 ▸ %	
☐ (No neutral color exists for Normal mode.)	

Figure 5.44 Check the Use Previous Layer To Create Clipping Mask box when you create the new Paint layer.

Take a large soft brush, sample colors from the blurred skin (Option/Alt+click to turn the cursor into an Eyedropper and sample a color), and paint with a very low opacity to gradually smooth out the color and tones (Figure 5.45).

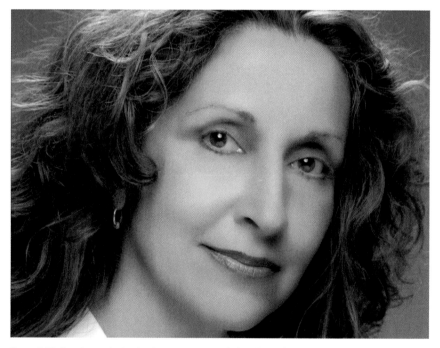

Figure 5.45 Use a large paint brush at low opacity to smooth the colors and even the tones.

At this point, you'll want to bring back some hint of the underlying skin. Select the Blur layer by clicking the thumbnail in the Layers panel. Push the Opacity slider to the left a bit to bring back some of the underlying layer (Figure 5.46).

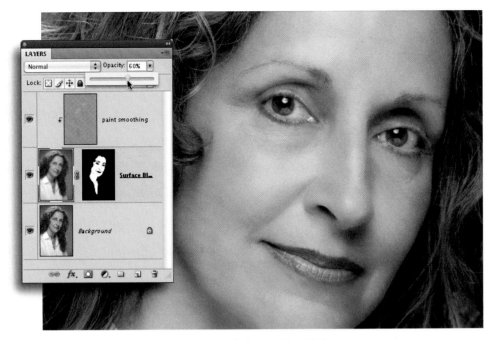

Figure 5.46 Reduce the opacity of the Blur layer to bring back some of the original texture.

Next, we'll use a technique similar to the one we used on my face at the beginning of this chapter. However, this time I've already covered the original skin with a blurred copy and paint. Now, I want to create a Dodge And Burn layer and dodge out any unattractive wrinkles that are left—this is very similar to what I did before—except that I will use Overlay instead of Soft Light. Option/Alt+click the New Layer icon at the bottom of the Layers panel. This will bring up the New Layer dialog. Change the Mode to Overlay, and then check the Fill With Overlay-Neutral Color box. This will fill the New Layer with 50 percent gray. Make sure you check the Use Previous Layer To Create Clipping Mask box. You want to keep using the mask you created with the Blur layer. Use the Dodge tool to dodge away wrinkles. In Figure 5.47, you can see what Overlay looks like if it is applied as a Normal layer. I'm using Overlay this time because the opacity of the underlying layers is less than 100 percent and we need the stronger application of dodging that Overlay provides.

The subject's skin now appears to be very smooth with just a hint of its original skin texture. To keep the image from looking too plastic, you'll need to add more texture to the skin. I've experimented with all kinds of different approaches and I've revised my approach to texturizing skin a bit since the first edition of the book—I have a few more tricks to share here.

All of these skin texture techniques share a basic idea that involves putting a texture into an Overlay or Soft Light layer. The basic one goes like this: first, create a new Gray Overlay layer. Option/Alt+click the New Layer icon at the bottom of the Layers panel to bring up the New Layer dialog. Check the Use Previous Layer To Create Clipping Mask box, select Overlay from the Mode drop-down, and check the Fill With Overlay Neutral Color (50% Gray) box (Figure 5.48).

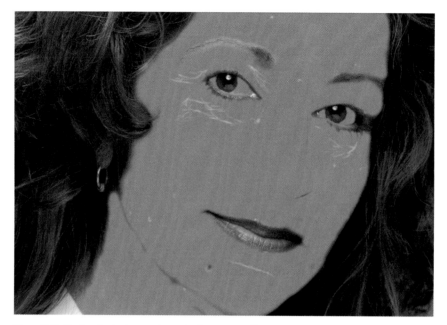

Figure 5.47 The Gray Overlay layer can be used to iron away wrinkles.

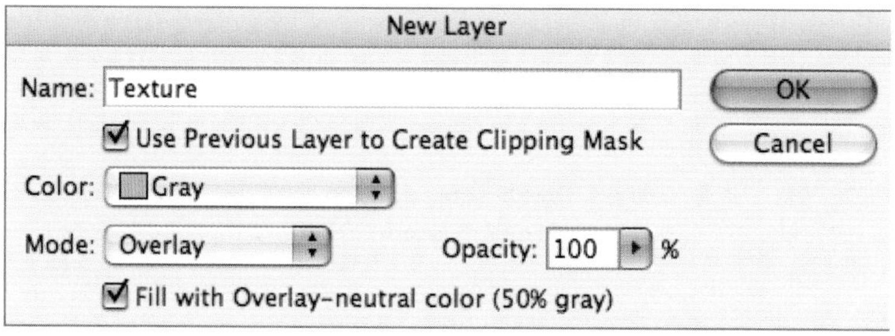

Figure 5.48 The Gray Overlay layer will have no effect on the image until you add texture to it.

The Layers panel should look like Figure 5.49. The last three layers created are being controlled by the opacity and layer mask of the Surface Blur layer. To get a better idea of how the Texture layer is going to affect things, temporarily push the Opacity slider for the Blur layer back to 100 percent. You won't see any of the original texture, but you will be able to see the new texture you are about to create. You will also see the dodge lines where you lightened the wrinkles; you can temporarily turn off the visibility of this layer if you find it distracting.

Select the Overlay Texture layer and run the Noise filter on it (Filter > Noise > Add Noise). Check the Uniform and Monochromatic boxes, and add enough noise to make the image look like an old fashioned, grainy, film image (Figure 5.50).

The ideal value in the filter dialogs depends on the size and resolution of the file. As such, no hard rules can apply to all images. You have to develop a feel for this, and sometimes you have to make a test print to judge a subtle effect such as noise. Remember that you can always change the opacity of the texture layer to reduce the intensity of the noise. What we're really looking for is the size of the grain. Don't go overboard because the size will swell somewhat in the next step, but don't be too timid either.

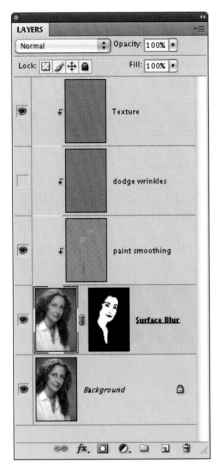

Figure 5.49
After you create the Overlay Texture layer, change the opacity of the Surface Blur layer back to 100 percent.

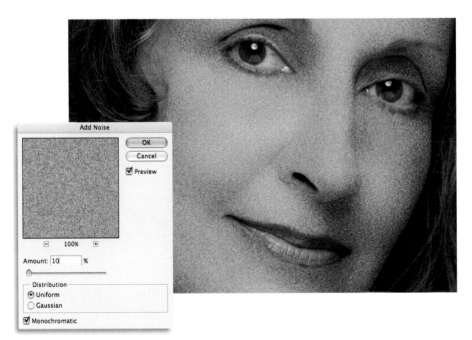

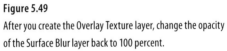

Figure 5.50 Add obvious noise.

Many photographers stop here, but this noise is too sharp for our purposes. With the Gray Overlay Texture still selected, run a Blur filter (Filter > Blur > Gaussian Blur). Use just enough Blur to soften the edges of the noise without completely smoothing it out (Figure 5.51).

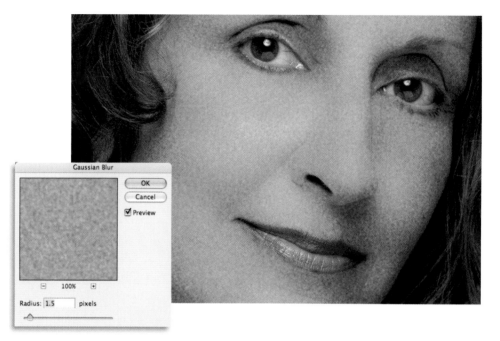

Figure 5.51 Soften the noise with a Gaussian Blur filter.

This texture can be used quite successfully by reducing the opacity of the texture as well as the smoothing layer. The interaction between the original texture and the new texture helps hide the original skin defects without rendering a plastic smoothness to the skin (Figure 5.52 bottom). Compare the results with the original (Figure 5.52 top) to see how effective this can be.

The problem here, as with all artificial skin textures, is that it is too uniform and consistent across the entire surface. Thus, it behooves you to create a library of different skin textures that can be applied to different areas of the face or body.

Let's start by saving this first skin texture as a pattern: first, remove the clipping mask from the Texture layer. (A quick way to do this is to Option/Alt+click on the line dividing the layer from its clipping layer (Figure 5.53). Notice that the cursor changes, indicating the clipping mask function (you can Option/Alt+click again to reclip). The Layer thumbnail will pop to the left in the layer stack—change the opacity to 100 percent and the apply mode to Normal. The Gray Texture layer will now completely cover the image.

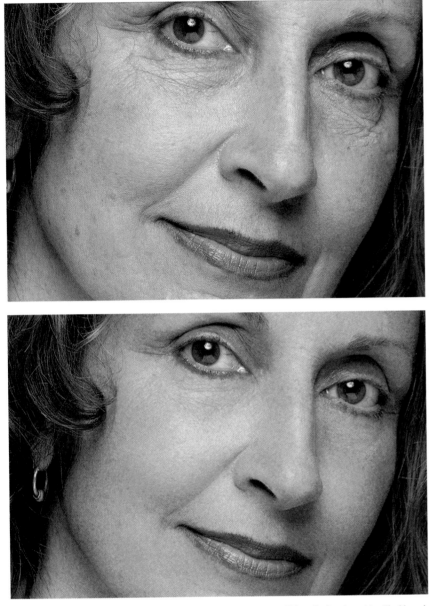

Figure 5.52 The original photo (top) shows that the subject has had a good life with a lot of sunshine. The blurred noise (bottom) creates a convincing texture.

Select all (Command/Ctrl+A) and then select Define Pattern from the Edit menu. When the Pattern Name dialog box opens, give the texture a meaningful name, as shown in Figure 5.54.

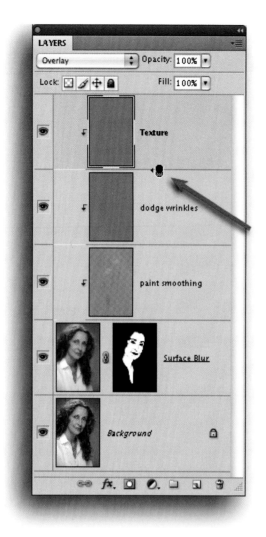

Figure 5.53 The Texture layer can be "unclipped" by Option/Alt+clicking on the dividing line between layers.

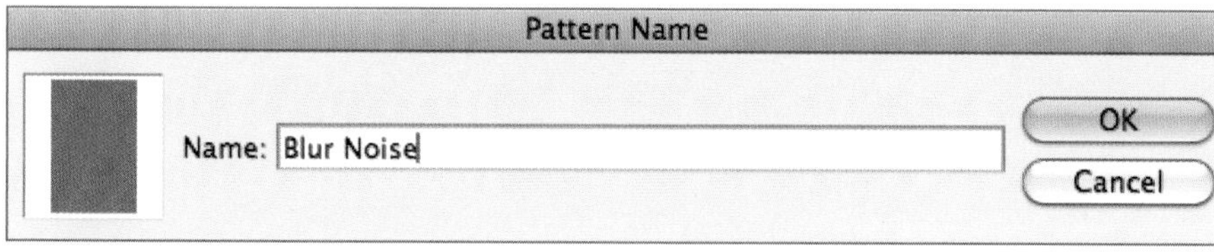

Pattern Name

Name: Blur Noise

OK

Cancel

Figure 5.54 Name the pattern something meaningful, so you can recall what it does.

Congratulations! You've made your first pattern. Turn off the visibility of this layer. (You will use it to create more texture patterns later; you can delete it after you're done making patterns.) To add the texture back in using the pattern you just created, hold down the Option/Alt key and select Pattern from the Adjustment Layer icon at the bottom of the Layers panel (Figure 5.55). Set your layer options the same way you did for the Gray Texture layer (Figure 5.56). Click the Pattern thumbnail in the Pattern Fill dialog and select your new gray pattern (Figure 5.57).

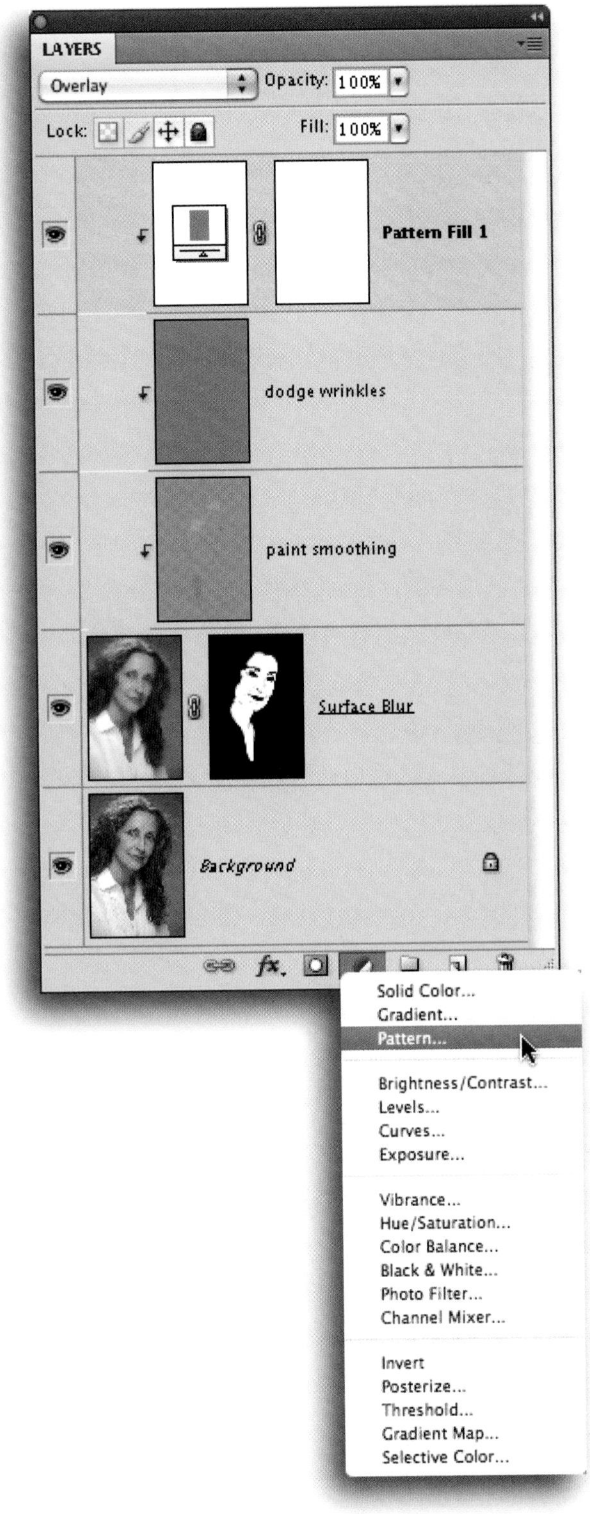

Figure 5.55 Select the Pattern adjustment layer.

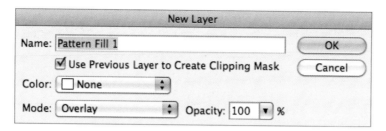

Figure 5.56 Set layer options to Overlay mode and check the Use Previous Layer To Create Clipping Mask box.

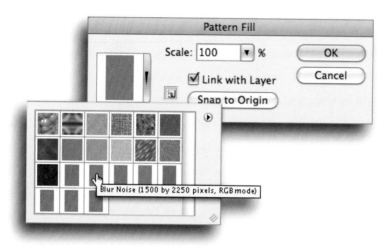

Figure 5.57 Select the new, gray texture pattern by clicking the thumbnails.

This pattern applies the texture the same way the original layer did. However, the beauty of using patterns, besides being able to recall them easily, is that you can scale them. Double-click the Pattern Fill Adjustment Layer thumbnail in the Layers panel and you'll return to the Pattern Fill dialog, where you can change the scale percentage to suit your needs; scale it up or down to size the texture to match the image. This scale factor can completely alter the look of the texture.

Let's make another pattern. Return to the Blurred Noise layer or create a new gray, blurred noise image, and then run the Emboss filter (Filter > Stylize > Emboss). This will generate a more three-dimensional effect. In many cases, you can introduce a subtle wrinkle into the texture (Figure 5.58).

Save this as a pattern, run a slight Gaussian Blur on the texture, and save that as a variation. Another thing I like to do immediately after running the Emboss filter is to select: Edit > Fade Emboss (Figure 5.59), then reduce the opacity of the emboss to return some of the original noise texture (Figure 5.60). Save this and try another one starting from the basic, blurred noise texture. Run the Emboss filter again and Fade, but this time change the mode to Lighten (Figure 5.61).

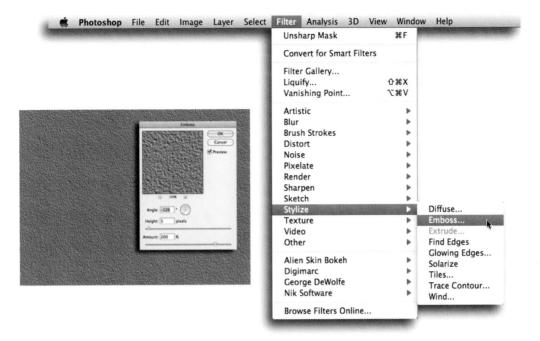

Figure 5.58 Run the Emboss filter to get a more three-dimensional effect. Sometimes the emboss generates interesting features into the texture.

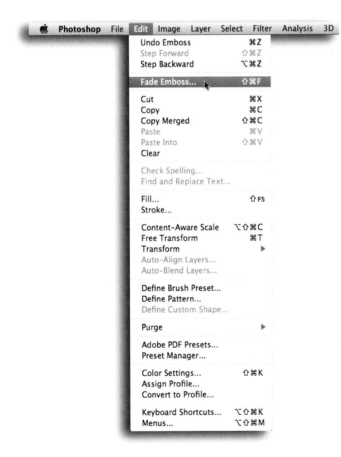

Figure 5.59 Select Fade Emboss.

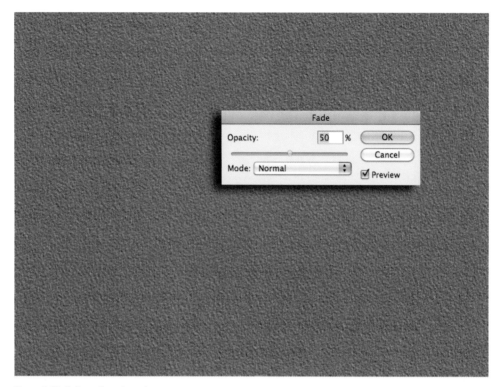

Figure 5.60 Fading softens the emboss texture.

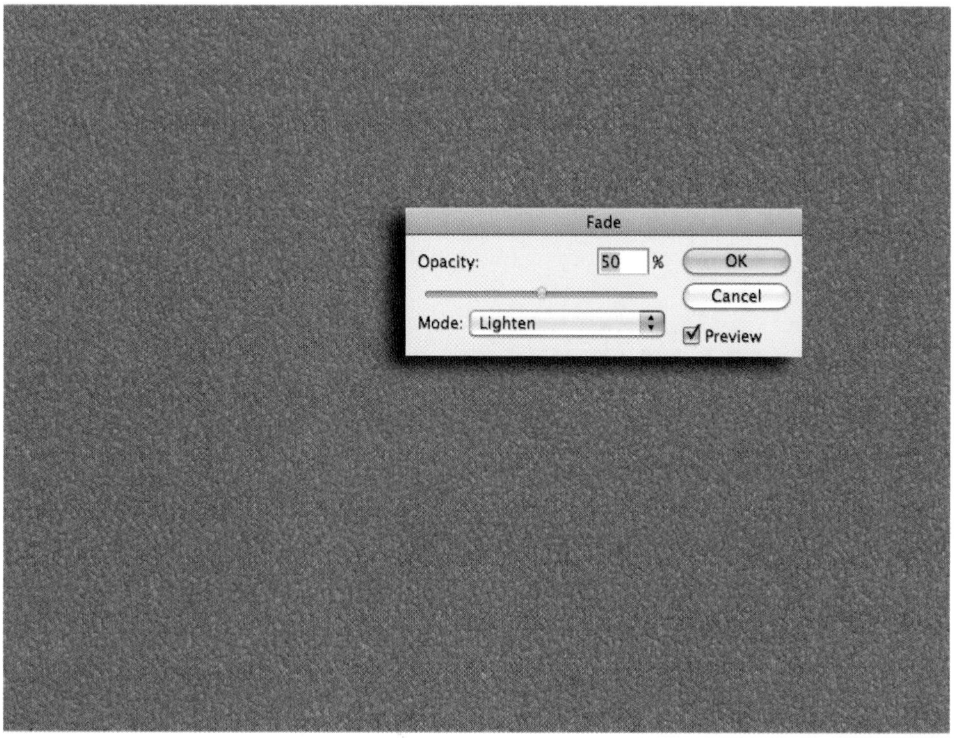

Figure 6.61 The Lighten fade has a realistic subtle texture.

These different textures can be used to give the smoothed skin some realistic variation in texture. Use different textures on the cheeks, neck, and chin. You should also vary the intensity of the texture across the face. The jaw line usually has less texture than the cheeks or around the mouth. The nose is also usually a lot smoother. Use a layer mask to introduce fine control over the opacity of the texture in different areas. Use the original skin texture as a guide for the relative strength of texture in the various parts of the face.

Note: A library of skin "patterns" is available on the website: www.varis.com/skinbook.

One last little trick! Often, with all this skin smoothing and retouching, we tend to lose or mute the subtle highlights on the skin. To enhance the natural sparkle, I use a technique I like to call "pixie dust." First, select the Blue channel in the Channels panel and drag the Channel thumbnail to the new Channel icon at the bottom of the Channels panel (Figure 5.62). This creates a new Alpha channel that you can use to create a selection for the highlights. The Blue channel is always the darkest for faces, and it is the perfect starting place for the high-contrast mask we're aiming for. Call up a curves adjustment while you have the new channel selected (Image > Adjustments > Curves). (See Figure 5.63.)

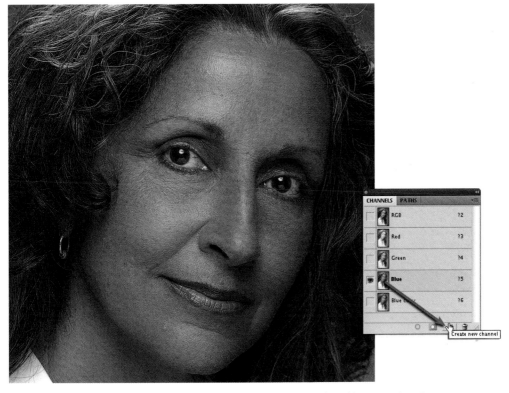

Figure 5.62 Duplicate the Blue channel to a new Alpha channel to create a Dark Blue channel for your starting point.

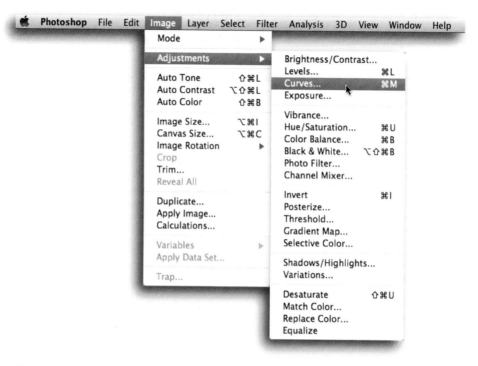

Figure 5.63 Run a Curves adjustment directly on the new channel.

Use a steep curve to create a very high-contrast effect. You want the major planes of the face to break to pure white and everything else to go very dark (Figure 5.64). Now, take a brush and paint everything that is not a skin highlight black. Paint white into areas you want to highlight more (Figure 5.65). Finally, run a Gaussian Blur to smooth out any texture (Figure 5.66).

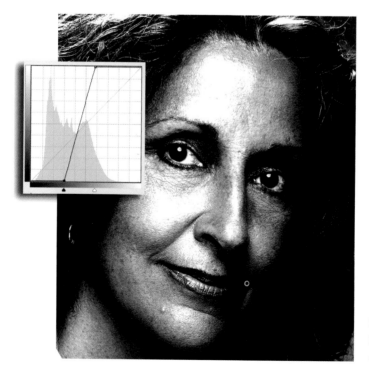

Figure 5.64
Run Curves to increase contrast.

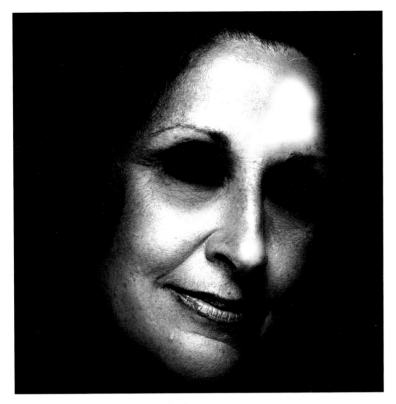

Figure 5.65 Paint non-highlight areas to black.

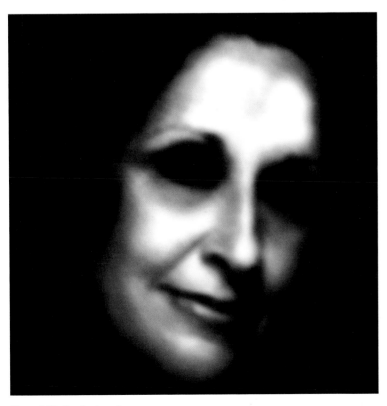

Figure 5.66 Blur the channel.

Reselect the RGB composite channel and Command/Ctrl+click the new Alpha channel to load a selection for the highlights (Figure 5.67). Then, create a new layer by clicking the icon at the bottom of the Layers panel and fill the selected area with white. If the highlights are too broad, you can "choke" them by clicking the Layer Mask icon at the bottom of the Layers panel while the selection is still active (Figure 5.68). The major planes of the face will take on a white glow (Figure 5.69). There are a number of different things you can do, including reduce the opacity and change the Apply mode to Overlay. I'll show you how to apply this in an unusual way.

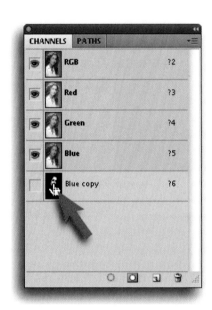

Figure 5.67 Command/Ctrl+click the Channel thumbnail to load the selection.

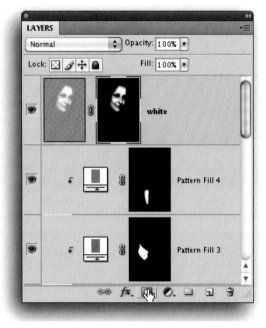

Figure 5.68 Add a layer mask from the selection to choke the highlights further.

Change the Apply mode of the White layer to Dissolve and reduce the opacity until the face is covered with a fine, even speckle (Figure 5.70). Select the layer right underneath this one and make a new Gray Overlay layer (Option/Alt+click on the New Layer icon at the bottom of the Layers panel and set up the resulting dialog with Overlay mode and "Fill with Overlay Neutral Color"). Name this layer **Pixie Dust** (Figure 5.71). Select the top "white" layer, and then select Merge Down from the Layer Options flyaway menu at the upper-right of the Layers panel (Figure 5.72).

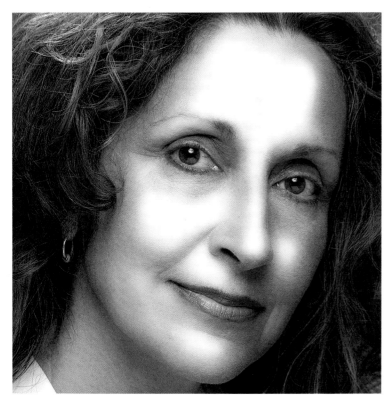

Figure 5.69 White covers the major planes of the face.

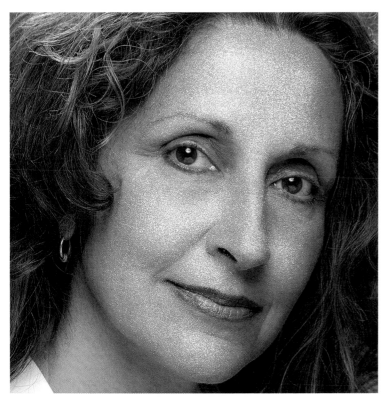

Figure 5.70 Lower the opacity until white speckles cover the face.

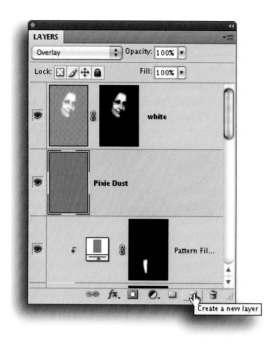

Figure 5.71 Create a new Gray Overlay layer.

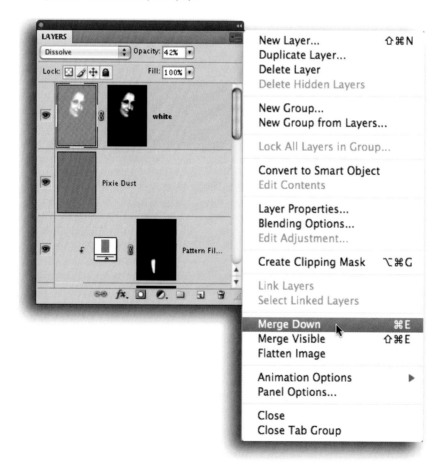

Figure 5.72 Merge the White layer down onto the Gray Overlay layer.

This is the last step; I promise. Run a Gaussian Blur on the Pixie Dust Overlay layer to just knock the edge off. Then, reduce the opacity to "dust" the highlights with a little sparkle. You want to keep this very subtle, and you might want to mask it off of more areas with a layer mask. I'm exaggerating it a bit in Figure 5.73 because I want to make sure you can see it. In practice, you want to keep this very subtle. The "dusting" adds just a little extra texture to the highlight areas that might have gone a bit flat.

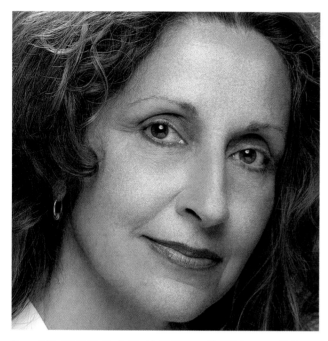

Figure 5.73 A light "dusting" of the highlights can add a little texture and bring up the highlights.

For the final retouched version (Figure 5.74), I brightened the eyes (enlarged the pupils), brushed in some subtle eye shadow color, and performed a little edge burning. (I'll tell you more about edge burning in Chapter 8, "Parting Shots.") Because all of the retouching was performed in layers that are controlled by the Surface Blur layer, you can reduce the opacity of that layer a little more if you want a more realistic rendering (Figure 5.75).

Note: The finished Photoshop document with all the layers is available on the www .varis.com/skinbook website.

Professional photographers are frequently asked to improve even young, classically beautiful models. Take a look at the results of this same sort of approach in Figure 5.76. (The original is on the left; the retouched version is on the right.)

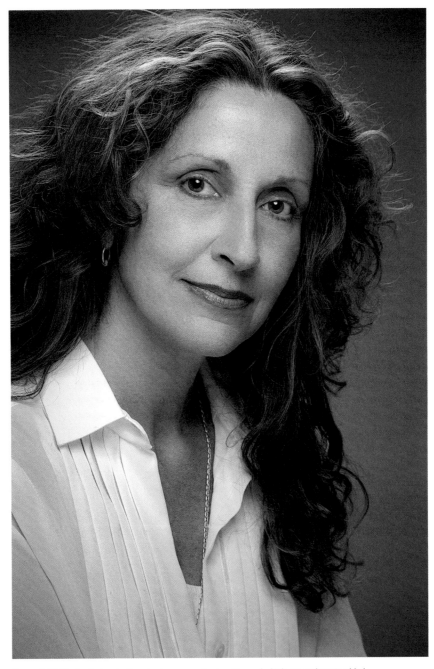

Figure 5.74 The final retouched version has some edge burning, and a little eye makeup is added.

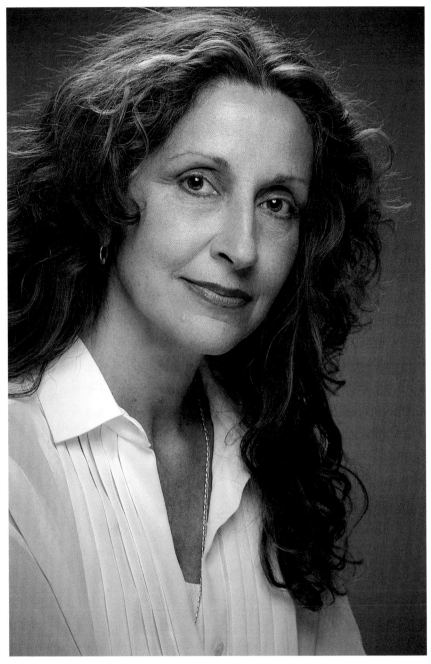

Figure 5.75 Reducing the opacity of the Surface Blur layer brings back some of the real skin and still manages to hide most of the wrinkles.

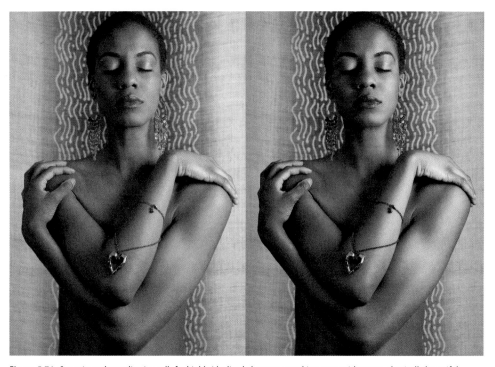

Figure 5.76 Sometimes the application calls for highly idealized glamour retouching, even with young, classically beautiful models.

Subtle Retouching

Extensive retouching is not always appropriate. For example, you aren't going to turn the sweet old lady in Figure 5.77 into a 20-year-old babe. You can enhance this image, but you certainly must resist any urge to remove wrinkles or other signs of aging because it would be perceived as undignified. In cases such as this, I prefer to simply adjust the skin color to give it a somewhat healthier tone. I might work on the makeup a bit and liven up the eyes by enlarging the pupils and catch lights; however, I don't want to make her look like anything other than what she is.

For the final version (Figure 5.78), I used a Hue/Saturation adjustment layer to equalize the skin color and increase the saturation in the skin and hair a bit to give it a healthy glow. I put a little light into her eyes, and I *very* slightly worked the wrinkles with a Soft Light layer. The finishing touch was the blur of the background. I did this by drag-copying the background into a new layer, running a Blur filter (you can use Gaussian Blur or even Lens Blur) and then hiding the blurred layer with a Black layer mask (Option/Alt+click the Layer Mask icon at the bottom of the Layers panel). I painted the blurred background over the underlying layer (use white to paint into the Black layer mask). We'll do more of this background blurring in Chapter 6, "Special Effects."

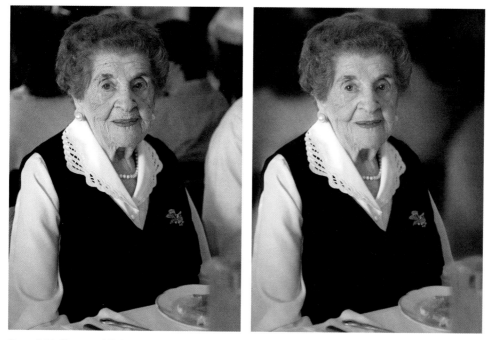

Figure 5.77 This sweet old lady is never going to look like a 20-year-old.

Figure 5.78 The final version enhances the overall image, without looking obvious.

When you are preparing this type of retouch for final printing, you should avoid sharpening the skin. We will go over sharpening techniques in Chapter 7, "Preparing for Print." For now, just be aware that you want to avoid sharpening wrinkled skin; this goes a long way toward minimizing the wrinkled look. In most cases for natural portraiture, less is more. Simple things, such as enlarging the pupils and working catch lights into the eyes (as discussed in Chapter 3, "The Color of Skin"), can work wonders without *looking* as though things were altered.

Subtlety is especially important for shots of mature men. Wrinkles are like war scars, badges of honor for someone who has lived a good life. Be very careful about removing them. The gentleman in Figure 5.79 has earned his wrinkles, and you might want to emphasize them.

When in doubt, ask. Some people are vainer than others, and even older men sometimes want to look younger. For the most part, however, you'll want to concentrate on obvious defects, such as red blotchy skin, and subtly minimize wrinkles.

In other situations, you might want to emphasize wrinkles for effect. This image from Audry Stein shows an older Hindu gentleman (Figure 5.80). He has clearly lived a good hard life in the sun, and you might be inclined to bring out the leathery quality of his skin. To achieve this, you can use a special type of sharpening. (I will cover more sharpening techniques in Chapter 7.) First, duplicate the Background layer and immediately desaturate the new duplicate (Image > Adjustments > Desaturate). (See

Figure 5.81.) Now, run the High Pass filter (Filter > Other > High Pass). Aim for a kind of bas-relief effect using higher radius settings of maybe 15 to 20 or so, depending on the resolution of the image (Figure 5.82). Change the Apply mode of this Gray layer to Overlay. The image takes on a lot of extra contrast (Figure 5.83).

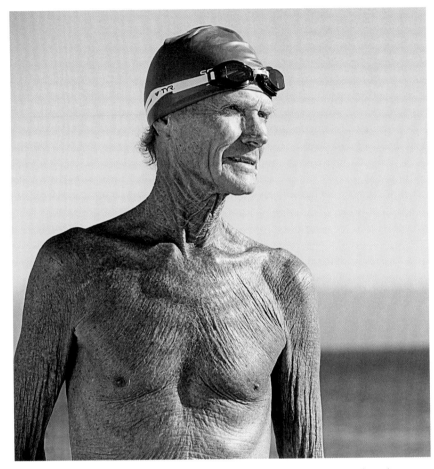

Figure 5.79 This gentleman is an athlete who has spent a lot of time in the sun. (Photo by Ken Chernus)

This man has fairly dark skin. You might want to prevent the Overlay effect from adding any darkening contrast and limit it to just lightening the highlights of the skin. To do this, you can use advanced blending options. Double-click into the area to the right of the High Pass Overlay Layer thumbnail in the Layers panel. This brings up the Layer Style dialog (Figure 5.84). Look in the Blend If area and move the This Layer gradient slider to the right until the setting changes to 128, the mid gray point. At this point, no effect occurs in the Overlay calculation. Only the lightening part of the Overlay layer will affect the underlying layer.

For the final image (Figure 5.85), I doubled up on the Overlay layer by duplicating it (dragging to the New Layer icon at the bottom of the Layers panel) a couple of times and masking to help equalize the highlights across the face (Figure 5.86). Compare it to the original image in Figure 5.80 to see how much extra texture we brought out in his face.

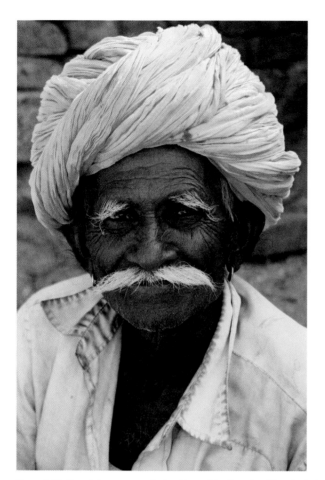

Figure 5.80 You might want to emphasize this man's leathery skin. (Photo by Audry Stein)

🍎 **Photoshop** File Edit **Image** Layer Select Filter Analysis 3D View Window Help		

Mode ▶

Adjustments ▶ | Brightness/Contrast...

Auto Tone   ⇧⌘L   Levels...   ⌘L
Auto Contrast ⌥⇧⌘L   Curves...   ⌘M
Auto Color   ⇧⌘B   Exposure...

Image Size...   ⌥⌘I   Vibrance...
Canvas Size... ⌥⌘C   Hue/Saturation... ⌘U
Image Rotation ▶   Color Balance...   ⌘B
Crop   Black & White... ⌥⇧⌘B
Trim...   Photo Filter...
Reveal All   Channel Mixer...

Duplicate...   Invert   ⌘I
Apply Image...   Posterize...
Calculations...   Threshold...
    Gradient Map...
Variables ▶   Selective Color...
Apply Data Set...
    Shadows/Highlights...
Trap...   Variations...

    Desaturate   ⇧⌘U
    Match Color...
    Replace Color...
    Equalize

Figure 5.81 Desaturate a duplicate layer.

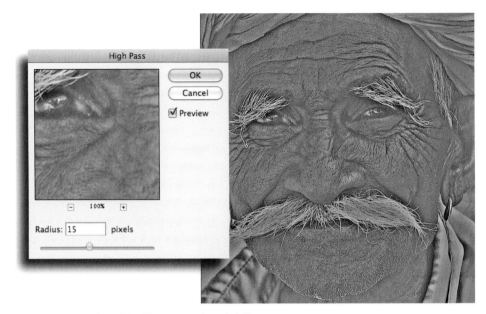

Figure 5.82 Run the High Pass filter to create a bas-relief effect.

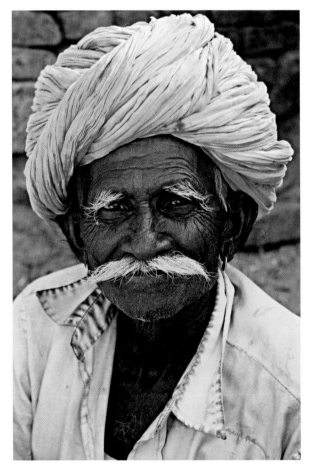

Figure 5.83 Added edge contrast is the result of changing to Overlay mode.

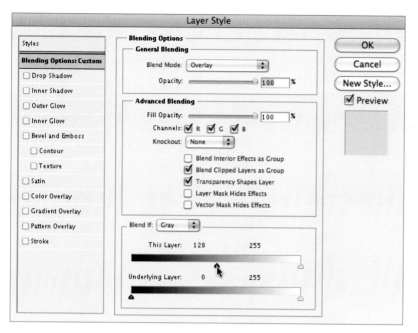

Figure 5.84 Move the Black slider to the right in the Layer Style dialog to limit the darkening contrast of the Overlay layer.

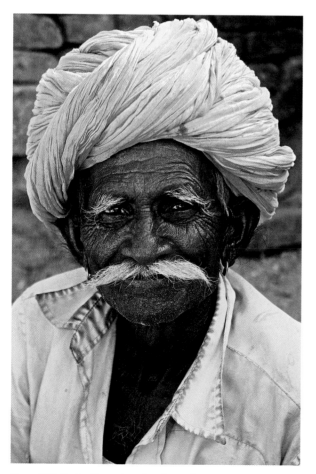

Figure 5.85 The final image shows lots of extra skin texture.

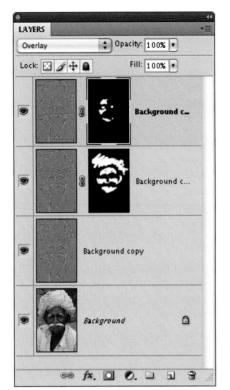

Figure 5.86
Doubling the High Pass Overlay
strengthens the effect.

Figure Thinning Techniques

"Make me look thinner!" Depending on the nature of the shot, a number of different techniques can be used for this very common request. Extreme cases involve a lot of re-illustrating, but the most common problems can be fixed very easily. Most people don't have perfect bodies; even attractive models can be captured in less-than-flattering angles and need some amount of corrective retouching.

One very simple approach can be illustrated by the example in Figure 5.87. This blackmail photo was taken on the occasion of my fiftieth-birthday party. I am making a fool of myself dancing with my daughter. (Yes, that's really my daughter.) I look a little wide in the hips here. It's been quite a while since I had a 30-inch waist, and I'd like to look a little thinner in this shot. This sort of situation, where you have a subject who isn't too bad but who wants to look thinner anyway, is very common.

To begin the digital makeover, make a simple rectangle selection around the figure and press Command+J/Ctrl+J to copy the figure into a new layer. Reselect it by Command/Ctrl+clicking the thumbnail in the Layers panel. Then do a free transform (Image > Transform > Free Transform). Squish and stretch the figure by pushing and pulling on the middle handles so that the figure becomes taller and thinner. A little bit goes a long way (Figure 5.88).

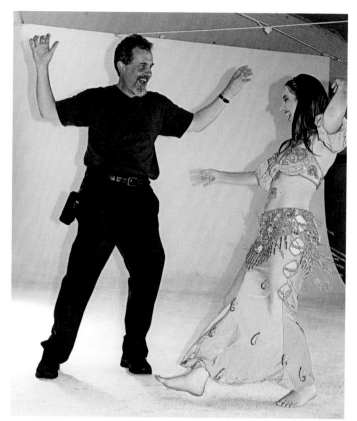

Figure 5.87
I'd like to look a little
thinner here.

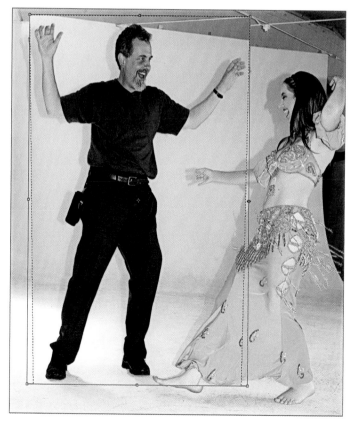

Figure 5.88
Stretch and squeeze
the figure.

The only thing that really gives away the trick is how squashed the head looks. To correct it, select the original head in the underlying layer and copy it into a new layer at the top. (Press Command+Option+J/Ctrl+Alt+J and drag to the top.) Position the original unsquashed head over the squished body, and voilà! You have a thinner me (Figure 5.89). Clone a little bit around the background to clean it up, and you'll get Figure 5.90.

The next example is more complex, but it is just as common (Figure 5.91). A simple *x-y* stretch will not correct the problem. The dancer really needs a tummy tuck. This type of retouching used to require a lot of careful work with the Clone Stamp tool. Fortunately, ever since Photoshop CS you have the Liquify tool, which works much better. The Liquify tool is actually a kind of super-filter with its own interface and set of tools.

Copy the background to a new layer and choose Filter > Liquify. A new window will appear with a preview of the image, a set of tools in the upper left, and a panel of controls at the right (Figure 5.92). By default, the Forward Warp tool is selected. You can use this tool to literally push in the tummy.

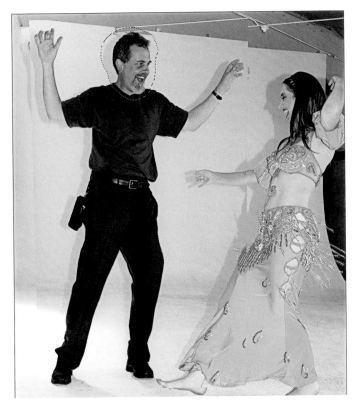

Figure 5.89 Copy the original head and place it above the squashed figure.

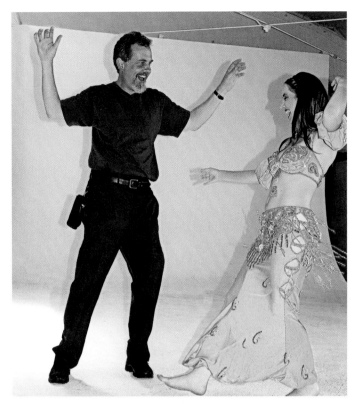

Figure 5.90
The final retouch

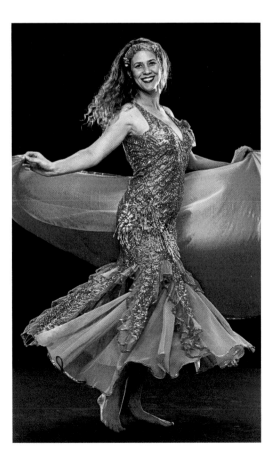

Figure 5.91
This beautiful dancer just had a baby and
needs just a little help with a tummy tuck.

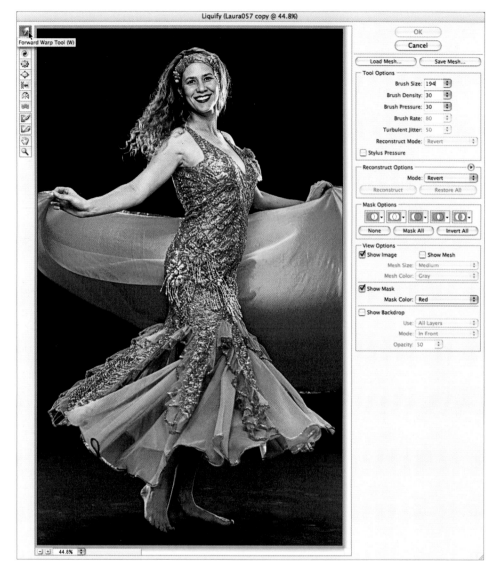

Figure 5.92 The Liquify filter has its own self-contained interface.

Adjust the brush size in the right-hand panel until it is big enough to, more or less, cover the stomach area. Reduce the Brush Density and Pressure to about 30 or even less; this will cause the tool to work more slowly and give you more control. Brush the stomach in, and you can magically push the image around as if it were plastic gel (Figure 5.93). If you work slowly and gradually push things into the final shape, you can avoid lumpy bumpy effects.

 Note: The normal keyboard navigation commands work inside the Liquify interface, so you can zoom in by pressing and holding spacebar+F/spacebar+Ctrl and clicking.

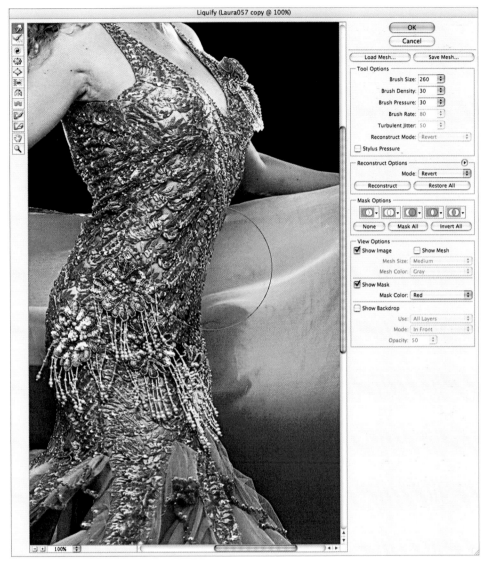

Figure 5.93 Push the tummy in with the Forward Warp tool.

You can do a lot of detailed reshaping using this technique. When you are satisfied with the results, press OK. That's it. For the final version (Figure 5.94), I also flipped the hair and trimmed her arm a bit; I did it all using the same Liquify brush.

This kind of retouch is so easy that I don't charge for it if my client is the subject. In fact, I often just go ahead and do this sort of thing without telling them. Your subjects will always be happy with the flattering version and typically compliment you on your excellent photography. (There is no need to spoil their illusions by showing them the unretouched version.) Of course, if the client is an ad agency, you should make sure they know you are doing the retouching. You can charge for it and get input on any other changes they might want. The more people who are involved in the decision making, the more nit-picky the retouching demands will be.

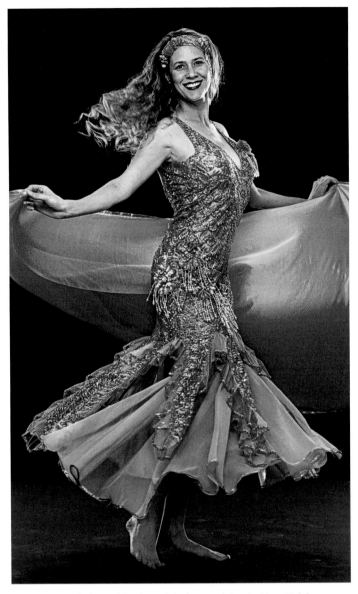

Figure 5.94 The final retouch has slimmed the dancer and given back her girlish figure.

Figure 5.95 is another example that demonstrates how much figure slimming you can perform with the Liquify tool.

I've shown you a number of different techniques using examples that are particularly suited to a specific technique. Most of the time, in the course of your regular work, you will need to use multiple techniques in different combinations for different parts of the image. Be on the lookout for novel solutions to unique problems. Perhaps the Liquify tools could be used to adjust an expression slightly, curl the lips subtly, or open a sleepy eye. Combine techniques in different ways. Adjust opacities more or less to suit a particular image. Use different kinds of noise or embossing effects in skin texture layers. Don't just apply the steps outlined here in a formulaic way. Keep experimenting and you'll discover your own techniques.

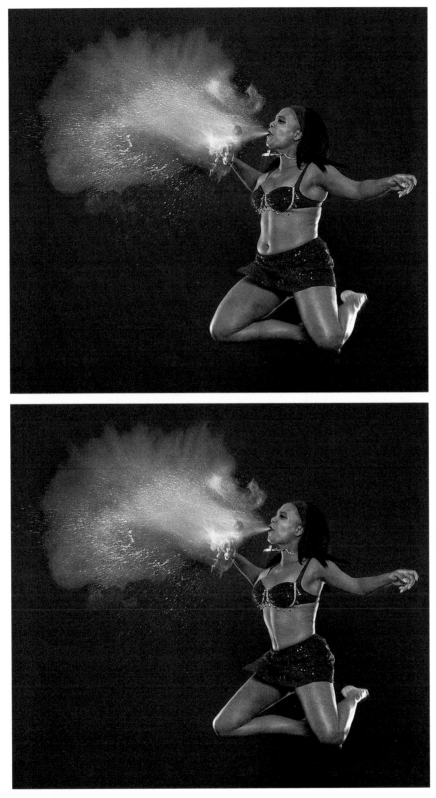

Figure 5.95 The original fire-eater could be slimmer; the Liquify tool can work wonders.

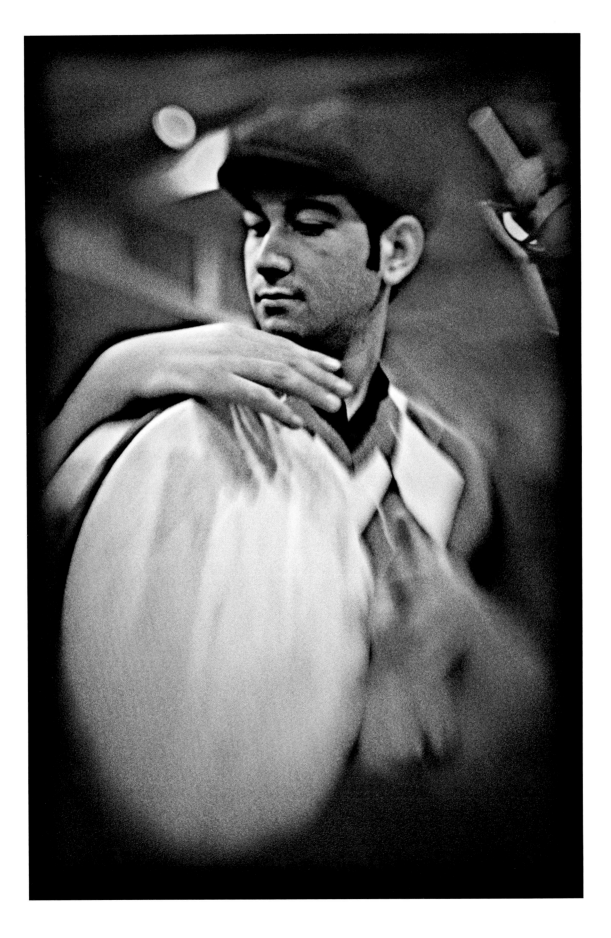

Special Effects

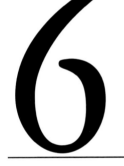

Ever since the movie Jurassic Park, *the general public has associated digital imagery of any kind with special effects. This is true with digital photography as well, and often people assume that some trick is involved just because an image was shot with a digital camera. Not all digital imagery involves trickery, but I certainly don't want to disappoint anyone hoping to learn a few special effects. This chapter will explore a few techniques that are uniquely digital, even though they may simulate traditional photographic effects. The focus will be on useful photographic effects commonly used with people photography.*

Chapter Contents
Soft Focus
Cross-Processing
Film Grain and Noise
Grunge
Tattoos

Soft Focus

Soft focus or diffusion effects have been used in photography since the earliest days when photographers sought to emulate impressionistic paintings (which were, in turn, influenced by the perspective rendering of the camera). Soft focus became very popular with people photography because it hid skin defects and suggested a sense of glamour and romance. Some Hollywood stars insisted on always being photographed with a diffusion filter. Photoshop has several ways to simulate the look of traditional diffusion filters, as well as some other soft-focus effects that go beyond what is possible with traditional methods. The biggest advantage to the digital approach, of course, is that you don't have to commit to a particular look at the time of exposure. Instead, you have the luxury of experimenting with different looks at your leisure after the shoot in a nondestructive way. We will explore a number of effects using the image in Figure 6.1.

Basic Diffusion Effect

All of the following soft-focus effects start with this basic technique.

1. Duplicate the background into a new layer by dragging the thumbnail to the New Layer icon at the bottom of the Layers panel (Figure 6.2).

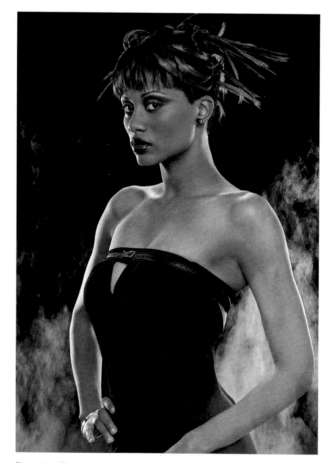

Figure 6.1 This sultry-model shot is the perfect starting point for glamour-enhancing soft-focus effects.

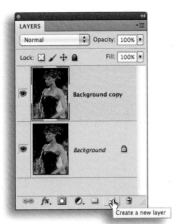

Figure 6.2
Duplicate the background into a new layer.

2. With this layer selected, choose Filter > Blur > Gaussian Blur. Set the radius high enough to get a good blur but still be able to identify the major features—eyes, lips, and general silhouette (Figure 6.3).

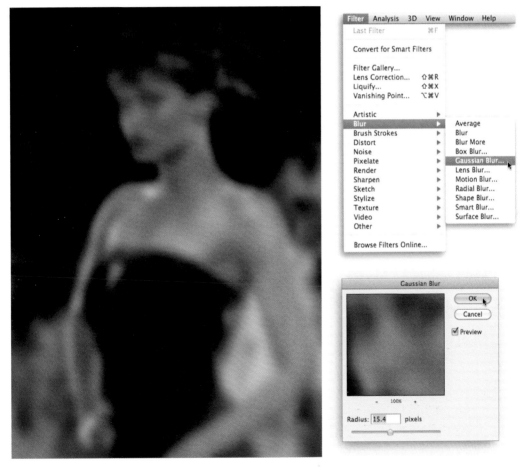

Figure 6.3 Run the Gaussian Blur filter on the duplicate layer.

3. Reduce the opacity of the blurred layer to bring back some of the sharp image underneath (Figure 6.4). This is very similar to what happens when you shoot with a diffusion filter on the lens. The only problem with this is that the blur also reduces the contrast of the image because shadows are blurred into highlights and highlights are blurred into shadows.

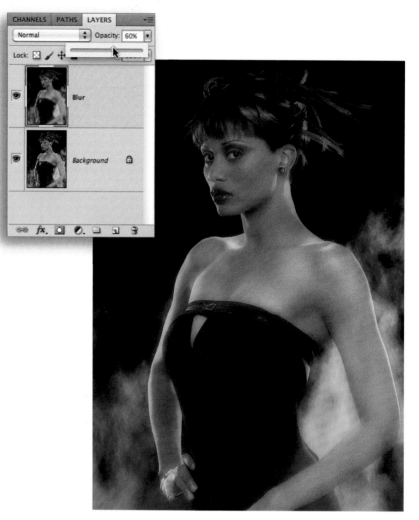

Figure 6.4 Reduce the opacity of the blurred layer.

You can compensate for this with a contrast-enhancing Curves adjustment layer on top of the Blur layer (Figure 6.5). Be careful with the curve; you don't want to eliminate the glow effect that the Blur layer gives you. In this example, returning the highlights to white is more important. If you try to bring the midtones back down to where they were, the glow effect of the blur will be hidden.

Steep S-curves such as this will also increase saturation in RGB. You might want to change the Layer mode for the curve to Luminosity (Figure 6.6). This will affect only the contrast of the image without affecting the color.

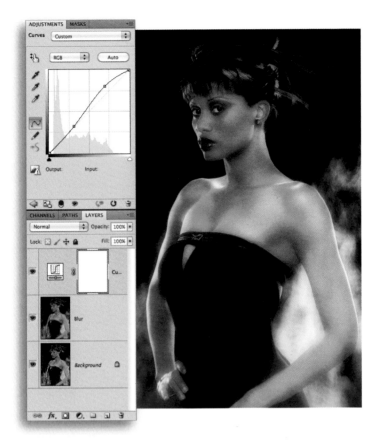

Figure 6.5
Bring back the
contrast with a Curves
adjustment.

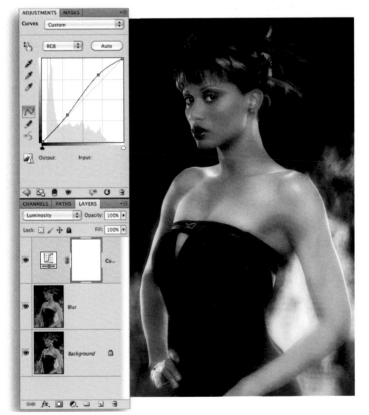

Figure 6.6
Change the Layer
mode to Luminosity
to eliminate the
oversaturated look.

If you would like to keep some of the increased saturation, you can duplicate the Curves layer, change the first one back to normal, and reduce the opacity to 40 percent. Reduce the duplicate to 60 percent; now you'll have the same contrast with just a little bit of the increased saturation (Figure 6.7).

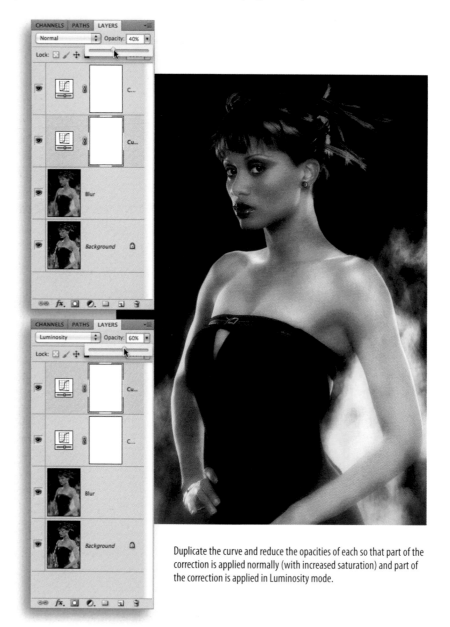

Duplicate the curve and reduce the opacities of each so that part of the correction is applied normally (with increased saturation) and part of the correction is applied in Luminosity mode.

Figure 6.7 You can keep some of the increased saturation.

Screen Diffusion

Let's return to the original two-layer version without Curves adjustment layers. Changing the mode of the blurred layer to Screen creates an interesting variation. Screen lightens the values in the underlying layer with the blur so you can change the opacity back to 100 percent and the sharp underlying image will be clearly visible. All the values are elevated with the highlights bleeding into the shadows (Figure 6.8).

A Curves adjustment is necessary to bring back the screen-lightened values. This time, to preserve the impact of the blurred highlights, place the Curves adjustment underneath the blurred layer: select the Background thumbnail in the Layers panel before creating the Curves adjustment layer (Figure 6.9).

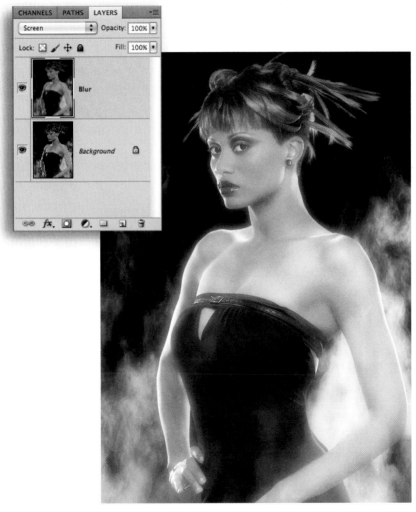

Figure 6.8 When the Blur Layer mode is changed to Screen mode, all values are lightened.

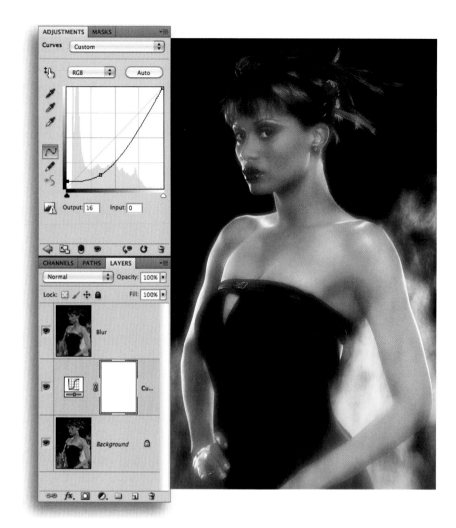

Figure 6.9 Place a darkening Curves adjustment layer beneath the Blur layer.

Note: In this example I've raised the black point of the curve because I don't want the black point in the image to go below a level of 15. (For more about black points, see Chapter 3, "The Color of Skin.")

Screen diffusion creates a more intense highlight glow than normal blur diffusion, and this can be quite attractive with certain images. However, achieving enough contrast by using a simple Curves adjustment can be difficult. You might need to mask off the effect from areas where you want detail to show. To accomplish this, put the blur and the curve adjustment into a group:

1. Select the Blur Layer thumbnail in the Layers panel. Press and hold the Shift key and then select the Curves adjustment layer. Both layers should be highlighted in the Layers panel.

2. Select New Group From Layers in the Layer Options flyaway menu at the upper right of the Layers panel (Figure 6.10). The two layers will be placed into a folder in the panel; this container can be treated as one unit in the Layers panel as if it were a single layer.

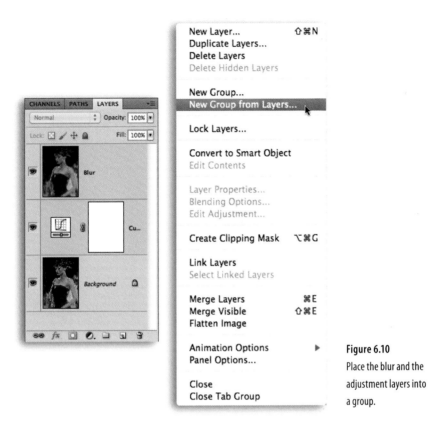

Figure 6.10
Place the blur and the adjustment layers into a group.

3. With the group selected, click the Add Layer Mask icon at the bottom of the Layers panel (Figure 6.11).

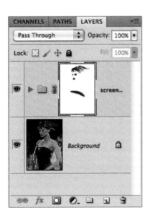

Figure 6.11
Make a layer mask for the group.

Once this layer mask is in place, paint into the mask with black over the areas through which you want the original sharp layer to show. In this example, I've masked off the eyes, lips, hair highlights, and other small details (Figure 6.12).

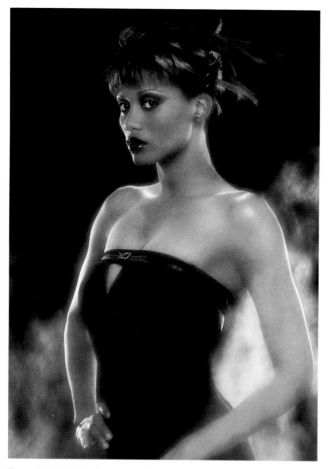

Figure 6.12 Paint into the mask with black where you want details to show through from the underlying sharp layer.

Multiply Diffusion

You may have guessed that you can also change the blending mode to Multiply. This, of course, has the opposite effect of Screen. The shadows bleed into highlights and all values are darkened. In this example, the subject is fairly *low key*, meaning that dark tones dominate the image. A Multiply blur would not have the same impact on such a dark image. It is worth experimenting with Multiply blur on lighter images where the subject is against a lighter background, such as the one in Figure 6.13. However, you would need to apply a lightening Curves adjustment to compensate for the darkening effect of Multiply (Figure 6.14).

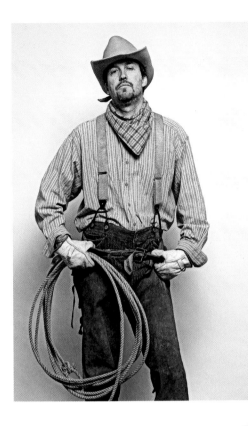

Figure 6.13
The original image

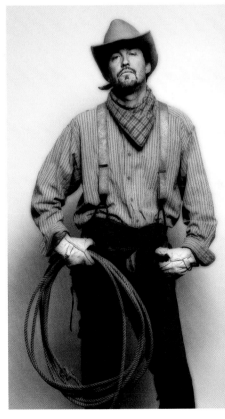

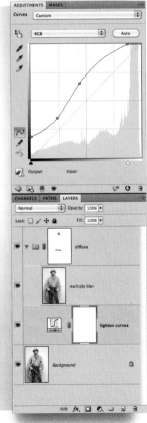

Figure 6.14
The image with
Multiply blur

Overlay Diffusion

Let's return to the sultry model for something a little different. I'll show you how to return to a two-layer version without Curves adjustments. All of the diffusion effects I've shown you have had a contrast-reducing effect. Something different happens when you change the Blur Layer mode to Overlay (Figure 6.15). You can see an increase in contrast and color saturation. The blur is now a very subtle glow.

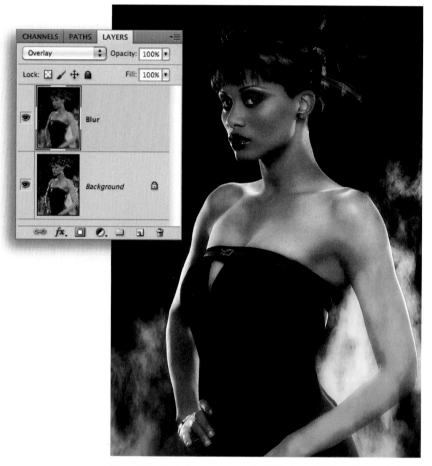

Figure 6.15 Overlay increases contrast by lightening with lighter blurs and darkening with darker blurs.

Curves are called for again, but this time we need to reduce the contrast. To maximize the impact of the Overlay blur, place the Curves adjustment layer underneath the Blur layer. You can work the curve while you watch the combined result with the Overlay on top. The inverse S-curve shape shown in the example reduces the midtone contrast and raises the low values to combat the increase in contrast that the Overlay layer supplies (Figure 6.16).

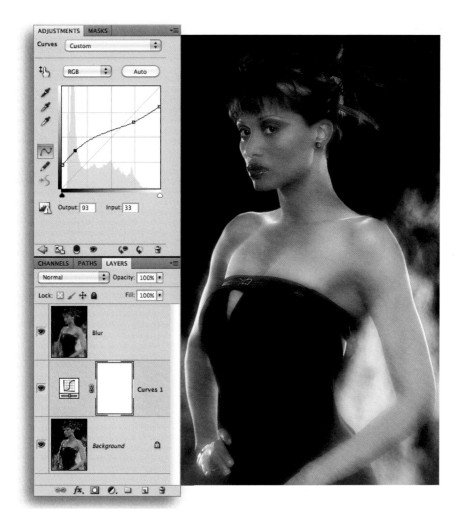

Figure 6.16 Reduce the contrast underneath the Overlay layer to return the image to a normal range.

For the final version, I placed a Hue/Saturation adjustment layer above the Blur layer to reduce the saturation a little. Then, all the layers above the background were grouped and a layer mask was used to bring back sharp details from the original background image (Figure 6.17).

Overlay blur creates a subtle glow effect that doesn't look blurred and has an interesting glamour-enhancing glow to it. It is also worth experimenting with other blending modes to achieve other variations on the basic blur-on-top effect. Clearly, you can use it to go well beyond simulating traditional filter effects using digital techniques. The power of layers and Layer Blending modes can be utilized in many different ways. Let's look once again at some traditional blur effects for more inspiration.

232

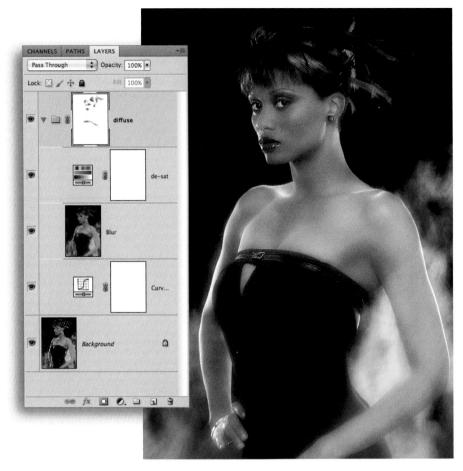

Figure 6.17 The final version reduces the saturation and brings back some sharp details from the original image.

Depth of Field Effects

Limited depth of field, where a very narrow plane of focus is used to provide visual interest, has a long tradition in portrait photography (Figure 6.18). The Japanese refer to the special quality of out-of-focus areas in a defocused lens as *bokeh*, and the subtle bokeh of certain lenses is very hard to simulate successfully with digital techniques. This portrait by Anthony Nex shows the bokeh effect most strongly at the upper-right corner in the hair and ear.

A very common use for the limited depth-of-field bokeh is to throw a background out of focus to help separate the subject from a busy background. This shot of my friends Rosa and Emil has a background that's a bit distracting (Figure 6.19). Ideally, it should be a little more out of focus, so we will use digital techniques to achieve this rather than reshoot.

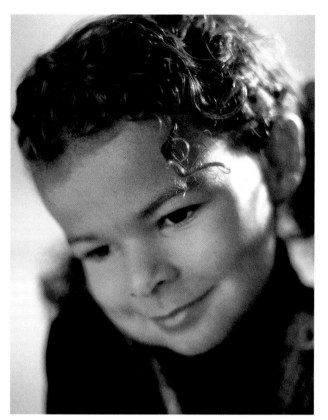

Figure 6.18
This beautiful child
portrait by Anthony Nex
shows true optical *bokeh*.

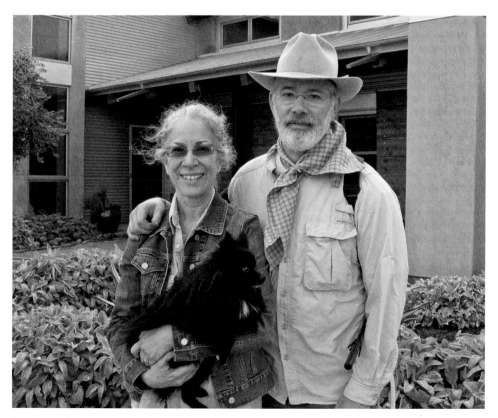

Figure 6.19 This shot could use a background that's just a little more out of focus.

The basic strategy is to duplicate the background into a new layer, as we did for the diffusion techniques, blur this duplicate, and use a layer mask to hide the areas of the image that we'd like to keep sharp:

1. Duplicate the background to a new layer by dragging the Background thumbnail to the New Layer icon at the bottom of the Layers panel (Figure 6.20).

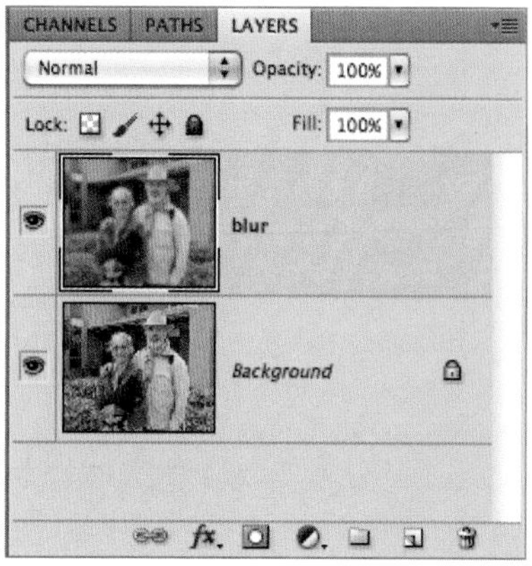

Figure 6.20 ■ Duplicate the background to prepare for the blur.

2. Select a blur filter. You could use the venerable Gaussian Blur filter (Figure 6.21), but this blur effect has no sense of bokeh. Everything is blurred in a uniform manner; it doesn't look like an out-of-focus lens capture.

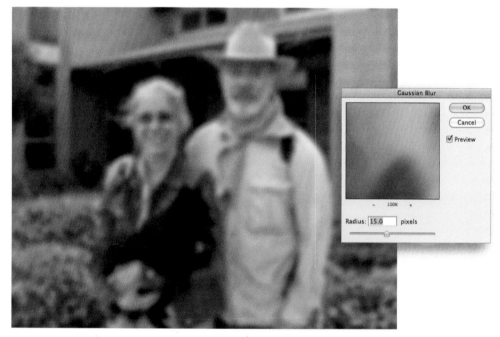

Figure 6.21 Gaussian Blur

Gaussian Blur would serve the purpose, but we are looking for more than just utility here. Let's stop for a moment and examine the other possibilities. The Lens Blur dialog (Filter > Blur > Lens Blur, Figure 6.22) has a very large preview and a number of advanced options that help simulate a lens blur effect.

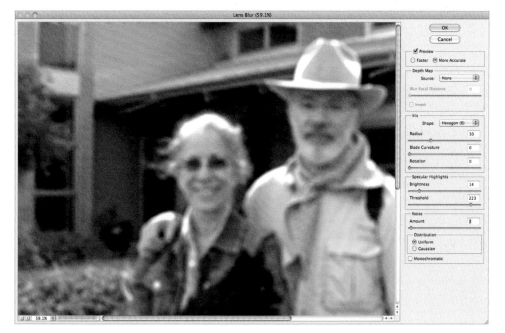

Figure 6.22 Lens Blur creates a better simulation of lens blur.

Faster and More Accurate   The Faster and More Accurate check boxes provide an option for slower machines or especially large files where you might not want to wait the extra time for the effect to render. The difference between the two options is subtle; however, if you have a fast machine, there's no reason not to use More Accurate.

Depth Map   Depth Map allows you to load an Alpha Channel mask to control where the blur is applied. This is sometimes a good option, but we're not going to take the time to build a mask for this example.

Iris   Iris is where you control the intensity and look of the effect; you can load different shapes meant to simulate the diffraction effects of the f-stop iris in a lens. This effect is most visible when there are small points of white highlights. The radius controls the intensity of the blur (higher radius equals more blur). Blade Curvature and Rotation affect how the iris image is rendered when it is visible in the effect.

Specular Highlights   Specular Highlights allows you to keep the brightness level up in highlights. Digital blur effects combine all pixel values together such that shadows bleed into highlights, reducing the brightness. Real lens optical blurs do not do this because the dynamic range of the real world is thousands and sometimes millions of times greater than what can be represented in typical digital file. The 256 levels and lower dynamic range of an 8-bit digital image cause highlights to absorb the blurred shadows and appear duller. The Brightness slider introduces brightness back into the highlights to compensate for this effect; Threshold sets the level at which this brightness is reintroduced.

Noise   Finally, because digital blurs can introduce banding, there is a Noise section where you can add banding-killing noise to the effect.

Despite all the sophistication of the Lens Blur filter, it still falls short of the subtle bokeh of real lens blur. Part of the magic of bokeh is the way real lens blur creates abstract geometrics and subtle double images. Notice the overlapping octagonal shapes in the real blur of Figure 6.23.

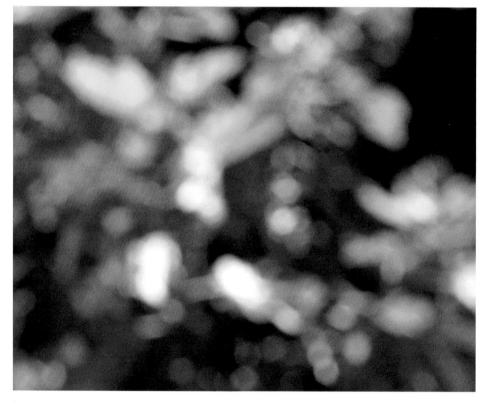

Figure 6.23 Real lens blur is not just soft; it contains lots of abstract shapes and double images.

Adobe introduced a number of new blur filters in Photoshop CS2, and one of the most interesting has great potential for simulating lens bokeh. The Shape Blur filter (Filter > Blur > Shape Blur) allows you to load a library of shapes to create abstract geometrics and double imagery based on a specific shape. The result can be used to approximate bokeh (Figure 6.24). Experiment with the various shapes to find a look that works with your specific image. Outline shapes have a more pronounced effect than solid shapes.

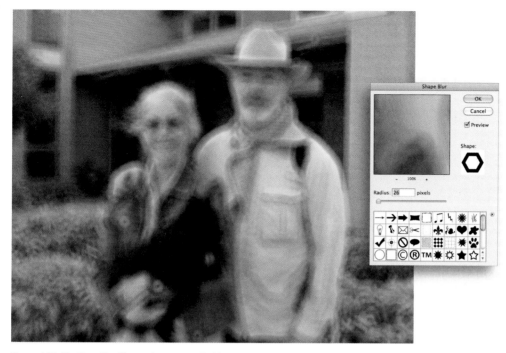

Figure 6.24 The Shape Blur filter produces unique double-image geometrics based on the chosen shape.

You can also use Motion Blur (Filter > Blur > Motion Blur); this filter creates an effect more like camera shake, but it is still a bit more interesting than Gaussian blur (Figure 6.25).

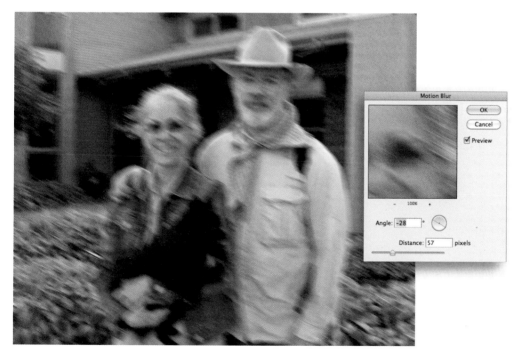

Figure 6.25 Motion Blur looks more like camera shake.

Let's return to the process of adding bokeh to your image.

3. Add a Blur layer, using your chosen blur method.

4. For maximum flexibility, make a mask for the subjects and put a copy of the sharp background layer on top of the Blur layer. You should now have three layers: the original background, the Blur layer, and the sharp subject layer with the subject masked from the background (Figure 6.26).

5. At this point, the image exhibits a problem that is common when the background is artificially blurred: there is a faint halo around the subjects where they have been blurred and spread into the background. It is best to fix this issue before you do the blur

Note: For readers who might have a hard time with basic masking, I have a number of tutorials on the book website (www.varis.com/skinbook) to help you along with these images.

6. Throw away the Blur layer and start over by duplicating the background into a new layer (drag the Background thumbnail onto the New Layer icon at the bottom of the layers panel). You should have a new layer between the Background and the masked subject layer. Turn off the visibility of the top layer by clicking on the Eye icon next to the thumbnail for the layer. Before you run the Blur filter, clone parts of the background into the edge of the subject. You want to make sure its edge won't bleed into the background once you blur it (Figure 6.27). You don't have to be extremely careful because you're going to blur the background anyway.

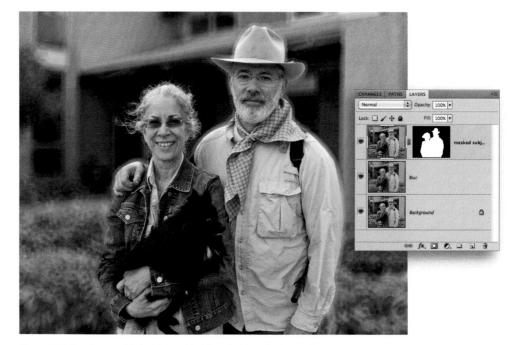

Figure 6.26 Use a layer mask to isolate the subject from the blurred background.

7. When you finish cloning, blur the background and turn on the top layer (Figure 6.28).

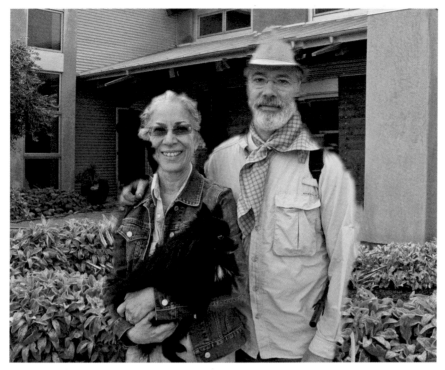

Figure 6.27 Clone into the edge of the figure to prepare for the blur.

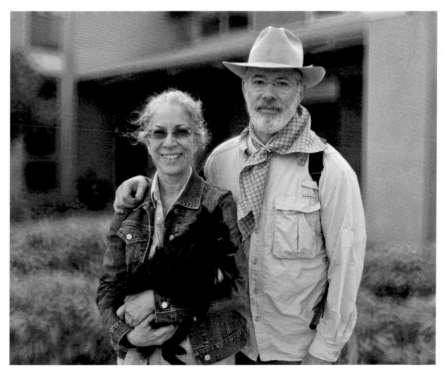

Figure 6.28 The Masked Subject layer sits on top of the blurred background.

There has been a lot of interest in the *bokeh* effect in the last couple of years, and now there are several new plug-in filters that offer better lens blur simulation than what is available inside Photoshop. Alien Skin's Bokeh (Figure 6.29) and OnOne's Focal Point (Figure 6.30) are two good examples that offer a lot of control as well as variety for the look of the out-of-focus regions.

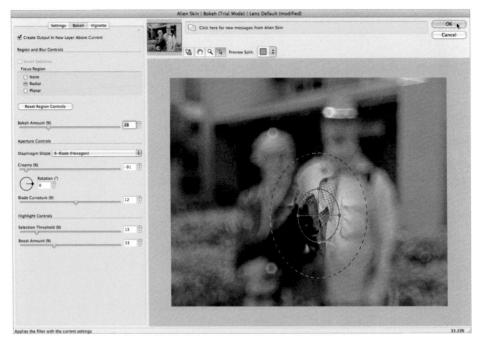

Figure 6.29 The Alien Skin Bokeh interface

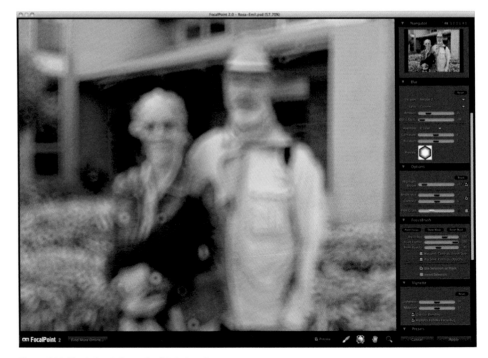

Figure 6.30 The OnOne Software Focal Point interface

My final version uses Alien Skin Bokeh for the blur and incorporates a gradient to preserve a little focus in the closer plants (Figure 6.31).

This might seem like a lot of trouble to go through just to blur the background—and it is. However, I still feel that the digital bokeh version is more beautiful than if I simply ran a Gaussian Blur on the background (Figure 6.32).

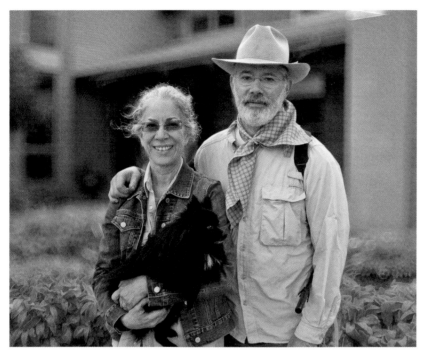

Figure 6.31 The final version utilizes the better Bokeh blur of the Alien Skin "Bokeh" filter.

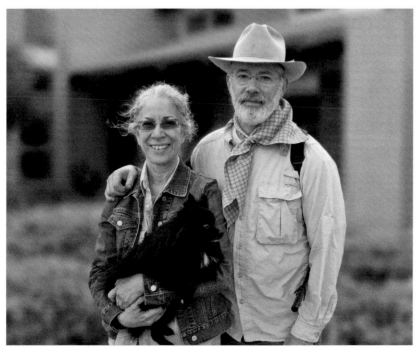

Figure 6.32 The Gaussian Blur background looks fake: it's too uniform and smooth.

Lens Tilt Effect

Another popular traditional technique to achieve a limited plane of focus is a lens tilt effect. Usually done with a view camera, it involves deliberately tilting the lens to place the plane of focus through a narrow area, such as the eyes, and throwing other areas more seriously out of focus than limited depth of field would normally accomplish. This is another effect that is difficult to simulate digitally. Figure 6.33 is an example of a digitally simulated lens tilt effect by Anthony Nex.

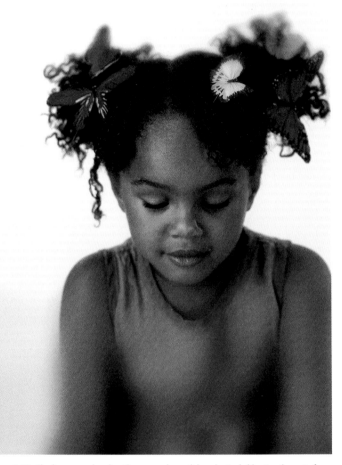

Figure 6.33 The focus was placed on the eyes and mouth by selectively blurring the rest of the image. (Photo by Anthony Nex)

Let's use the image in Figure 6.34 to look at one method to achieve this effect. I'd like to place the plane of focus through her eyes. If I were using a view camera, I would tilt the lens forward and adjust the focus until only the eyes were sharp. The top of her head would go out slightly, and the focus would fall off gradually down her body until it was very soft by her waist.

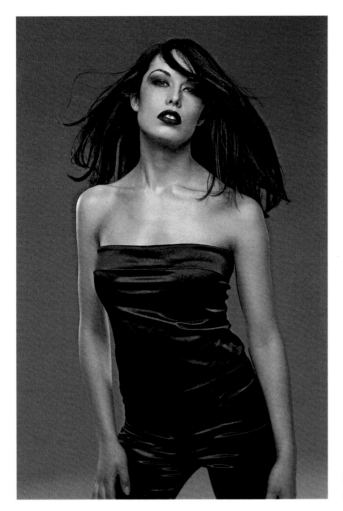

Figure 6.34
Original sharp image

Again, the basic approach to digital blurs is to duplicate the background and blur the copy so you can blend back to the original if necessary (Figure 6.35).

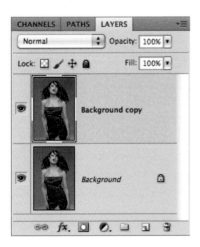

Figure 6.35
Duplicate the background to prepare for the blur.

You want to achieve a gradual transition from sharp to blurry; Lens Blur has the tools to create this effect using only one dialog box. To prepare for the effect, however, you'll need to make a special gradient mask. Add a layer mask to the duplicate layer by clicking the Layer Mask icon at the bottom of the Layers panel. The idea is to create a gradient in the mask that is black where the eyes are and gradually transitions to white at the lower third and lightens toward the top of the head (Figure 6.36). The black area will be protected from the application of the blur, white will receive the full blur, and gray areas will be partially blurred.

Figure 6.36 The gradient to be used for the layer mask

To create the gradient, first make sure the layer mask is selected, and then select the Gradient tool from the Tool panel or press the G key. Set the Tool options with black as the foreground color and choose the Foreground To Transparent gradient (Figure 6.37).

Place the cursor at the eyes, press and hold the Shift key (to constrain the direction to 90 degrees), and drag down to about her waist. Switch the foreground and background colors so that white is the foreground color (press the X key) and drag from the top of her head to her eyes (Figure 6.38).

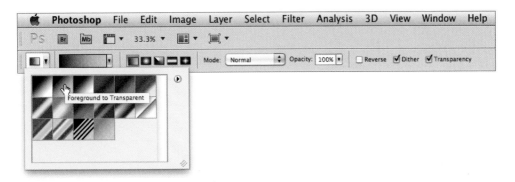

Figure 6.37 Choose the Gradient options.

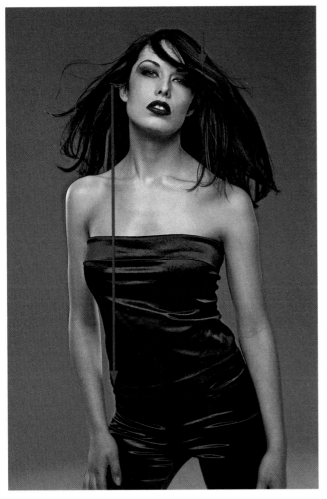

Figure 6.38 To create the gradient, drag into the layer mask in the direction of the arrows.

You can turn off the bottom layer to visualize the parts of the image that will receive the blur (Figure 6.39). The more transparent areas will receive less blur. If you think some areas should be blurrier, you can revise the mask by painting into it with white. The more visible an area is, the more it will be affected.

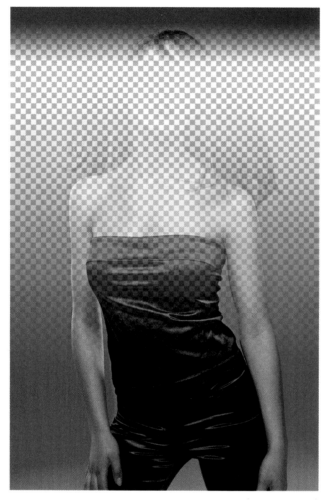

Figure 6.39 The more visible parts of the image will be more strongly affected by the Lens Blur filter.

Select the Image thumbnail in the Layers panel (so that the mask is no longer selected) and select the Lens Blur filter (Filter > Blur > Lens Blur). See Figure 6.40.

Select Layer Mask from the Depth Map drop-down menu. The gradient you just created will be used to control where the blur is applied to the image. The Blur Focal Distance slider determines the value where the blur will start; leave it set at zero (black in the mask) to begin and gradually increase the blur until it's at full strength at 255 (white in the mask). Different settings will push the blur into different areas of the mask and can lead to unexpected results. You can use this to fine-tune where the blur starts and stops in the image. In this example, because there are essentially two gradients in the mask, the blur will be difficult to control successfully, so you should leave the slider at zero. Set the Radius slider to the desired blur strength and add a small amount of noise to the image to control possible banding. When everything is set and you're happy with the preview, click OK.

When you return to the image, you can throw away the layer mask—it is unnecessarily masking part of the effect. Drag the layer mask from the top Blur layer to the Trash icon at the bottom of the Layers panel, and select Delete when you are asked to apply the mask. Now you can see the full extent of the blur (Figure 6.41). Unlike using the layer mask to partially hide a one-level blur in the layer, the Lens Blur is applied at progressively higher intensity depending on the value in the mask.

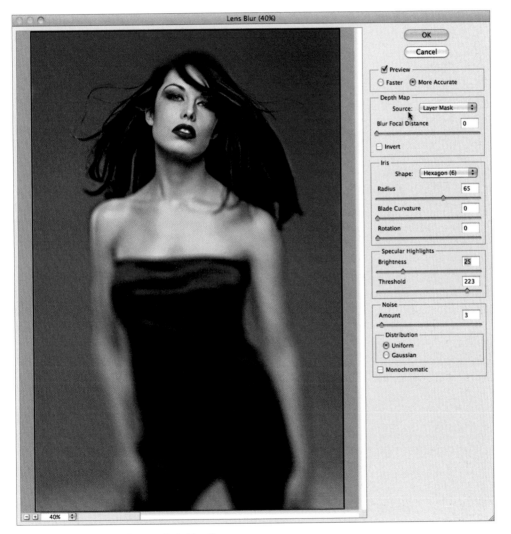

Figure 6.40 The Lens Blur dialog controls the blur effect.

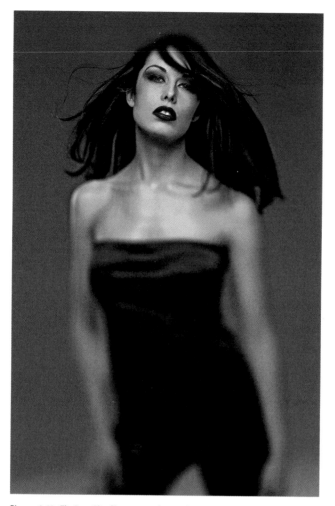

Figure 6.41 The Lens Blur filter was used to apply a progressive blur to simulate the lens tilt effect.

If any areas in the image are too blurry, you can selectively mask them off with a new layer mask to reveal the sharp image underneath; I did this with the lips. Reduce the opacity of this progressive Blur layer to generate a progressive diffusion effect. You can combine diffusion with the progressive blur for all kinds of interesting variations. Here is one that uses Overlay Blur Diffusion (Figure 6.42).

The new blur filter plug-ins turn this multistep process into an easy application of a filter in one step. Besides offering more control over the look of the blur, they also allow for gradient application with feathering and directional ramping through interactive slider controls. This alone makes these filters worth the price of admission (Figure 6.43 and Figure 6.44).

I created the final image using Alien Skin Bokeh (Figure 6.45). Compare this version with the Photoshop Lens Blur in Figure 6.41.

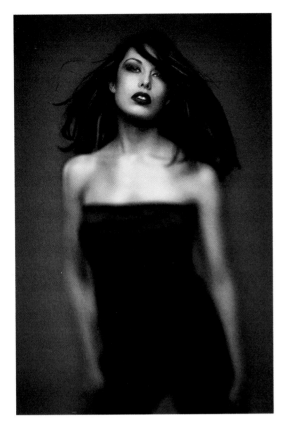

Figure 6.42
Overlay Diffusion adds another
dimension to the effect.

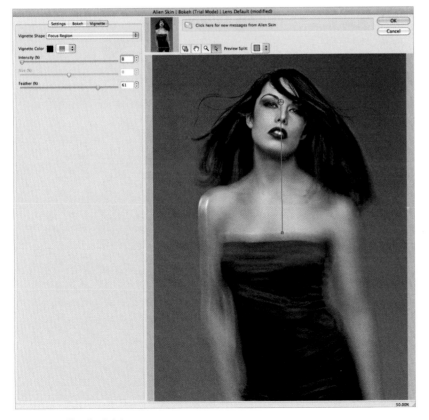

Figure 6.43 Alien Skin Bokeh

CHAPTER 6: SPECIAL EFFECTS ■

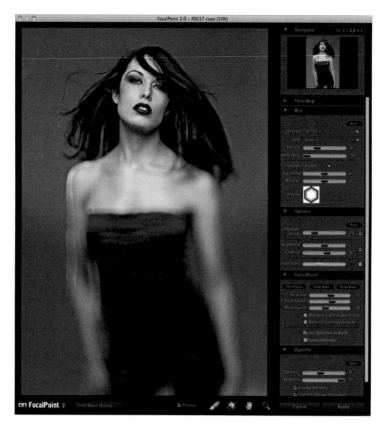

Figure 6.44
OnOne Software
Focalpoint

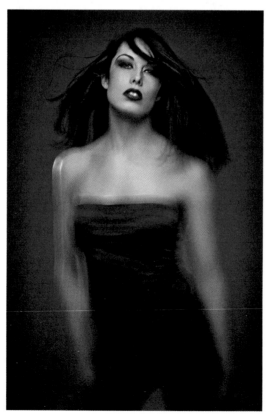

Figure 6.45
Alien Skin Bokeh used to
simulate a shift tilt lens

Film Grain and Noise

Digital photography is known for being smooth and grainless. Mostly this is considered to be an advantage. Still, there is something to be said for the subtle pointillist quality of film grain, and there are times when grain or noise can be used for artistic effects. Grain or noise can also be handy for eliminating banding and smoothing gradients. I'm going to look at a few examples to illustrate the best techniques for adding grain to a digital image.

The image in Figure 6.46 was captured digitally using a special Lensbaby soft-focus lens. The selective focus of the image enhances the mood and conveys a sense of mystery, but it still seems just a little too soft to me. Some selective sharpening helps (I'll go over sharpening in Chapter 7, "Preparing for Print"), but the image could still use something else (Figure 6.47).

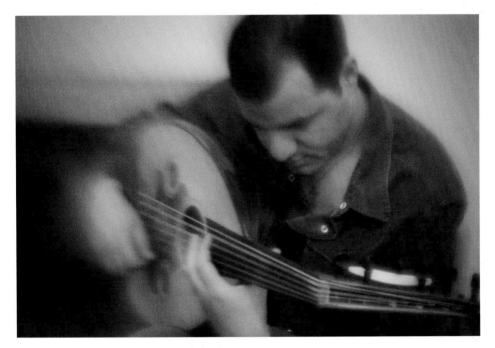

Figure 6.46 This shot of an oud player is just a little soft.

Grain can enhance the apparent sharpness of an image, so let's add some to this image and see what happens. Noise is the digital equivalent of grain, and most people would simply use the Noise filter (Filter > Noise > Add Noise). However, film grain does not look the same as digital noise. If you simply run an Add Noise filter on the image, you'll get Figure 6.48—a sort of dirty haze that reduces the image contrast because light noise covers the shadows and dark noise covers the highlights.

To combat this, use the following technique. Hold down the Option/Alt key and click the New Layer icon at the bottom of the Layers panel. This will bring up the New Layer Options dialog (Figure 6.49). Make sure you change the Mode to Overlay and check the Fill With Overlay-Neutral Color (50% Gray) check box.

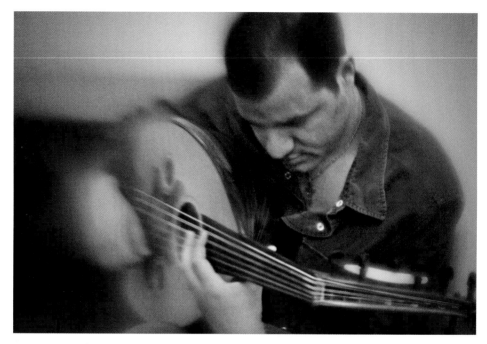

Figure 6.47 The sharper version still needs some help.

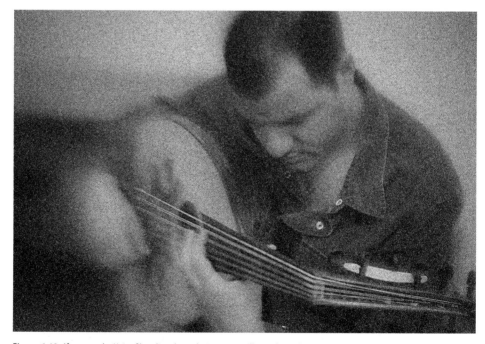

Figure 6.48 If you run the Noise filter directly on the image, you'll get a haze that reduces the contrast of the image.

There will be no change in the image because Overlay will affect the image only when values in the layer deviate from gray. Now, run the Add Noise filter on this gray Overlay layer. Zoom the image to 50 percent magnification to get a better sense of how the noise level will look in print.

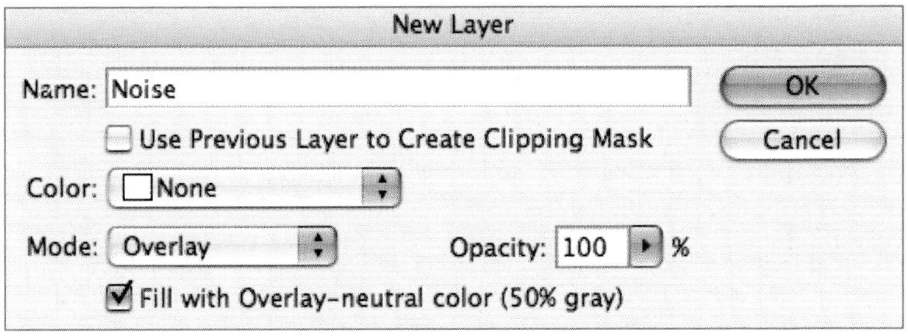

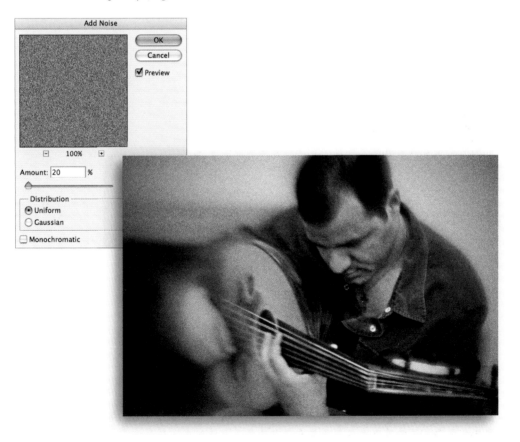

Figure 6.49 Set the New Layer mode to Overlay and Fill With Overlay-Neutral Color.

Overlay noise looks a lot more like film grain: the noise ramps off in the shadows and highlights. This approximates what happens when grain plugs up in the shadows and thins out in the clear highlights. The Noise Dialog options control the character and intensity of the noise. The Amount slider controls the intensity, but the radio buttons have a large impact on the look of the noise. Uniform noise is smoother and more even (Figure 6.50).

Gaussian noise is clumpy and more organic looking (Figure 6.51).

The Monochromatic check box creates noise that is even clumpier and doesn't have the random color component. Perhaps best suited to B+W imagery, it has a more-intense contrast quality (Figure 6.52

Figure 6.50 Uniform noise is more even.

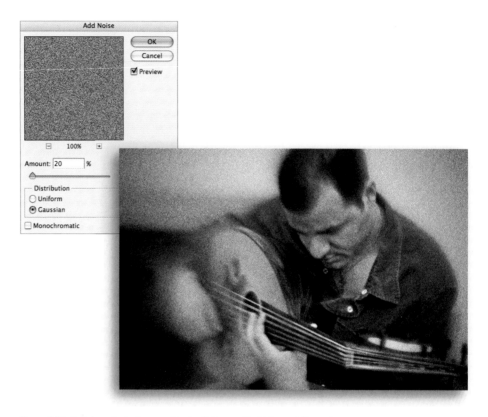

Figure 6.51 Gaussian noise is clumpy and looks a little more like high-speed film grain.

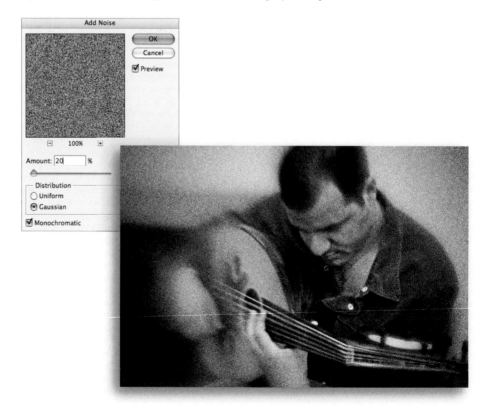

Figure 6.52 Monochromatic noise has a more aggressive look without additional color.

Another strategy is to add a high level of noise but reduce the opacity of the Overlay layer (Figure 6.53).

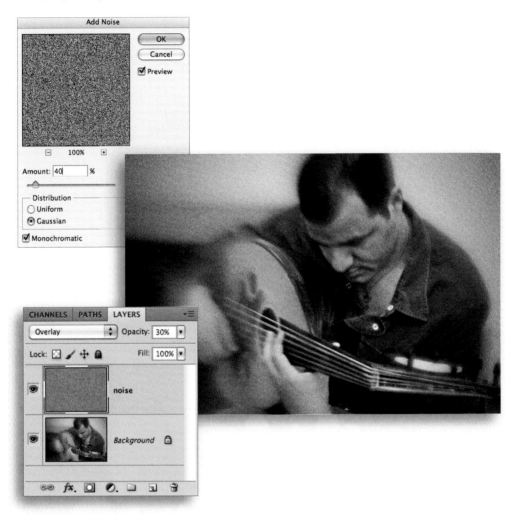

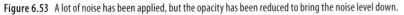

Figure 6.53 A lot of noise has been applied, but the opacity has been reduced to bring the noise level down.

Let's look at some more noise techniques with this colorful image by Aaron Rapoport (Figure 6.54).

If you want something more like color negative noise, you can blur the noise slightly. To take the edge off the noise, run the Gaussian Blur filter at less than 1 pixel (Figure 6.55).

Change the Layer mode from Overlay to Soft Light for a more subdued effect (Figure 6.56).

Apply a Motion Blur on the Noise layer to create an interesting illustration variation. Choose Filter > Blur > Motion Blur and apply a 100-pixel diagonal blur. Then apply Unsharp Mask (Filter > Sharpen > Unsharp Mask) to increase the contrast for an interesting texture effect (Figure 6.57).

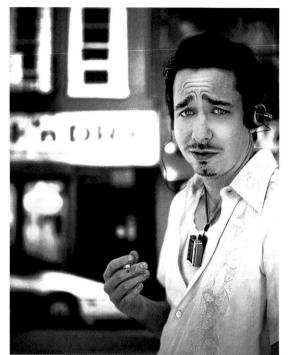

Figure 6.54
The original image by
Aaron Rapoport has a
low level of noise.

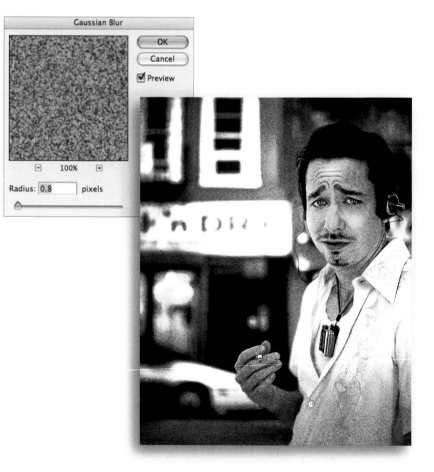

Figure 6.55 Blurred noise looks a little more like soft-gelatin film grain.

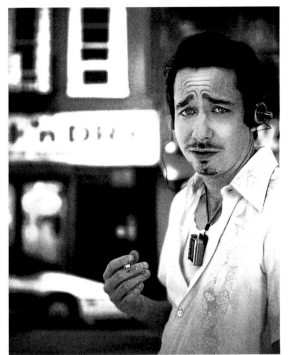

Figure 6.56
Soft Light gives a
more subdued effect.

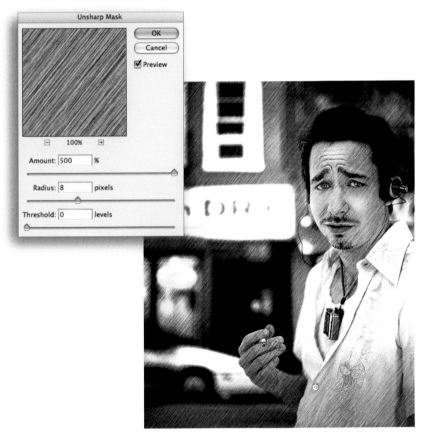

Figure 6.57 Sharpened Motion Blur noise creates an interesting illustrative effect.

Cross-Processing

Another traditional technique comes from the world of chemistry. *Cross-processing*, a technique that is very popular with fashion photographers, involves processing either transparency or negative film in the opposite type of chemistry. The most popular type of cross-processing uses transparency or slide film processed as a negative. With this technique, photographers rate their slide film at high ISO (plus two stops or so) and then process the film in C-41 or color negative chemistry. This results in a grainy negative with very saturated colors and no orange base color. When printed, the images have lurid colors with odd crossover colors in the shadows and lots of contrast. The exact effect is very hard to predict, and many photographers have their own secret way of exposing and printing the cross-process look.

This is another difficult effect to simulate digitally, but I have developed a method that gives you a lot of flexibility and control with the same kind of happy accident discovery as the traditional wet chemistry technique. This technique is fairly involved, so follow along closely.

1. Duplicate the background to a new layer by dragging the thumbnail to the New Layer icon at the bottom of the Layers panel (Figure 6.58).

2. We're going to mimic the look of slide film processed in negative chemistry and printed as a positive, so let's start by turning the image into a negative. With the new layer selected, press ⌘ + I/Ctrl + I to invert the values in the image (Figure 6.59).

3. Now, make it look more like a color negative. Press and hold the Option/ Alt key and click the Adjustment Layer icon to select a Levels adjustment. In the resulting Layer Options dialog, check the Use Previous Layer To Create Clipping Mask box (Figure 6.60). When the Levels dialog opens, set the Output Levels in the Red channel, Black slider to 90; in the Green channel, Black slider to 40; and in the Blue channel, White slider to 180. The results are a good approximation of a color negative (Figure 6.61).

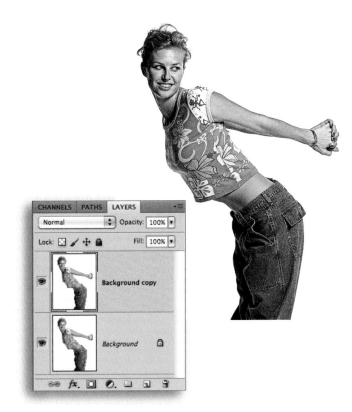

Figure 6.58 Duplicate the background to a layer.

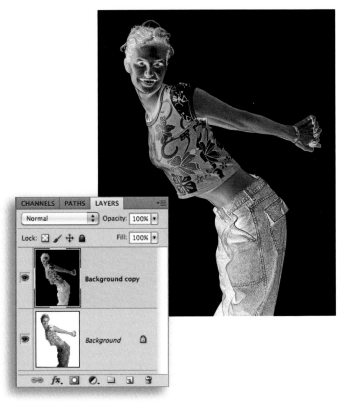

Figure 6.59 Invert the image in the top layer.

4. Reselect the Background copy layer and change the Mode to Difference (Figure 6.62).

5. Duplicate the Background layer again, drag it to the top of the layer stack, and change the Mode to Luminosity (Figure 6.63). The original tonal values are restored, but with odd color crossovers.

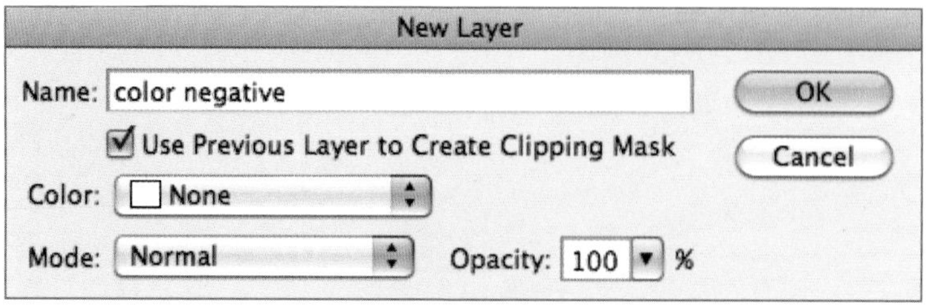

Figure 6.60 Set the Layer options to create a clipping mask for the Levels adjustment.

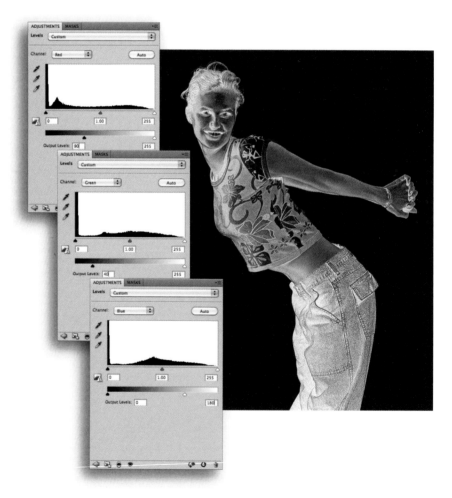

Figure 6.61 Turn the layer into a color negative.

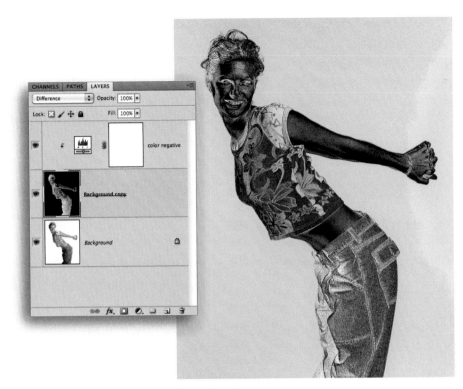

Figure 6.62 The Difference mode introduces wacky colors.

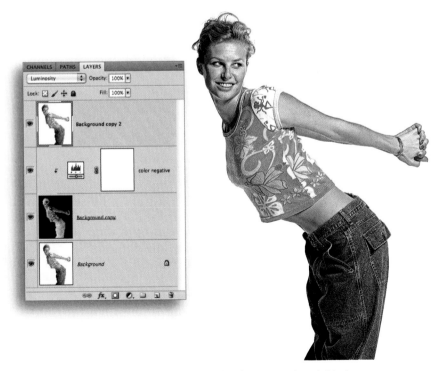

Figure 6.63 Duplicate the background again and apply its luminosity to the underlying layers.

6. Make a Curves adjustment layer on top of everything, but simply click OK without changing anything. Change the Mode to Overlay. Overlay applies the normal image on top of itself, resulting in the enhanced contrast that is typical of the cross-processed look. At this point, you can play around with the Overlay Curves to get the tone, color, and contrast you want for the effect (Figure 6.64).

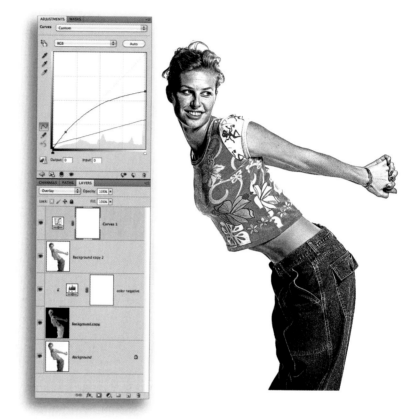

Figure 6.64 Adjust the Overlay Curves to get the look you're after.

7. You can also return to the Levels layer and tweak the effect of the color negative to modify the colors. Everything is available for revision—you can change layer opacities, change the Overlay layer to Soft Light, Hard Light, or whatever, and watch what happens. You can put a Hue/Saturation adjustment layer at the top to further modify the color

8. Because the effect is created in layers, you can mask off specific parts of the image. Select the top layers and place them in a group. Add a layer mask for the group and paint out the effect where you want to bring back the original image, as I did for her face and arms (Figure 6.65). The chapter opener is another example where a cross-process look was masked from the face.

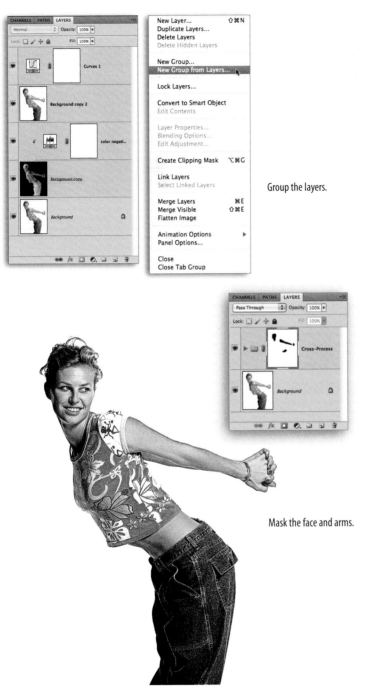

Group the layers.

Mask the face and arms.

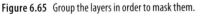

Figure 6.65 Group the layers in order to mask them.

The cross-process look doesn't have to be extreme; you can use it to simply generate some cross-over shadow colors and subtly alter hues for an interesting look (Figure 6.66 and Figure 6.67).

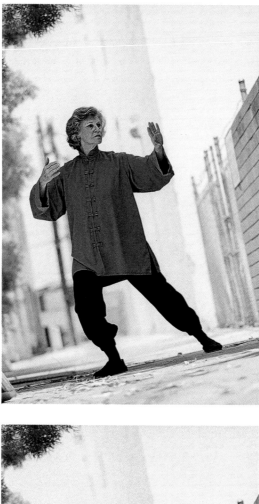

Figure 6.66
The original tai chi lady
(Photo by Ken Chernus)

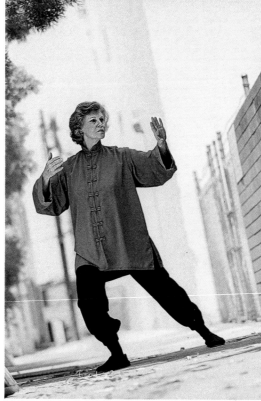

Figure 6.67
The cross-process version
shifts the colors in the
background and on the jacket.

Grunge

The *grunge look* has become very popular in the last few years, perhaps due to the influence of movies like *Sin City*, *300*, and other highly stylized, digitally rendered productions. The effect is characterized by a high-contrast, compressed tonal range where a lot of textural detail is revealed by extreme midtone contrast, usually combined with reduced saturation. This is often enhanced with dramatic rim lighting, but the basic effect depends on tonal adjustments in Photoshop.

I'll explore some techniques for generating this effect using this image of the lovely Zorka (Figure 6.68).

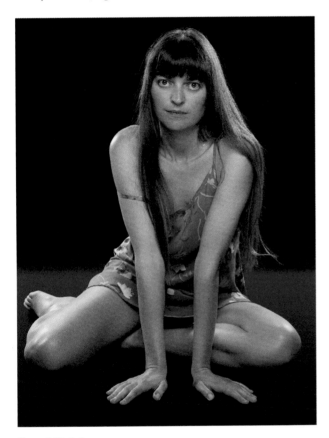

Zorka was shot with standard beauty lighting: medium softbox with two umbrellas at right and left rear to provide soft rim lighting.

Figure 6.68 Zorka

The easiest way to experiment with the grunge look is to use the new HDR Toning adjustment in Photoshop CS5. First, duplicate the document because HDR Toning works only on flat documents and we want to have a copy to blend back into as necessary. Then select Image > Adjustments > HDR Toning (Figure 6.69).

When the HDR Toning dialog box opens, set the Method to Local Adaption. You can examine the presets; but the exact nature of the effect is very image dependent, so its usually best to just start wiggling the various sliders until you find a look that you like (Figure 6.70).

Edge Glow   Radius and Strength affect the overall sculpting of the effect—smaller Radius settings give a less rounded look. Most of the action happens in the Tone and Detail sliders.

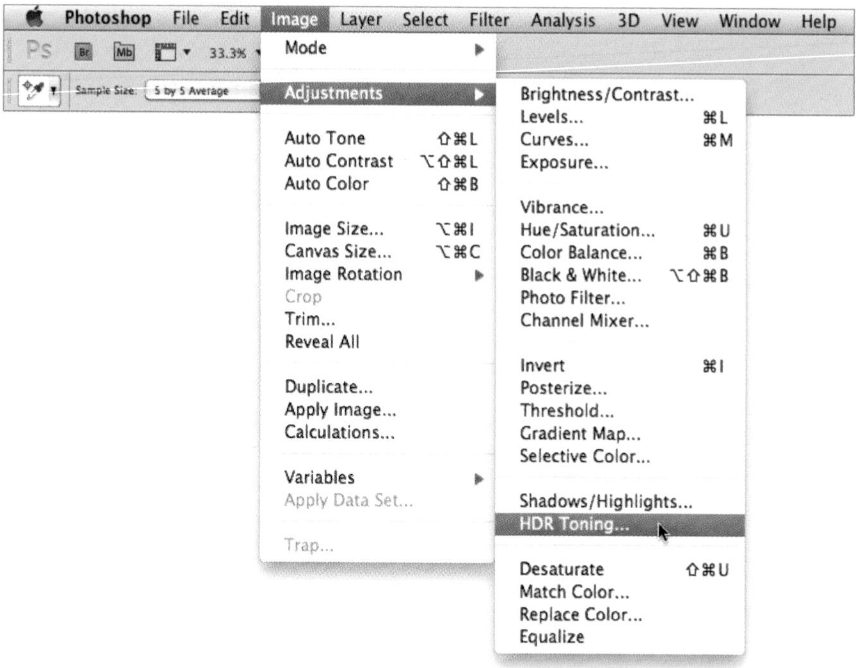

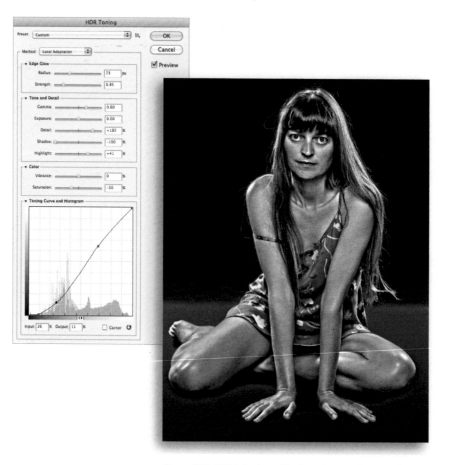

Figure 6.69 Select HDR Toning.

Figure 6.70 HDR Toning is capable of a wide range of grunge effects.

Tone and Detail   Higher Detail settings provide the kind of exaggerated texture that is a feature of the grunge look. Gamma affects the overall lightness and contrast, where exposure acts more like a White Point slider and can be used to introduce some clipping into the highlights or shadows. Work the gamma and exposure together to get the overall contrast. The Shadow and Highlight sliders boost or suppress highlights or shadows and can be used to fine-tune the contrast.

Color   The Color sliders operate much like the Vibrance and Saturation controls in Adobe Camera Raw or Lightroom. You'll find that you have to bounce back and forth among the sliders a bit to craft the look you're after. I often find that it's better to blend different versions together later rather than trying to get exactly the right look in one go.

Figure 6.71 represents a variation with a darker background but harsher contrast. I layered the two versions together and blended for Figure 6.72.

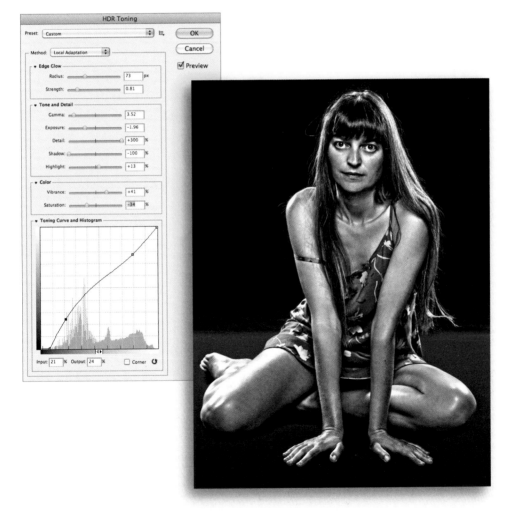

Figure 6.71 Different settings can yield very different results.

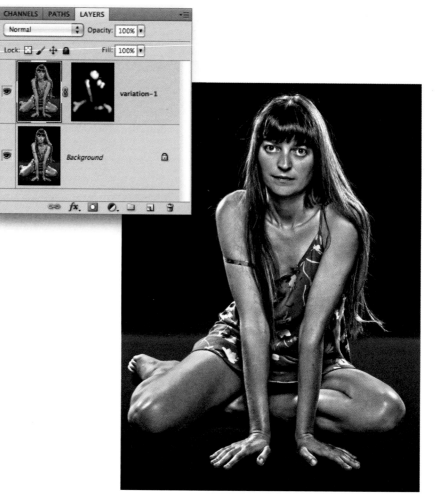

Figure 6.72 Two versions blended together

Sometimes, after the grunge look has been pushed really far, it's worth considering blending back into the original starting place, as shown in Figure 6.73 (a 50/50 blend between Figure 6.68 and Figure 6.72).

Another relatively easy way of getting a similar grunge effect can be done in Lightroom (Figure 6.74). Set the basic sliders to:

- Recovery: 100%

- Fill Light: 100%

- Contrast: 100%

- Clarity: 100%

- Blacks: adjust for contrast

- Brightness, Vibrance, and Saturation: adjust to taste

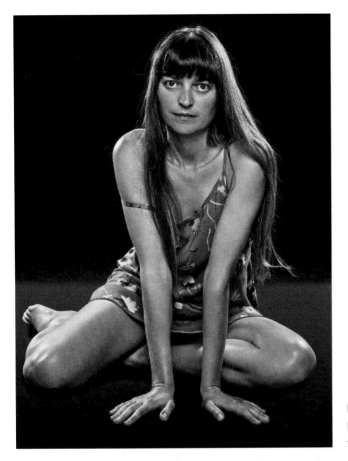

Figure 6.73
Blend back into the original
to soften the effect.

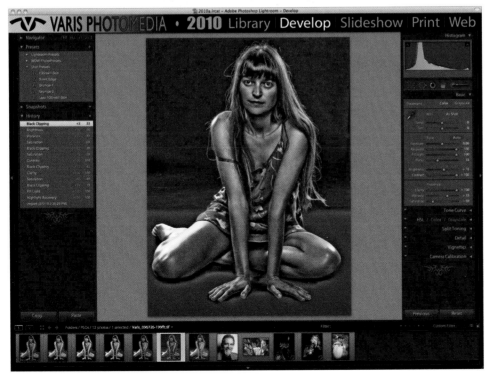

Figure 6.74 You can achieve a similar grunge look in Lightroom.

You don't have the same flexibility in Lightroom as you do with HDR Toning in Photoshop, but it can be a very convenient way of experimenting with the effect especially if you are dealing with RAW files. You can render out two versions and blend together, as shown in Figure 6.75.

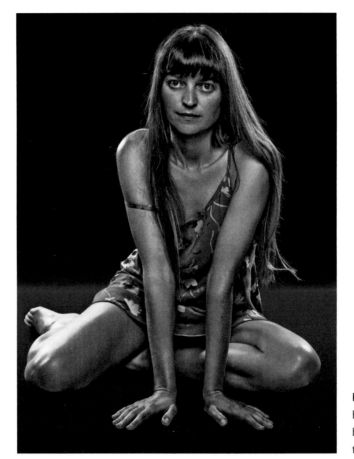

Figure 6.75
Blend the Lightroom version back into the original to fine-tune the effect.

Tattoos

Tattoos can provide some interesting challenges. In many cases, photographers simply accept what the camera captures. Photographing tattoos is just like photographing a normal subject (Figure 6.76). Making sure the tattoos have as much color and contrast as possible becomes very important when the clients are the ones with the tattoos. They are often more interested in how the tattoos render rather than the overall impression of the photographs. Let's look at a few tricks to enhance the tattoos on this subject.

Enhancing Existing Tattoos

First, duplicate the background into a new layer. Tattoos almost always look more faded than their owner would like. For this project, the black lines of the tattoo need to appear darker. Change the Mode to Multiply to get the changes in Figure 6.77.

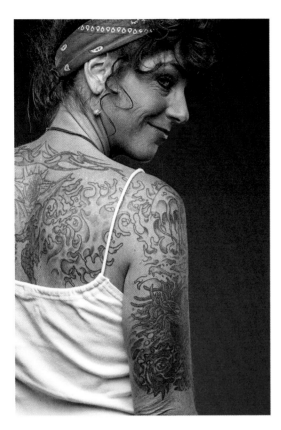

Figure 6.76
The tattooed subject is treated just
like any other portrait model.

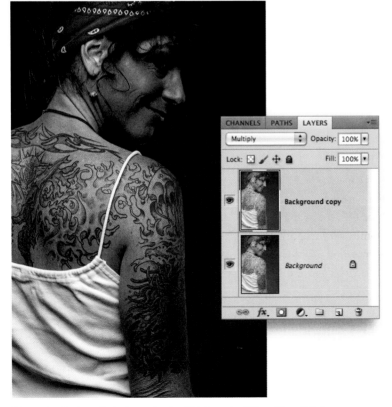

Figure 6.77 Duplicate the background and multiply it over itself. Everything will darken.

The tattoos are darker, but so is everything else. We need to keep the non-tattooed skin from getting darker. Double-click the Multiply layer to bring up the Layer Styles/Blending Options dialog. Change the Blend If drop-down to Red and move the White slider (in either layer) to the left until the lighter skin from the underlying layer starts to appear.

To soften the harsh transitions, reduce the posterized look, and bring back more of the lighter skin, split the slider. Press and hold the Option/Alt key and push the left half of the slider to the left until most of the lighter skin appears (Figure 6.78).

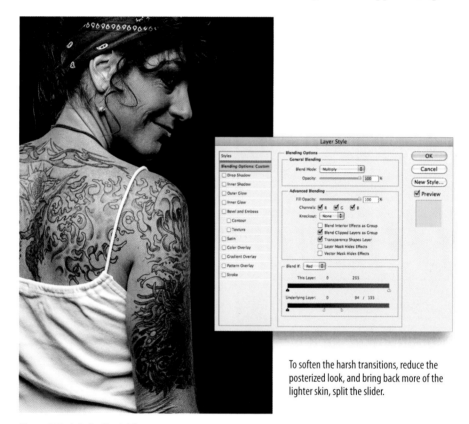

To soften the harsh transitions, reduce the posterized look, and bring back more of the lighter skin, split the slider.

Figure 6.78 Split the Blend slider.

Hide this whole layer with a layer mask: Hold down the Option/Alt key and click the Layer Mask icon at the bottom of the Layers panel. This will create a Black Layer mask and hide the effects of this layer. Select the Brush tool and, using a low opacity, gradually brush over the tattoo with white (into the mask) to darken the lines. Some areas will need to be darkened more than others; the more solidly colored section on her arm won't need to be darkened as much. Build up slowly and try to even out the darkness in the lines (Figure 6.79).

If you want more darkening, you can apply a darkening Curves adjustment to the layer as you look at the combined result. The lines are certainly darker now, but I'd also like to enhance the colors and add more saturation. I don't want to add any saturation to the skin color, however. To achieve this, we'll use a trick in the Lab color space. Choose Image > Duplicate and check Duplicate Merged Layers Only in the dialog (Figure 6.80).

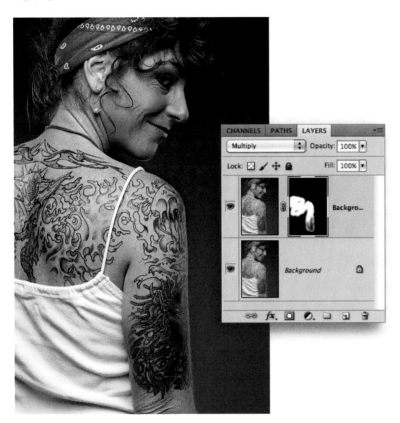

Figure 6.79 Hide the layer with a mask and paint back into the mask over the tattoo to darken the lines.

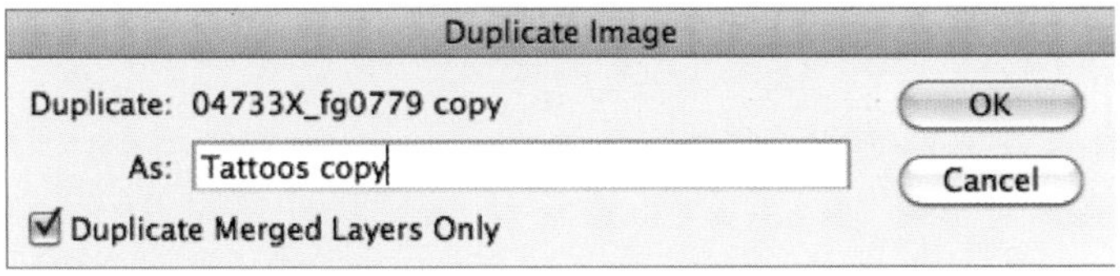

Duplicate Image

Duplicate: 04733X_fg0779 copy

As: Tattoos copy

☑ Duplicate Merged Layers Only

OK

Cancel

Figure 6.80 Duplicate the document and check Duplicate Merged Layers Only.

You'll get a duplicate document that is the result of the work done so far. Change this document to Lab (Image > Mode > Color). Lab is a great color space for manipulating color saturation. Make a Curves adjustment layer by selecting from the Adjustment Layer icon at the bottom of the Layers panel. Select the *a* channel in the Channel drop-down. Take the Target Adjustment tool in the Curves panel (the little Finger icon) and click in the image on an area of light skin; this will place a point on the *a* curve where the color of skin lives. We will leave this point unchanged and steepen the curve above and below that point to increase the saturation in every color that is different than the color of skin. Pull the end points of the curve into a pronounced vertical line without moving the original point. Do the same thing for the *b* channel (Figure 6.81).

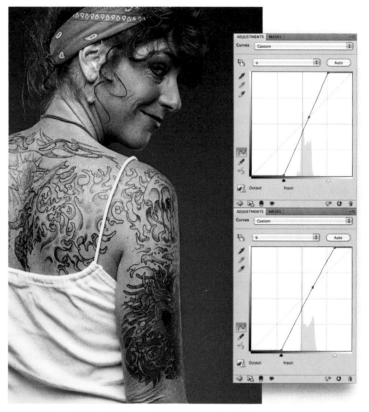

Adjusting the a and b channels increases saturation. The center point in the curve is the anchored skin color.

Figure 6.81 Make a Curves adjustment in the *a* and *b* channels.

Increasing the contrast in the *a* and *b* channels amplified the saturation. Even though you anchored the skin color with a point, some additional saturation crept into the skin color. To remedy this, you need to flatten the curve through that center point. Place two more points on the curve near the original anchor points and drag them to flatten the line near that point (Figure 6.82).

This amount of saturation is needed only in the tattoos, not everywhere. Hide the Curves adjustment by inverting the layer mask. Make sure the mask for the Curves adjustment is selected in the Layers panel, and then press ⌘ + I/Ctrl + I. This changes the layer mask for the Curves adjustment to black. All you have to do is paint white over the colored areas of the tattoo in the mask (Figure 6.83).

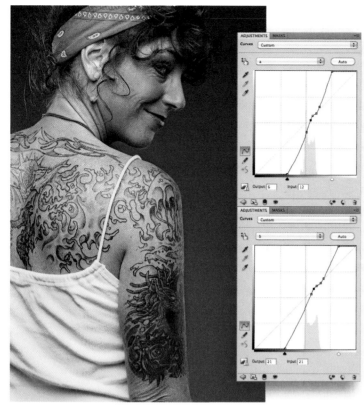

Figure 6.82
Flatten the curve through the anchor point to fix the skin color.

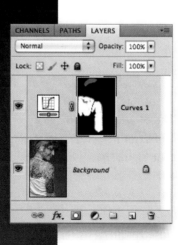

Figure 6.83
Normal color is restored everywhere except where you paint in the Curves adjustment mask with white.

At this point, you could stop, convert the Lab document back into your regular RGB workspace, and call it a day. I like to save a layered version with everything in it so I can revise things later if necessary. For maximize flexibility, put everything into one document with all layers intact. First, save the Lab document with the Curve. Then, flatten the Lab document. Press and hold the Shift key (this ensures that the documents will be aligned properly) and, using the move tool, drag this document on top of the original RGB document. If you are using the Application Frame in CS5, your documents will be in the tabs along the top of the frame. In this case, drag from inside the document window to the tab for the document you want to drop onto. Again, remember to hold down the Shift key. Change the Mode to Color so you can reduce the opacity of the top layer if the saturation is too much or revise the interaction of the underlying layers if you need different contrast (Figure 6.84).

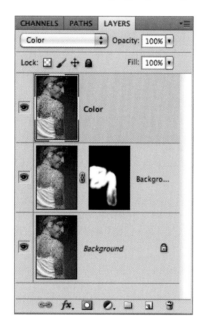

Figure 6.84
This layer structure allows for maximum flexibility.

Faking Tattoos

What if you want to know what a tattoo would look like before you go to all the trouble (and pain) of having one applied for real? Yes, you could have a henna tattoo, but you couldn't necessarily see the tattoo the way others could. There are other uses for fake tattoos in photographs as well; fake tattoos have been used in movie posters. It is actually easier to blend a tattoo image into a photograph than it is to enhance an existing tattoo.

We'll start with this shot of a young woman's back and a dragon tattoo design (Figure 6.85).

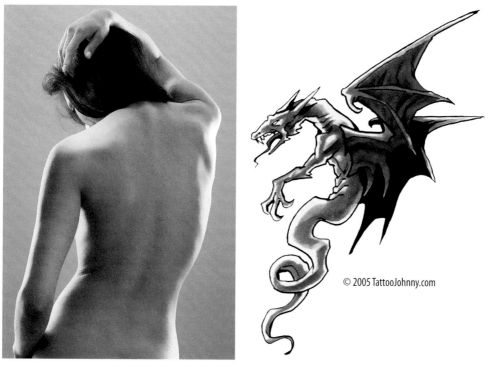

© 2005 TattooJohnny.com

Figure 6.85 Ready for the application of a tattoo

There are many sources for tattoo designs, including some online. (Check the licensing requirements before downloading and using images or *flash*, as they're known in the tattoo trade.) This dragon design was downloaded as a JPEG file. I applied a small amount of Overlay noise to smooth it out and add a sense of skin texture.

Drag the dragon-design document on top of the woman's back and change the mode to Multiply (Figure 6.86). The tattoo ink only makes skin darker; therefore, multiplying anything darker than white in the Tattoo layer makes the underlying image darker too. As a result, the tattoo automatically blends in with the image.

Reduce the Layer opacity a bit, and resize the Tattoo layer: choose Edit > Free Transform (or press ⌘ + T/Ctrl + T) and drag the corner handles until the tattoo is sized correctly. At this point, the wings of the dragon will extend past the woman's right shoulder (Figure 6.87).

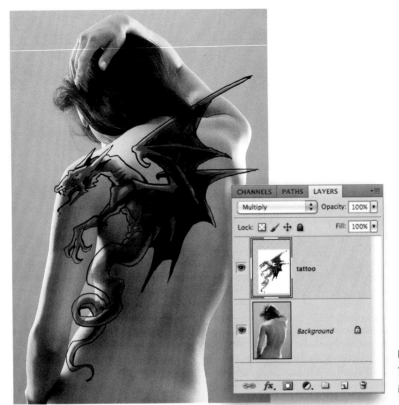

Figure 6.86
The tattoo is placed
in a Multiply layer.

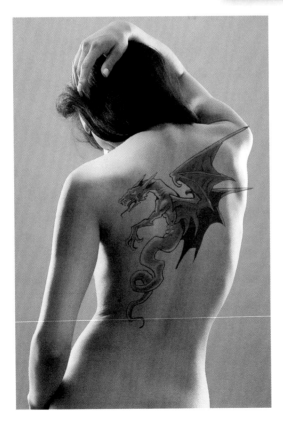

Figure 6.87
Resize the design.

If the tattoo were really on the woman's body, the design would curve toward the shoulder and dip at the shoulder blade. You can use Liquify to shape the tattoo to follow the contours of the body. Choose Filter > Liquify. When the dialog comes up, make sure you check Show Backdrop at the bottom right so you can see how the design fits on the body. Use the Forward Warp Tool (Distort Brush in CS4 and earlier versions) to push the dragon design to fit (Figure 6.88).

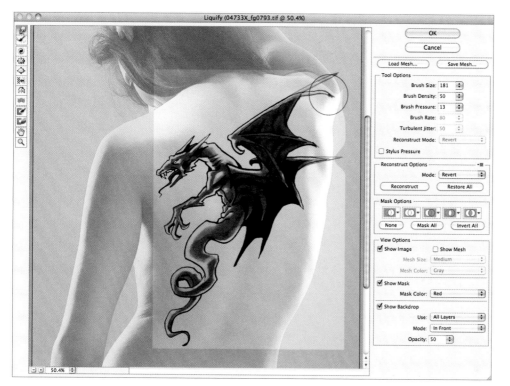

Figure 6.88 Use Liquify to push the design to fit the body.

To finish, I added a White layer mask (click the Layer Mask icon at the bottom of the Layers panel) and added some blurred noise to add texture to the black areas of the tattoo. I also blurred the dragon design slightly to suggest the way tattoo ink bleeds into skin (Figure 6.89). You can adjust the Layer opacity to give you a freshly inked or a faded-and-aged look.

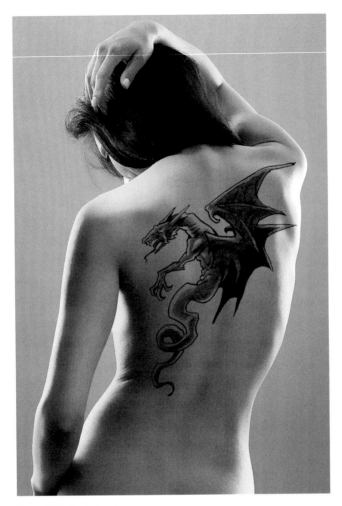

Figure 6.89 The final version

Final Notes

Hopefully, these few techniques can serve as a starting point for further explorations. Remember that all of the techniques I presented in this chapter can be mashed up in different combinations and blended together to create something new, such as the image that opens this chapter. I will finish with this final image by Michele Eve Sandberg (Figure 6.90). Here you'll find a combination of Channel-Mixer B+W, HDR Toning-Grunge, plus Lab color enhancement for the tattoo. It's all about playfully experimenting with the idiosyncrasies of digital image construction—channels, layers, blending modes, and color spaces—these are your friends!

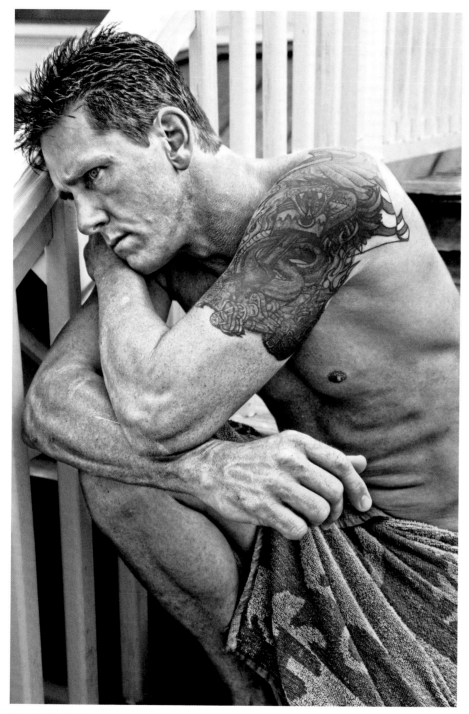

Figure 6.90 John (© 2009 by Michele Eve Sandberg)

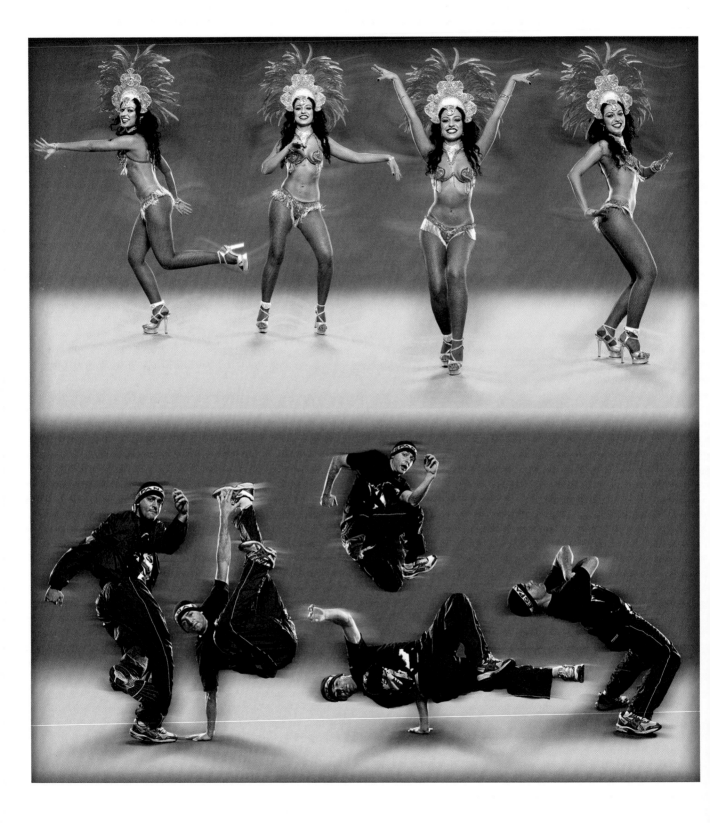

Preparing for Print

The final form of a digital image is often a print of some kind. To prepare for this eventuality, or at least make the image good enough to print, digital photographers must do a number of things aside from using all the creative techniques employed when working with the image on the monitor. Last minute tweaks frequently make the difference between a great print and a mediocre one. This chapter covers techniques that are particularly important in people pictures including:

7

Chapter Contents
Sharpening
Color Management for Print
Soft Proofing
Desktop Printing
Creative Print Finishing

Sharpening

Whether they are scans from film or direct digital captures from a digital camera, all digital images require some level of sharpening. Often, some sharpening is applied automatically by the scanning software or in-camera processing. Sharpening is critical for CMYK offset lithography because the line screen has a fairly drastic diffusing effect on photographic imagery. People photographs printed with high-quality inkjet printers often don't need as much sharpening as other photographs, and many times the soft effect is desirable to hide skin texture. Perhaps because of this, most photographers of people tend to ignore sharpening or, at best, treat it as an afterthought, applied as some kind of default setting based on camera model.

Sharpening is an art in itself. Good sharpening techniques can enhance almost any image and elevate an ordinary photo to an arresting image that jumps off the page. Really sharp images have a three-dimensional quality that is almost impossible to achieve without using some kind of edge-enhancing technique. Sharpening techniques were employed by the old master painters of the Renaissance. They placed dark lines next to light edge highlights to visually carve important detail into an image. Modern photographers use *unsharp masking*, a technique pioneered by astrophotographers, whereby a blurred negative was sandwiched with a positive to enhance edge details in images of distant galaxies. Although the modern version of this technique involves complex digital-image-processing algorithms, the principle is the same. Sharpening is best done after the image is sized for final output, often as the last step before printing. We will examine a couple of the best Photoshop sharpening techniques that are the most pertinent for our work with people in digital photography.

Unsharp Mask

Let's begin our exploration of sharpening from the Filter menu with the Unsharp Mask—rather than Sharpen, Sharpen More, or Sharpen Edges—because Unsharp Mask offers useful adjustable parameters that the others don't.

The Unsharp Mask filter detects edge transitions and applies dark and light halos around these edges. Most beginners simply run the filter directly on the image. This often results in enhanced saturation in dark and light halos around colored edges, and it makes the artificial sharpening more obvious. You can see this saturation effect in this image (Figure 7.1) in the direct-apply version on the left. The version on the right was applied to affect luminosity only. In order to avoid the saturation enhancement, you can convert the image to Lab and sharpen the L channel or you can "fade" to luminance (Edit > Fade > Unsharp Mask, choose Luminosity in the dialog) right after running the filter. Another approach is to run your sharpening filter in a duplicate layer set to Luminosity. These methods prevent sharpening halos from acquiring saturated colors. When you sharpen in a separate layer, you gain the benefit of extra control over how that sharpening is applied through the use of layer masks.

Let's set up a basic sharpening routine for this image of a jazz musician. First, let's set up a Luminosity Sharpen layer—drag the Background thumbnail to the New Layer icon at the bottom of the Layers panel to duplicate it—and then select

Luminosity from the Blending mode drop-down menu just under the Layers tab (Figure 7.2). After doing that, we will zoom to the best magnification to judge our sharpening effect.

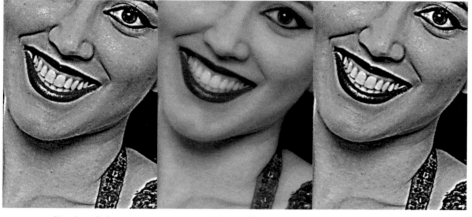

Directly applied   Unsharpened   Luminosity only

Figure 7.1 The close-up in the center is unsharpened. An Unsharp Mask was applied to the versions on both sides.

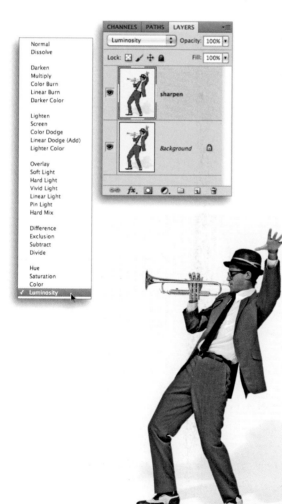

Figure 7.2

To set up sharpening, place a duplicate in a layer and change the Layer Blending mode to Luminosity.

Many experts will advise you to view the effect of the Sharpen filter at 100 percent—I used to do this myself. The sharpening effect at this magnification will appear at lot more drastic than it will appear at the final printed size. I prefer to judge the effect of sharpening at 50 percent.

Note: Because the image appears so much bigger than it will actually print, most photographers tend to undersharpen when they view an image at 100 percent onscreen. When you zoom to 50 percent, you are viewing the image at approximately 150 pixels per inch. Most of the time, you will be sharpening for size at 300 pixels per inch. By viewing the effect of sharpening at the 150 ppi size, you can partially compensate for the lower screen resolution of 72 ppi.

Once you've zoomed to a 50 percent view, select the Unsharp Mask filter (Filter > Sharpen > Unsharp Mask). Compare the effect inside the dialog (where it is displayed at 100 percent) with the 50 percent zoomed view (Figure 7.3).

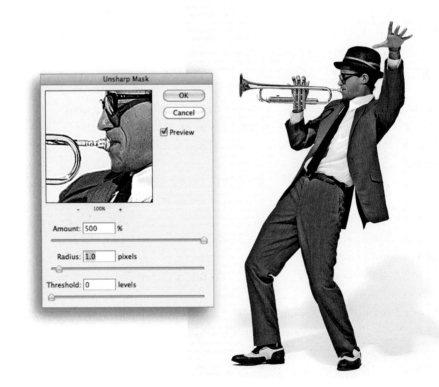

Figure 7.3 The dialog allows you to view sharpening at 100 percent, but always check the effect at 50 percent as well.

Unsharp Mask works by enhancing the contrast of rapid tonal transitions; we perceive this as light and dark halos around edges. The sliders in the Unsharp Mask dialog give you some level of control over the size and intensity of these halos. The Threshold slider sets the value change necessary before sharpening halos are applied.

This is primarily used with images scanned from film to prevent the sharpening of grain. For most digitally captured images, grain is a nonissue, so you can leave the Threshold slider set at zero. Noise, however, can be present in digital files, especially when the camera was set to a high ISO. Therefore, the Threshold slider can be used to minimize sharpening of noise (push the slider to the right until you reach a setting where noise isn't impacted). You can set the amount slider all the way to 500 percent because you are applying the sharpening to a duplicate layer, and you can use the layer opacity to control the amount. At this intensity, you can clearly see what the halos are doing to the image.

The whole trick with using the Unsharp Mask filter is to set the Radius high enough to adequately sharpen without being obvious at the desired print size. You might be surprised by how much you can get away with; I almost always sharpen more than what I think looks good onscreen. Adjust the layer opacity to bring the intensity down so the effect doesn't overpower the image.

A uniform level of sharpening everywhere in the image often looks unnatural; you can use a layer mask on the Sharpen layer to refine how the sharpening is applied across the image. Try painting with black into the mask to remove sharpening from skin texture for instance. Our example image suffers a little bit from this uniform level of sharpening The edges of the figure against the white background are a little too sharp, lending the figure a cut-out look! You can remedy this with a layer mask.

Make a selection for the figure in the sharpened layer. Here it is easy to use the Magic Wand tool to select the background (click on the white background). Shift+click to add areas that didn't get selected. When the whole background is selected, go to the Select menu and choose Inverse. The selection will reverse and you'll end up with the figure selected.

The idea here is to mask the figure so that the sharpened edges of the figure are hidden by the layer mask, allowing the original unsharpened edges to be revealed in the underlying layer. To accomplish this, we need to "choke" the mask. I'll use a new feature in CS5. From the Select menu, choose Refine Edge. When the Refine Edge dialog box opens, you'll find advanced controls for adjusting the edge of the selection. First, select On Black (B) from the View Mode drop-down (Figure 7.4). This reveals that the selection includes the white (and, therefore, the black) halos—you can see a white edge around most of the figure.

Check the Smart Radius check box under Edge Detection, and push the slider to the right until most of the white halo disappears. Smart Radius automatically finds the actual edge of the figure based on the distance from the original selection you set in the slider. To really choke the selection, I'll set the Shift Edge slider to a negative value and contract the selection further (Figure 7.5). The beauty of the Refine Edge dialog is that you can adjust where the edge is while viewing the effect of the adjustment against the higher contrast of the temporary black background. Click OK and you'll return to the marching ants view of the selection.

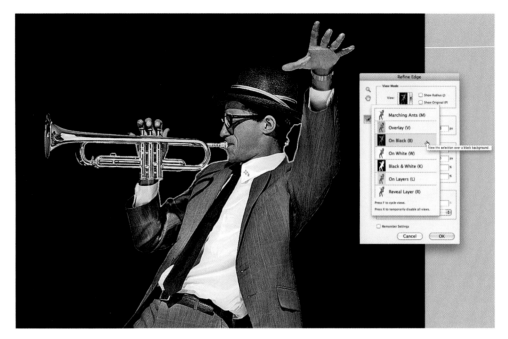

Figure 7.4 View the figure On Black to see the halo around the edge of the figure.

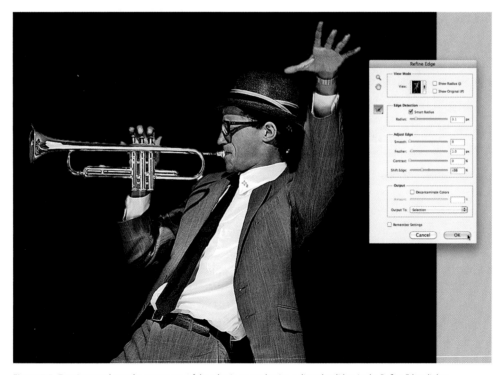

Figure 7.5 To gain control over the appearance of the edge in your selection, adjust the sliders in the Refine Edge dialog.

Now, to hide the sharp edge, click the Layer Mask icon at the bottom of the Layers panel (Figure 7.6). The newly contracted selection will be converted into a layer mask that hides the sharp edge and reveals the original unsharpened edge. The effect is subtle but a little more realistic because the figure now looks more like it is in the environment instead of pasted on top of it.

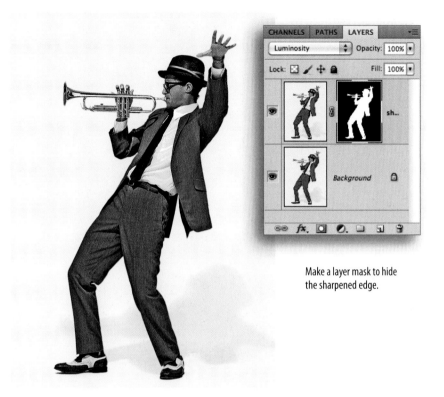

Make a layer mask to hide the sharpened edge.

Figure 7.6 The final image is sharp, but the edge blends into the background better.

To really appreciate the effect of sharpening, you should make test prints. It is often quite amazing how even a small amount of sharpening can enhance an image. Compare the sharpened version to the original unsharpened version shown back in Figure 7.2.

Smart Sharpen

Sharpening can supply a lot of sparkle to an image. This effect is the result of the lightening halos. Unfortunately, if an image contains a lot of high-frequency transitions such as tiny details, texture, or fine lines (hair), this "sparkle" can be distracting. The shot of the belly dancer in Figure 7.7 has this issue. If you apply a regular Unsharp Mask (right), you run the risk of turning the sequins into a riot of white speckles. Ideally, you want to apply more dark halos than light. Photoshop CS2 introduced the Smart Sharpen filter that allows you to do just that. As always, make a duplicate layer to use to apply the sharpening. Choose Filter > Sharpen > Smart Sharpen, and you will be presented with a larger dialog that contains some additional features (Figure 7.8).

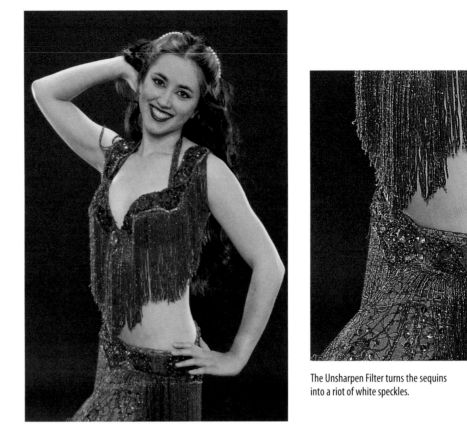

The Unsharpen Filter turns the sequins into a riot of white speckles.

The original image

Figure 7.7 Notice the distracting white halos that appear when a regular Unsharp Mask is used.

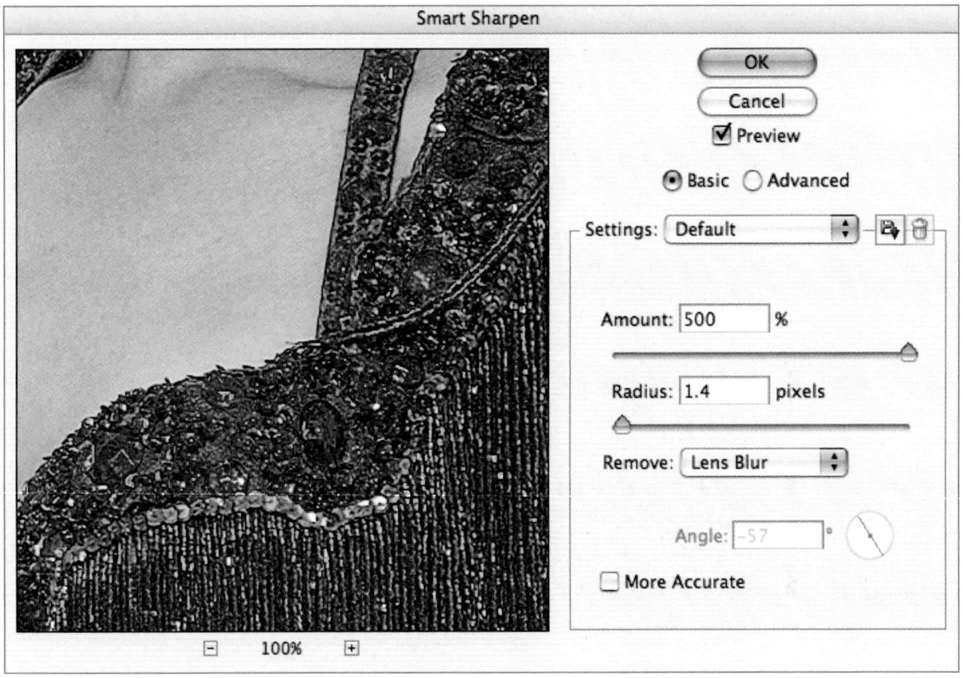

Figure 7.8 The Smart Sharpen dialog presents a large preview.

When the Basic radio button is selected, you can access the Amount and Radius sliders that control intensity and halo width, respectively. Just below these sliders, the Remove drop-down changes the sharpening effect to accommodate Gaussian Blur, Lens Blur, and Motion Blur. Gaussian Blur gives you very much the same effect as straight Unsharp Mask. Lens Blur offers a tighter halo with some built-in Threshold to minimize texture sharpening in a subtle way. Motion Blur activates the angle control and applies the Sharpen halos along the axis perpendicular to the angle setting; line up the angle with the direction of the Motion Blur to remove the blur. Finally, at the bottom of the dialog is a More Accurate check box. This is perhaps a misnomer; checking this changes the sharpening algorithm to generate an intense edge sharpening that has the tendency to introduce double edges and strange texture effects. I am still looking for an image that is suited to the More Accurate approach. So far, I've found that leaving this box unchecked yields the most natural-looking effects.

The big advantage of Smart Sharpen appears when you check the Advanced radio button; this option adds a Shadow and Highlight tab. Selecting the Shadow tab reveals three sliders: Fade Amount, Tonal Width, and Radius (Figure 7.9). The interaction of these sliders is not obvious. Fade determines by how much the darken halos are reduced in intensity. Tonal Width determines the degree of darkening to remove; if your Tonal Width setting is low, only very subtle darkening halos will be removed. This works kind of like the Threshold slider in Unsharp Mask. Higher Width settings remove darker halos; lower Width settings leave the darker halos alone and remove halos that are less dark. Setting the Fade Amount to 100 and the Tonal Width to zero will have no effect; neither will setting the Fade Amount to zero and Tonal Width to

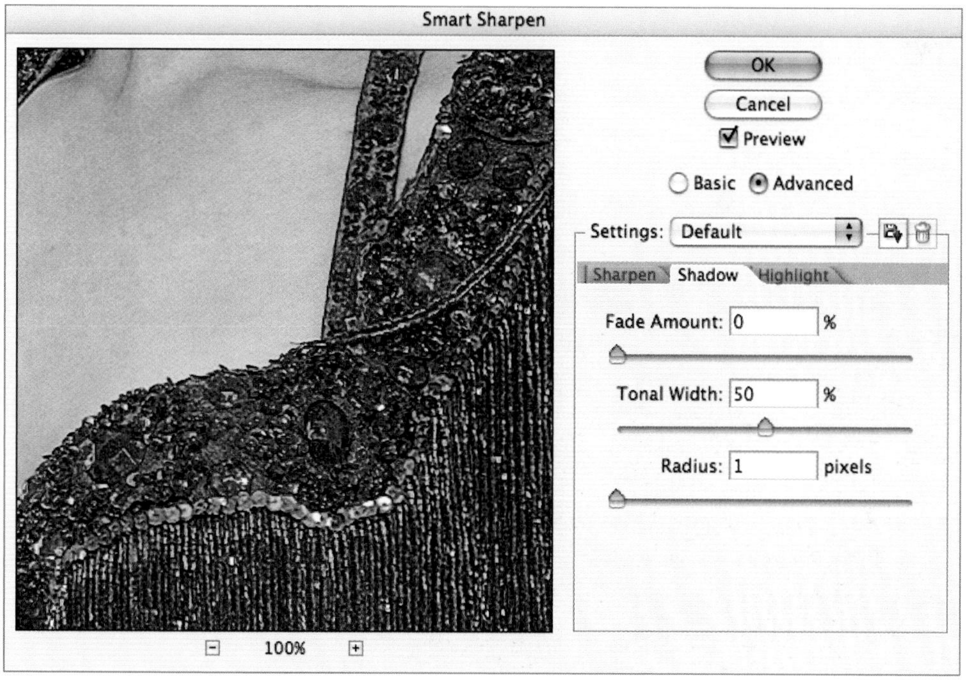

Figure 7.9 The Advanced settings Shadow options

100. Radius appears to work relative to the basic Sharpen radius, and determining exactly what it's doing is difficult. The Highlight tab works the same way with lightening halos (Figure 7.10). The best results for our example are seen with the Shadow Fade at zero and the Highlight Fade at 100. This doesn't seem to remove all the lightening halos, but it reduces the ratio of lighten to darken halos by half. You still get significant sharpening with this approach, but the light "sparkle" doesn't overwhelm the image.

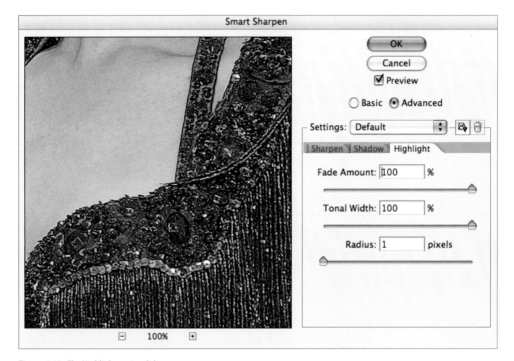

Figure 7.10 The Highlight option sliders

Multiple Sharpening Layers

Although it is convenient to control darkening and lightening halos in one dialog, I find it much more flexible to achieve similar results using two Sharpen layers with different blending modes. The idea is to apply regular Unsharp Mask to a duplicate layer, copy the sharpened layer, and use Lighten and Darken modes on these layers. The Sharpen effect will then be in two layers that can be controlled separately. This approach preserves the ability to apply sharpening with a Threshold slider, as well as Lighten and Darken.

1. Return to the unsharpened version and again duplicate the background into a layer. Run Unsharp Mask: Amount 500, Radius 1.3, Threshold 6 (Figure 7.11). This Threshold setting is just enough to keep the skin smooth.

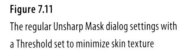

Figure 7.11

The regular Unsharp Mask dialog settings with
a Threshold set to minimize skin texture

2. Immediately after running the filter, choose Edit > Fade Unsharp Mask. You
   will be presented with a small dialog where you can change the Blending mode
   of the filter to Luminosity (Figure 7.12).

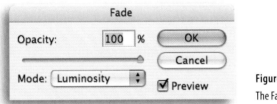

Figure 7.12

The Fade dialog set for Luminosity

3. Now you can use the Layer Blending modes to control Lighten and Darken
   effects. Duplicate the sharpened layer and turn off its visibility by clicking the
   Eye icon in the Layers panel. Target the original Sharpen layer and change the
   Layer Blending mode to Darken (Figure 7.13). The image will now have only
   darkening halos.

4. Turn on the top layer and change the Blending mode to Lighten; reduce the
   layer opacity to 50 percent (Figure 7.14).

The resulting version of the image is very similar to the Smart Sharpen version,
but you can more easily modify the balance of lighten to darken without having to run
the filter again—and you have the added benefit of being able to use layer masks to
modify the lighten and darken layers independently.

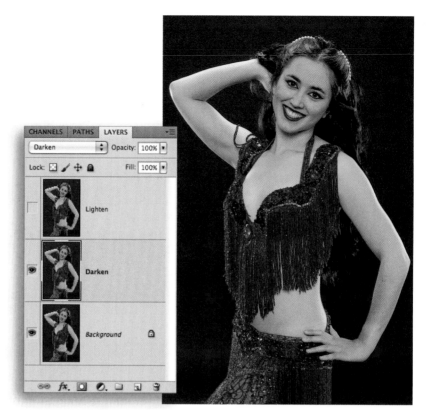

Figure 7.13 Target the first Sharpen layer and change the Blending mode to Darken.

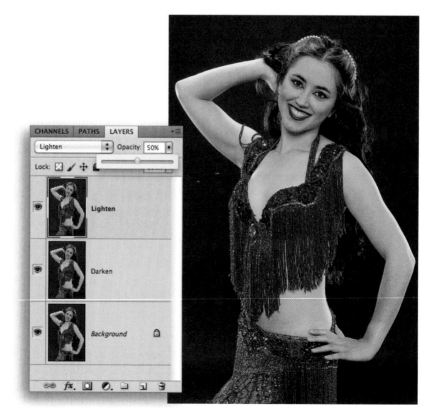

Figure 7.14 Target the second Sharpen layer and change the Blending mode to Lighten.

Octave Sharpening

The idea of multiple Sharpen layers has a unique application when you need a more intense Sharpen effect and need to minimize the visibility of wide halos. I call this technique *octave sharpening* because it applies ever-widening Sharpen halos in diminishing opacities similar to the overtones of a musical note. The net effect of this approach is to create ramped halos that fade as they move away from the edge.

Creating the Ramped Halos

My sample image is from a session I conducted with swing dancers. Focusing on moving subjects is difficult, and the dancers managed to move just outside of the ideal focus range (Figure 7.15). We'll begin this example the same way we began all the other examples. First, zoom in to 50 percent to evaluate the sharpening. Make a duplicate layer and change the Blending mode to Luminosity. Now make three additional duplicates.

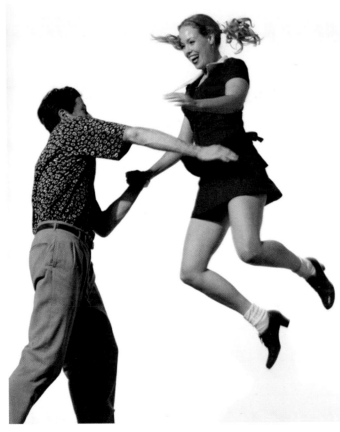

Figure 7.15 Original unsharpened version

The idea is to apply progressively wider radius sharpening in successive layers with decreasing opacity. Wide-radius sharpening gets low layer opacity, and as the Sharpen halos get tighter, opacity increases until the tightest halo is at 100 percent. We will start with the first duplicate layer and the tightest halo. Turn off the other duplicates above this layer by clicking the Eye icon to the left of the Layer thumbnail. Make sure the Blending mode is set to Luminosity and call up the Unsharp Mask filter. Set the Amount to 500 percent, Radius to 0.5, and Threshold to 0. This creates a very small but intense halo that will increase the sharpening effect but be almost imperceptible at print size. Leave the Opacity slider for this layer at 100 percent (Figure 7.16).

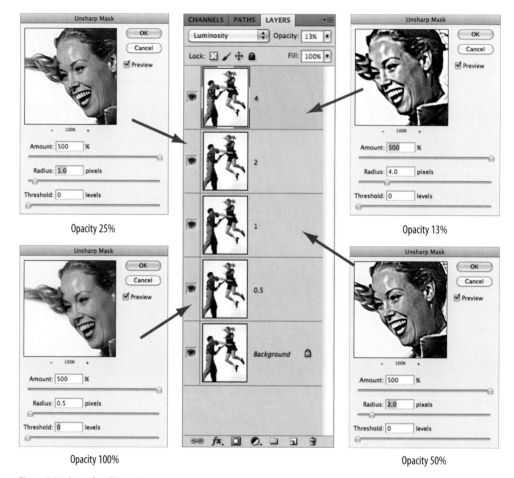

Figure 7.16 Set up four Sharpen layers.

The next layer up gets an Unsharp Mask Radius of 1 pixel, but you should reduce the opacity of the layer to 50 percent. The next layer gets a Radius of 2 pixels with an opacity of 25 percent.

The last layer gets an Unsharp Mask Radius of 4 pixels, but you should reduce the opacity of the layer to 13 percent.

Masking Multiple Layers for Sharpening

At this point, you would normally be done, but this particular image suffers from the same sharpening problem as the earlier trumpet player example. The dark-edge halos around the figures are exposed against the white background, lending a cutout appearance to the figures (Figure 7.17).

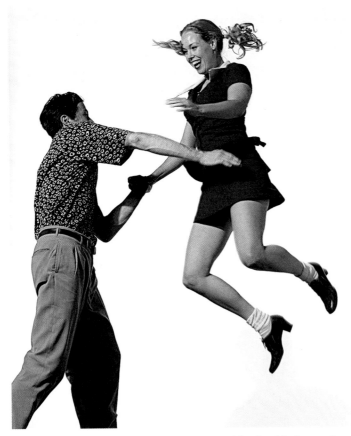

Figure 7.17 The sharpened version looks extra sharp around the edge of the figures and has a cutout look.

You will need to use the same layer mask trick to *trim off* the edges. The problem is that you have four layers to mask. There is a solution. You can use one mask to control all four layers if you put the layers into a group. Start by selecting all the sharpened layers (Shift+click all the Sharpen layers). Once this is done, choose New Group From Layers from the Layer Options menu at the upper-right corner of the Layers panel (Figure 7.18).

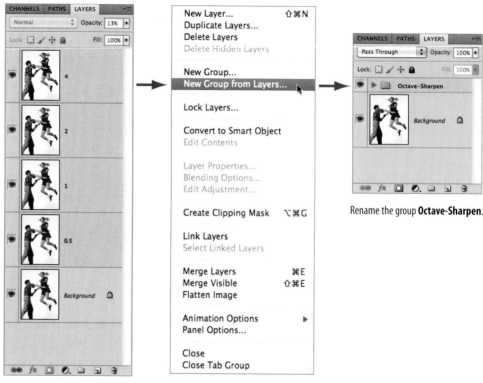

Select all four sharpen layers.

Create a new group from the layers.

Figure 7.18 Select all the Sharpen layers and group them.

Name the new group **Octave-Sharpen**, leave the Blending mode at Pass Through and the Opacity at 100 percent. All the linked layers are now contained in a folder in the Layers panel. This Sharpen folder can be treated as an individual layer by adding a layer mask to it.

Use the same procedure as outlined before to mask off the over-shape edge:

1. Use the Magic Wand tool to make a selection of the background.

2. Choose Select > Inverse to reverse the selection so the figures are selected.

3. Choose Select > Refine Edge to bring up the Refine Edge dialog.

4. Adjust the sliders to choke the selection and click OK (Figure 7.19).

Now, simply target the Sharpen Group and click the New Mask icon at the bottom of the Layers panel to create a mask that trims off the outer dark edge of the Sharpen effect. The mask can be further refined and extra-dark or light halos can be *painted out* using black in the mask. Compare the result in Figure 7.20 with the original sharpened version in Figure 7.17. The difference is subtle, but now the edges are more rounded, and they seem to be more part of the background.

You'll be amazed at what you can do to rescue some out-of-focus images using this technique. The image in Figure 7.21 was taken using a Lensbaby soft-focus lens. When the octave-sharpening techniques are used, much of the apparent detail is restored.

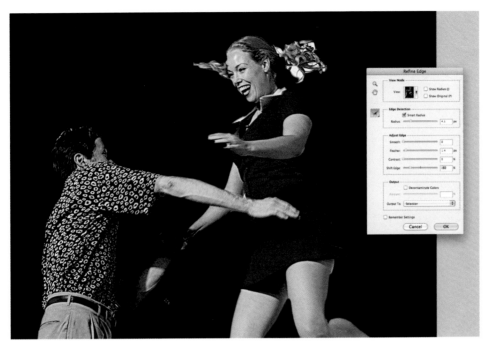

Figure 7.19 After shrinking, the selection will be just inside the edge of the figures.

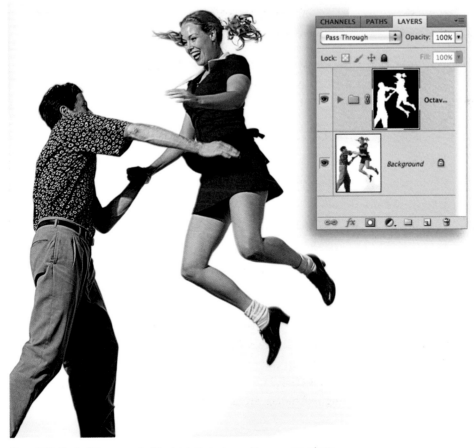

Figure 7.20 The final Sharpen version blends into the background in a more natural way.

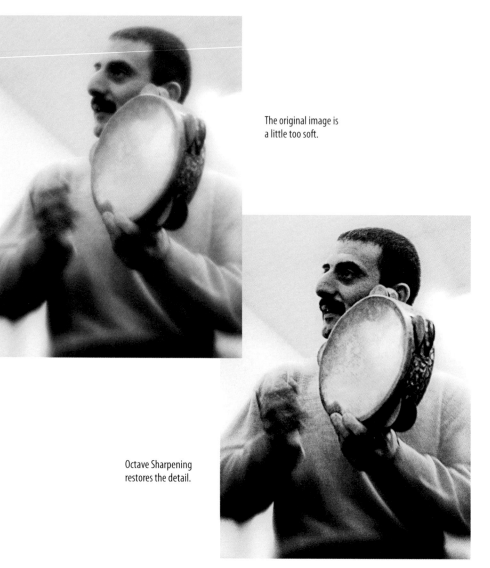

The original image is
a little too soft.

Octave Sharpening
restores the detail.

Figure 7.21 This Middle Eastern drummer has a more detailed look after Octave Sharpening is used.

Overlay Sharpening and High-Radius Effects

There is one more sharpening technique I'd like to cover. There are two basic kinds of Unsharp Mask sharpening. The first, a Low-Radius Unsharp Mask applied with a relatively high Amount, is what we've been practicing. The second kind, a high Radius with a low Amount, is the inverse. This second type is what Dan Margulis has called *HIRALOAM sharpening* in his books and magazine articles. The nature of this effect is different from regular sharpening. It tends to create a sculpted light, almost three-dimensional effect that can add shape and form to an image with relatively flat lighting.

Rather than use a regular Unsharp Mask for this effect, I like to use a special Overlay Sharpening technique that achieves a similar but better result. Let's examine this technique using an image of a swordsman in period costume at a Society for Creative Anachronism event (Figure 7.22). I will gradually build up the sharpening, bring the figure away from the background, and create some stronger shape to prepare for final printing. The first few steps are similar to what we did in the previous examples.

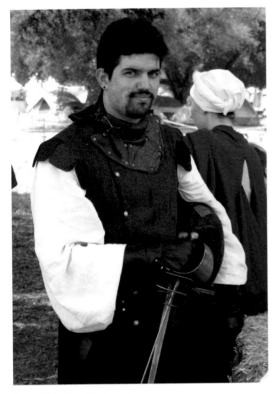

Figure 7.22 The original swordsman photo

First, create a Lighten and Darken sharpening group (similar to what I did for Figure 7.18 and mask the sharpening effect from the background (Figure 7.23).

Next, create a contrast-reducing Curves adjustment layer with a mask that applies the effect only to the background. Use the layer mask from the sharpen group to make the mask for this Curves adjustment layer (Cmd/Ctrl+click on the mask thumbnail to load it as a selection. Then, choose Select > Inverse to reverse it and select the background. Now, click the Curves icon in the Adjustment panel and flatten the curve (Figure 7.24). This helps to bring the figure forward, but I'd still like more contrast and shape in the face and hair. The soft open-shade lighting doesn't help here.

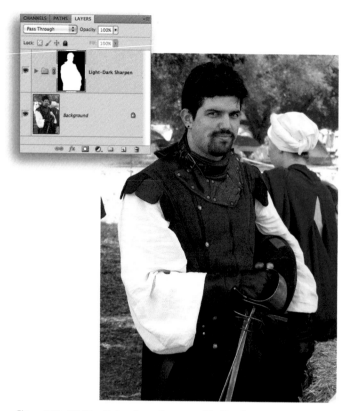

Figure 7.23 A Lighten-Darken sharpening group adds a basic level of sharpening.

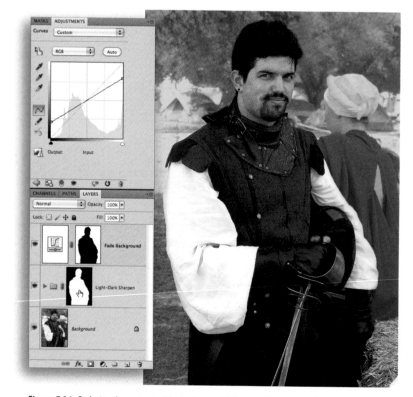

Figure 7.24 Reducing the contrast of the background brings the figure forward.

For the Overlay Sharpen technique, create a new layer by pressing and holding Option/Alt and then choosing Merge Visible from the Layers Panel Options flyaway. This places a merged copy of all the layers into this empty layer at the top of the layer stack (Figure 7.25). You will use this layer to sharpen the figure only—so, to prepare for this, copy the mask from the Sharpening Layer group.

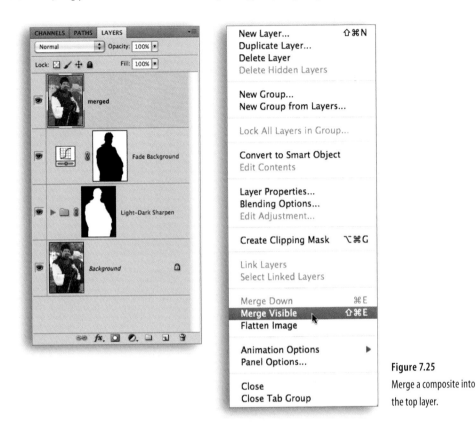

Figure 7.25
Merge a composite into the top layer.

Press and hold the Option/Alt key and drag the Layer Mask thumbnail from the Sharpen group to the merged layer. This duplicates the mask into this layer. Select the image thumbnail and choose Image > Adjustments > Hue/Saturation; desaturate the image by pushing the Saturation slider all the way to the left. You'll end up with the image shown in Figure 7.26. The reason we're doing this will become clear in a moment.

With the image thumbnail still highlighted, select Filter > Other > High Pass.

High Pass is an odd filter that reduces contrast to medium gray everywhere except where there is an edge transition based on the Radius setting in the dialog. We desaturate the image first so that the edge transitions have no color. As soon as we change the Apply mode to Overlay, we'll get a sharpening effect. If there is any color at the edge, we'll amplify colors along edges in the image—something we want to avoid. Low Radius settings preserve contrast only at narrow edges. The effect will be very similar to Unsharp Mask. In this case, we'll use a high Radius setting to produce an almost *bas-relief* effect (Figure 7.27). The High Pass filter has a built-in soft ramping effect that helps hide the edge halos most visible around the shirt.

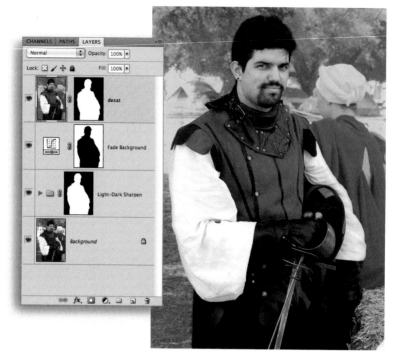

Figure 7.26 Mask the layer from the background and desaturate.

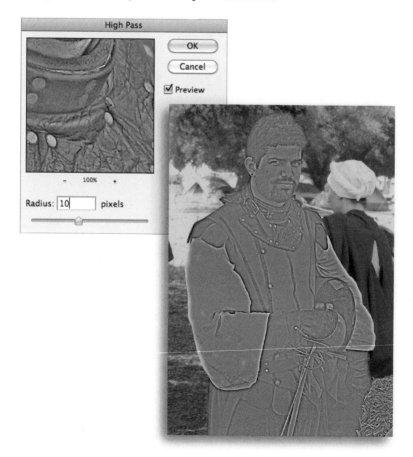

Figure 7.27 A high-radius High Pass filter creates a kind of bas-relief effect that simplifies the edge contrast.

Change the Layer mode to Overlay and you'll finally be able to see the sharpening effect (Figure 7.28). Notice the increase in contrast and shape in the face and hair. There is a better sense of texture in the neck protector and the clothing in general. In this example, the Overlay layer is used at 100 percent; however, you might need to reduce the opacity so the effect doesn't overpower the image.

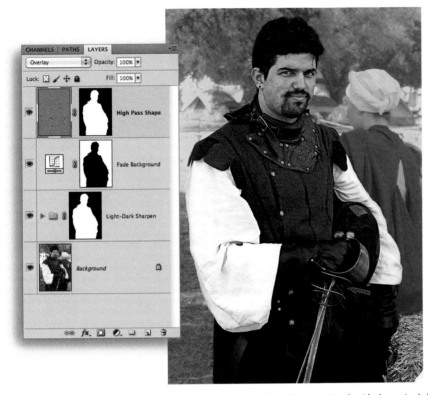

Figure 7.28 The final sharpening effect adds shape and texture without showing seriously wide sharpening halos.

Let's look at another example of this method. Remember the skin-lightening corrections we applied in Chapter 4, "Tone and Contrast: Color and B+W"? The image in Figure 7.29 is the next-to-last step in the process, after luminosity-blending lightened the skin. After duplicating the background into a new layer, desaturating, and running a 20-pixel Radius High Pass filter, we get Figure 7.30.

Change the Layer mode to Overlay to get Figure 7.31. The highlights on the face and arms are strengthened, but so are the shadows—and we don't want to make anything darker than it already is. By selecting Blending Options from the Layer Options flyaway menu, you can set the Blend If sliders to blend back the original shadow values so you get only the lightening effect of the High Pass Overlay layer (Figure 7.32).

Blending back the low values using this technique works the same as applying lighten-only Sharpen halos. The final result adds highlight shape to the image without also darkening it (Figure 7.33).

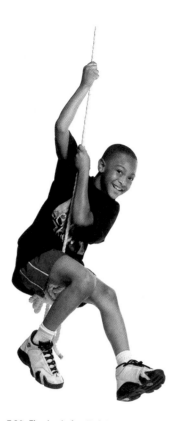

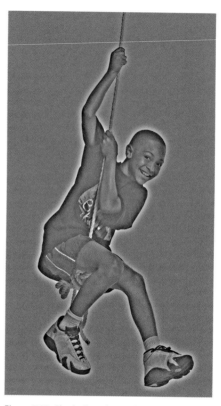

Figure 7.29 The shot before High Pass Overlay sharpening.

Figure 7.30 The duplicate layer is desaturated, and a 20-pixel Radius High Pass filter is applied.

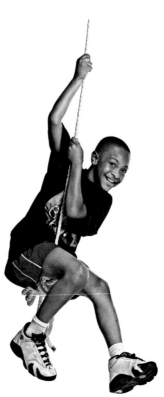

Figure 7.31
The High Pass Overlay effect lightens and darkens the image.

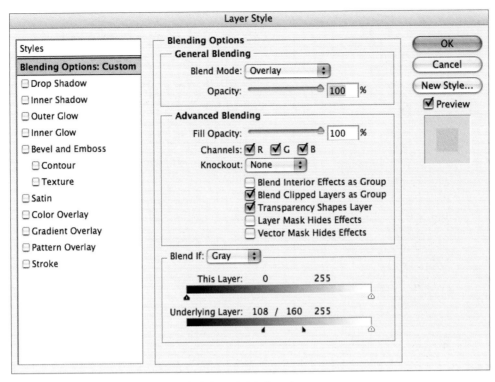

Figure 7.32 Blending Options are used to bring back the original shadow values.

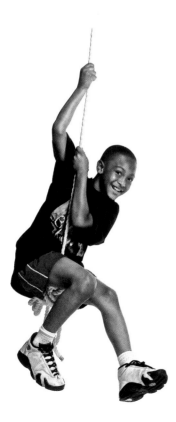

Figure 7.33
High Pass Overlay now supplies only enhanced highlights.

Color Management for Print

After your image is sized and sharpened, it is ready for you to make a print. So far, we have been working with a backlit display with vivid RGB colors that exceed the saturation and brightness of anything we can put on paper. Now the moment of truth arrives, and you need to translate what you see on the monitor to a print that can convey the same feeling. The problem is much the same as it was when photographers shot transparency film: There is still a huge discrepancy between the dynamic range and color gamut that can be represented with a glowing backlit monitor image and what can be printed on paper, where the brightest thing is the white paper. Another major issue is the way images are constructed in the two different media. RGB images on the monitor exist in an additive color space: Red, green, and blue light is added together to make white. CMYK images, which form the bulk of paper-based output, use cyan, magenta, yellow, and black to subtract from paper white to make a color image.

 Note: Tim Grey explains this well in *Color Confidence: The Digital Photographer's Guide to Color Management, Second Edition* (Wiley, 2006).

Translating from RGB to CMYK

Typically, all of our corrections and edits are made in RGB, and the majority of printed outputs are in CMYK. This includes desktop inkjet printers that are designed to receive RGB files. These printers internally transform RGB input into some kind of CcMmYKk-type color for the specific inkset that the printer uses. Even true RGB output devices, such as a LightJet printer, do not actually have a standard RGB workspace color gamut. Therefore, all prints require a color transformation to occur from the workspace (editing color space) to the output (printing color space) for optimum results. All such transformations are handled by the color management system. Photoshop uses ICC (International Color Consortium) profiles to manage color inside the application. Effective color management requires profiles that describe every device used in the image creation workflow from workspace to monitor to printer. I select default profiles for my RGB workspace and CMYK workspace in Photoshop color settings. Frequently, the default CMYK workspace is used for generic CMYK output. Ideally, the color transformations necessary for printing to a specific printer utilize a profile for that specific device. Fortunately, most modern desktop printers provide reasonable profiles that are installed with the device drivers, and we can use these profiles to control the color transforms for printing.

Profiles and Look-Up Tables

Understanding what a profile is will help you fully comprehend what happens in color-managed transformations. An ICC profile is a standard way of numerically defining the way a particular device (a scanner, camera, printer, or monitor) renders color for a human observer under average daylight conditions. Color management involves linking these various device profiles together in a way that allows us to control the appearance of colors from one device to another. In order for this to work, a profile must reference the observable colors from a device to a device-independent model, a sort of absolute definition of color. Profiles are static definitions, and the dynamic calculations that move an image file through various profiles to arrive at the final output are handled by a color management module (CMM) that is the mathematical engine for all the transforms.

Therefore, a profile is a special number transformer, a kind of black box called a look-up table (LUT) or more often a color look-up table (CLUT), that takes a set of numbers and returns another set of numbers. The first set of numbers can be from any kind of color device (RGB, CMYK, or grayscale); the second set of numbers is the Lab definition of the color represented by the first set (Figure 7.34).

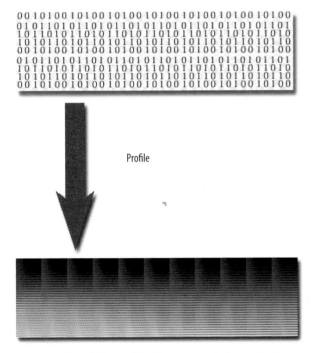

Device/Workspace Numbers

Profile

Lab Color

Figure 7.34 A profile "looks up" the Lab value for a color in a specific color space.

You can think of Lab numbers as being independent of any particular device but representative of colors observable under D50 graphics industry standard lighting. Therefore, a profile gives us a real color definition of the numbers from a digital file—in D50 light.

Some profiles are relatively simple rules based on a matrix with a few points defining a larger set of colors. Other profiles are larger plots of all possible colors in a particular set. Matrix profiles are commonly used for Photoshop's working spaces and monitor profiles. Printer profiles are most commonly larger CLUTs, sometimes referred to as table-based profiles. The math surrounding all this is staggering. For the artist, a profile is merely a definition of the color rendered by a device translated into

Lab. When photographers need to transform one set of device numbers into numbers for another device, they use profiles to "look up" the Lab colors and generate new numbers for the next device based on those colors (Figure 7.35).

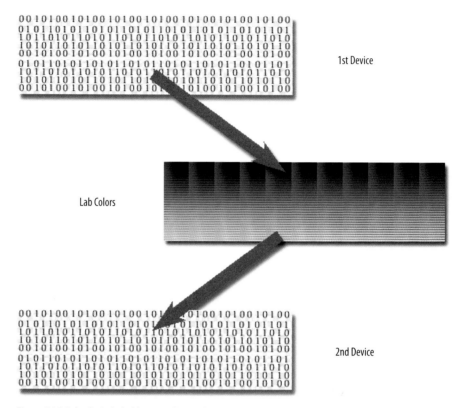

1st Device

Lab Colors

2nd Device

Figure 7.35 Lab color is the link between the two device numbers.

When the profiles for the devices you are using are installed, you simply have to select the appropriate profile at the right time to manage the necessary color transforms. The rest of this chapter will go over the steps necessary to get the most out of profiles in your color management system.

Soft Proofing

Photoshop includes a method for previsualizing the effect that gamut reduction in the output has on the image. You can find this preview, often referred to as a *soft proof*, under the View menu. Select Proof Colors under the View menu or press ⌘ +Y/Ctrl+Y to toggle the soft proof on or off. This changes the screen to simulate the appearance of the print. The default proof color is Working CMYK; you can select your CMYK color space in Photoshop Color Settings.

You can change the proof colors to match the output you are going to use. Go to View > Proof Setup > Custom. You will get a dialog that allows you to select a profile for a printer and a rendering intent for your transformation (Figure 7.36). You can select any output profile you want; you aren't restricted to working with CMYK or any of the default selections such as Monitor RGB or Windows/Macintosh RGB. If you have a profile for an Epson printer, you can select it here.

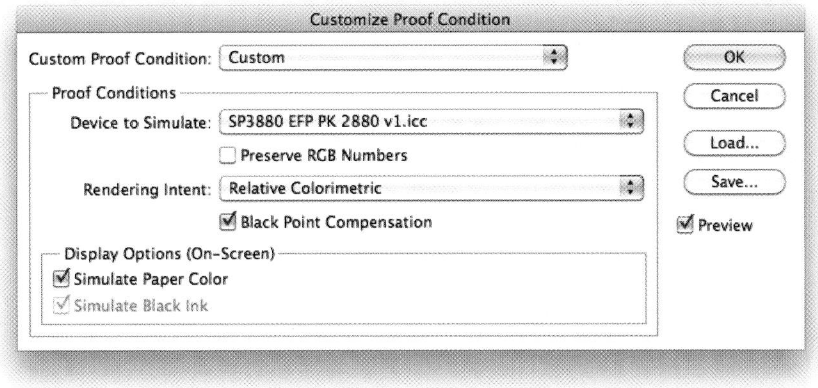

Customize Proof Condition

Custom Proof Condition: Custom

Proof Conditions
Device to Simulate: SP3880 EFP PK 2880 v1.icc
☐ Preserve RGB Numbers
Rendering Intent: Relative Colorimetric
☑ Black Point Compensation
Display Options (On-Screen)
☑ Simulate Paper Color
☑ Simulate Black Ink

OK
Cancel
Load...
Save...
☑ Preview

Figure 7.36 Select View > Proof Setup to change the output device you want to simulate.

The Simulate check boxes at the bottom of this dialog are particularly interesting. The Simulate options allow you to see a more accurate preview and force an absolute color match to the screen. However, evaluating the color this way requires a little practice. When you select Proof Setup and check the Preview box, you might observe a very slight change in appearance depending on the color gamut of the original. Normally, you'll see very little change. When you select Ink Black, the preview changes to reflect the actual intensity of the black ink on the paper to be printed. This can make the image seem a little dull, but it still is not entirely accurate. To be accurate, you need to select Paper White. This often results in a very dull rendition—yuck! (See Figure 7.37).

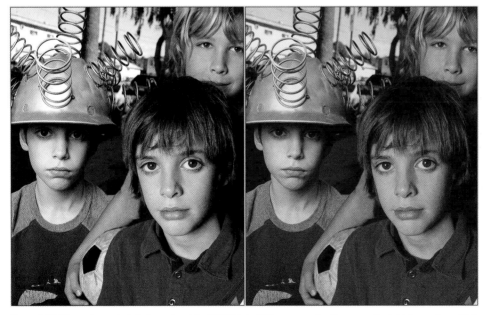

Figure 7.37 The version on the left shows the original RGB (Adobe RGB) screen version. The one on the right shows a Paper White simulation of CMYK (U.S. Web Coated—SWOP v2).

Note: When all the options for your soft proof are set up, click Save. You can recall the setup from the drop-down at the top of the dialog or go right to it from the Proof Setup menu.

Paper White is not as white as a backlit monitor. Once you understand that, you can begin to see how this simulation might be useful. The problem is that our eyes are confused by all the white in the interface visible on the monitor. You can mitigate the effect of all this white by toggling to Full Screen mode. Press the F key to hide the desktop and place the image on a gray background. Press the F key again to get a black background, and press the Tab key to hide the panels. Without the white reference of the interface, the duller image doesn't look that bad. In many cases, with desktop inkjet printers, the simulation will be only slightly duller; however, it can give you a heads-up warning about how the contrast will change—low values might get muddy and highlights might get less intense.

To most people, the screen simulation looks worse than the final print because matching the visual context of the print for screen viewing is very difficult. However, the simulation is still quite useful because it helps you get enough contrast in the image to produce a good print. You can leave Proof Colors on and use any adjustment tools to optimize the image for your output. Usually, simple Curves can be used to add extra contrast to punch up the image for the more-limited dynamic range of the typical output. Many photographers leave the simulation on when they display images on the monitor to their clients. This reduces the clients' expectations, and they have fewer problems accepting a final print.

Note: By working with the print corrections in a layer, you can save the adjustment for your printer and apply it to other documents. You can simply drag it onto the new documents. You can keep saved corrections available for different printer outputs and apply them at the last minute before printing.

Desktop Printing

After you finish sharpening, previewing, and adjusting the image, the moment of truth will finally arrive when you have to make an actual print. Even if you are sending the file to a commercial printer, you'll want to make a desktop print to use as a *rough proof* or *aim print*. As a digital photographer, you'll probably be printing from Photoshop. For your first step in the final sequence, go to the File menu (File > Print).

Print Options

When the print dialog comes up, make sure you have Color Management selected in the drop-down at the upper-right corner—most of the important printing options for our purposes are in this area (Figure 7.38). This is where you set up all the Profile options for your prints.

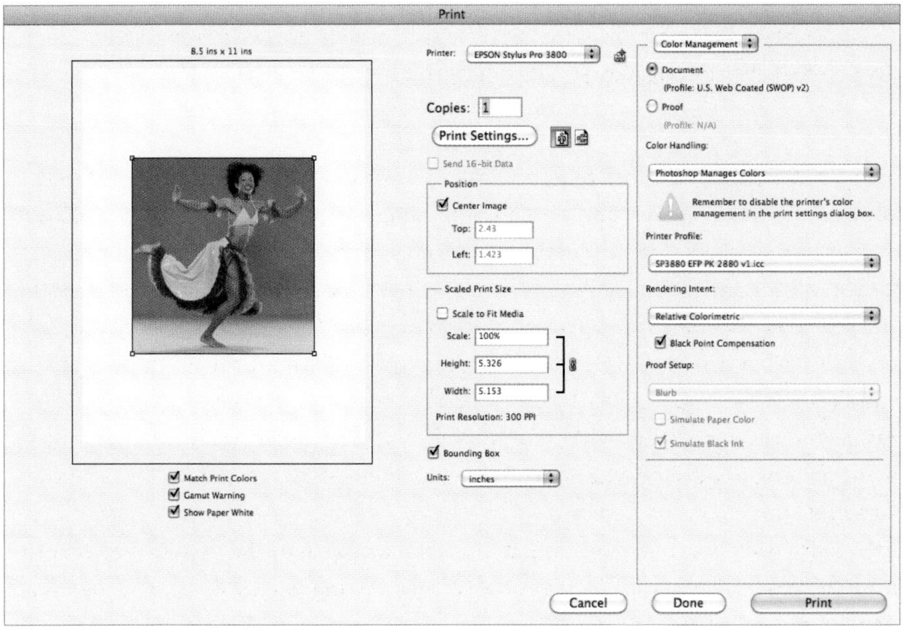

Figure 7.38 Select Color Management in the drop-down at the upper right.

At the center of the dialog, Position controls how the image lays out on the page. The Center Image check box provides a quick way to place the image. Directly below that is the Scaled Print Size area; by default, this is set up for 100 percent. If the image is way too small or way too big on the page preview, click the Print Settings button and make sure you're using the right size paper. Checking the Scale To Fit Media check box is a quick and dirty method of sizing the image to fit the paper—just beware that your quality will suffer if the reported Scale percentage is overly high. It is far better to set the size properly in Photoshop before using the dialog. The Bounding Box check box is useful when you have an area of white canvas in your image—the bounding box shows the edges of the image against the white of the paper.

The important color settings reside in the right third of the dialog box. The two radio buttons directly under the Color Management drop-down identify whether you are going to print the document directly or generate a simulation proof; if you are making prints for your portfolio or to sell to a client, you probably will check Document because this will generally provide the highest quality print for your image. This sets the profile to the document color space and determines where the color starts from in its journey to the print. (We'll cover the Proof setting later.)

Next, is the Color Handling area. For RGB images, the Color Handling drop-down shows Photoshop Manages Colors, Printer manages Colors, or Separations.

Photoshop Manages Colors Selecting Photoshop Manages Colors allows you to select the Printer Profile in the drop-down menu just below this one. This is the most straightforward way to set up color management for the print. If you select Photoshop Manages Colors, remember to turn off color management in the printer dialog!

Printer Manages Colors If you select Printer Manages Colors, the Print Profile option is grayed out and you will have to set the Color Management options in the printer driver. The Printer Driver dialogs are usually a lot more confusing in this regard, so you'd be wise to stick with Photoshop. (Don't forget to turn off the printer's color management.) The Printer Profile drop-down shows all the profiles installed on your system to which you have access. If the printer driver is installed properly, a profile for your printer and media can be selected here.

Separations   Separations will be available only if you are printing from a CMYK document; otherwise it will be grayed out. This option is used only when printing separate cyan, magenta, yellow and black "plates" or simulations; for the most part, you can ignore it.

The last choice is Rendering Intent. Here you can choose: Perceptual, Saturation, Relative Colorimetric, or Absolute Colorimetric. Ninety percent of the time Relative Colorimetric will give you the best result. Occasionally, certain very saturated colors will tend to posterize and lose detail in the print. If this is the case, you can try to solve the problem with Perceptual rendering. Generally though, Perceptual rendering will give a less saturated color in the print, and your skin tones could become dull. The other renderings are applicable for custom profiles and unusual circumstances; however, for the most part, you can ignore them with people images.

Beginning with Photoshop CS5, the large preview in the dialog is color managed and has some check box controls underneath the preview. Checking Match Print Colors, by default, checks the other two boxes—you can uncheck them if you desire. Gamut Warning renders flat areas of gray over any color that is out of gamut for the selected printer profile. Show Paper White puts a tone into the white areas of the preview in an attempt to simulate the effect of the paper color on the image (much as you can with the Custom Proof Setup under the View Menu). The preview can also be used to reposition the image directly. If you uncheck the Center Image check box in the Position area, you can click the image preview and move it around on the page and/or rescale it by dragging on the corner handles in the bounding box (if you uncheck Bounding Box you won't be able to do this).

Note: The Color Management options continue to generate a lot of confusion in Photoshop. Adobe has changed the user interface and the terminology used in the Print dialog for every version of Photoshop since version 4 (pre-CS). Much time has been spent in development of CS5 to make the dialog easier to comprehend, but I suspect that this area will continue to evolve in subsequent versions. Pay attention to the development of color management concepts and you should be able to decipher the controls laid out in the printer dialog.

Once all your options are set, you are free to click Print. The only additional thing you need to remember is that if your color management options are being set in Photoshop, you have to turn off any such options in the Printer Driver dialog. All of the color transformations will have already taken place in Photoshop before the data hits the printer driver, so make sure you do not "double color manage" and introduce an additional transformation. Every printer driver is a little different, but yours will have some option to select no color management in the printer driver.

Output Simulations

Moving directly from the document color space to the printer will give you the most faithful rendering of your image file. Sometimes you might want to simulate another kind of output with your desktop printer. The final use for the image may be in offset lithography or some other type of commercial output, but you will be delivering an RGB file and you may need to know how it will look in the final output. By selecting the Proof radio button in the Color Management section of the dialog, you will generate this kind of output simulation for your desktop printer (Figure 7.39).

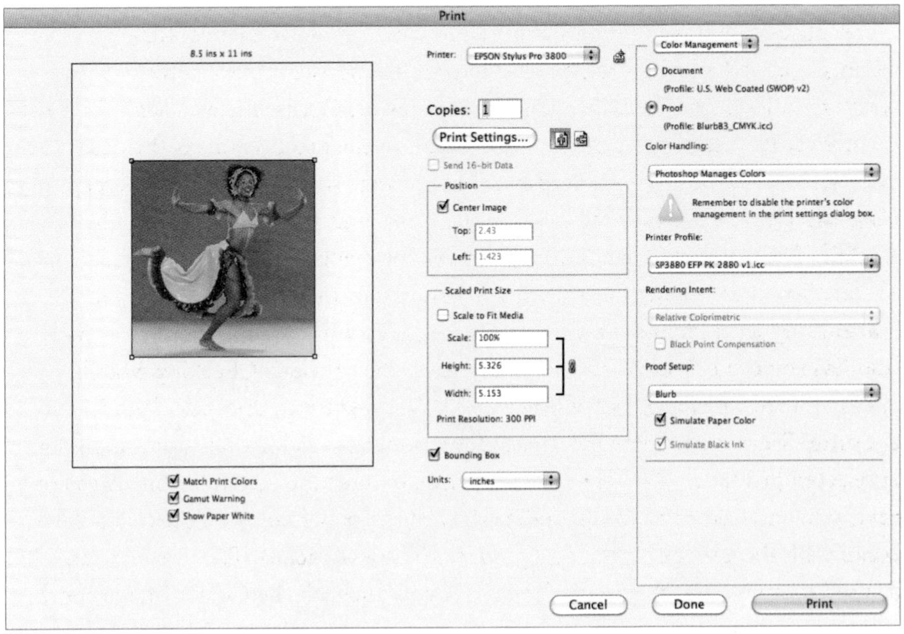

Figure 7.39 Use the Proof option to simulate another type of output on your desktop printer.

The Proof profile is determined by your Proof Setup under the View menu in Photoshop. If you use a custom proof setup that includes a paper white simulation, you can check Simulate Paper Color and this will print a tone into the white paper of your print. The tone may look off if you see it against the normal white of the paper, so be sure and trim off all the plain paper before showing it to a client. Whether you use the paper simulation feature or not, you should leave Simulate Black Ink checked to get a better idea of the contrast of your final output in your proof print.

Creative Print Finishing

Let's return to the Output options in the Print dialog. When you select Output from the drop-down at the upper right, a number of different options appear. Most of these are only of interest to commercial printers, but two of the options can provide some print enhancement features. Before you explore these options, uncheck the Center Image check box and enter a smaller value in the Top position. If you are going to print with page space around the image, you might want to have the image just above center on the page. Sometimes called the visual center; placing images in this area prevents the image from looking as if it is falling off the page (Figure 7.40).

Click on the Border button to bring up a dialog where you can create a thin, black keyline around the image on the page (Figure 8.41).

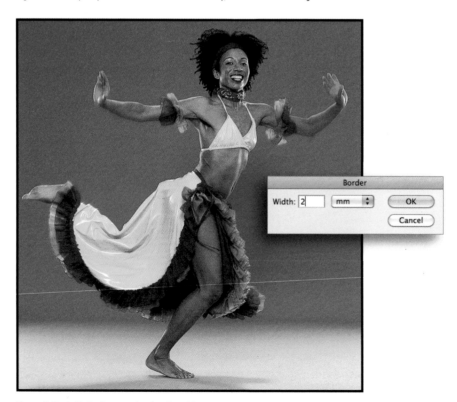

Figure 7.40 Output options can be used to enhance the presentation of the image.

Figure 7.41 A thin keyline contains the edge of the image.

Background and Canvas Options

The Background button calls up the Color Picker. With it, you can set a color value to print into the page background (Figure 7.42). You can achieve a very subtle effect with this option. By selecting a tone just slightly grayer than white (L=95 is a good starting place), you create the illusion that the paper white areas inside the image are brighter than they really are. Your eye catches the surrounding matte area as the white point, and small areas of white in the image appear as light sources. This is a subtle but real optical illusion. If your printer does not print to the edge of the paper, trim off any border before displaying the print.

The image that opens this chapter employs this effect in a slightly different way. The area surrounding the image at first appears to be the paper white, but it actually has a slight gray tone. The tiny white highlights in the image look just a little brighter, and this gives the image a little more sparkle. The surround was created using Canvas Size in Photoshop (Image > Canvas Size). To select a gray color in the Color Picker, set the Canvas Extension in the resulting dialog (Figure 7.42) and click the small square to the right of the Canvas Extension Color drop-down. You can generate many different rough-edge effects when you have some canvas area with which to work. You can also "sign" your work with the Text tool in the matte area just below the image.

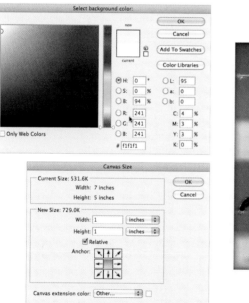
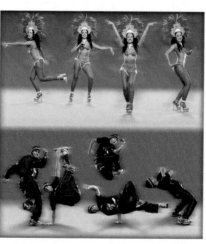

The tiny, white highlights in the image look just a little brighter and give the image a little more sparkle.

Figure 7.42 Use the Background button to pick a color slightly darker than white for the image matte. Add space around the image with the Canvas Size dialog.

Edge Treatments

Here is a simple technique to create a rough-edge effect. After creating your canvas area matte, as in the preceding steps, select the Pen tool or the Rectangle Path tool and draw a path just inside the edge of the image (Figure 7.43). Now, select the Brush tool. You are going to stroke the path with a rough brush.

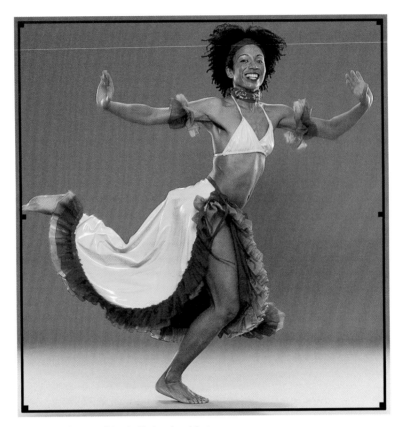

Figure 7.43 Draw a path just inside the edge of the image.

You can use any brush you want; I used one in the Dry Media Brushes preset. To load these brushes, go to the Tool Options bar and click the Brush drop-down. Then click the triangle at the upper right of the Brush Selector menu to load the preset brushes, select Dry Media Brushes from the drop-down menu, and click Append in the resulting dialog (Figure 7.44). Scroll down until you find the Soft Pastel Large brush—you can display the Stroke Thumbnail to help you find the brush you like. Set a diameter large enough to create a rough edge—in this example, I used 60 pixels.

Option/Alt+click the matte area and make sure the off-white color of the matte is the foreground color for the brush. Next, make a new empty layer in the Layers panel. Now you are ready to stroke!

Select Stroke Path from the Paths panel by clicking on the Panel Options triangle at the upper right of the Paths panel. You will get a dialog where you can select a Painting tool; make sure the brush is selected and click OK. The selected brush is *stroked* along the path, obscuring the hard edge of the original image (Figure 7.45).

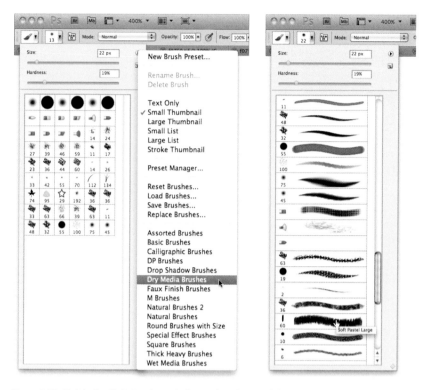

Figure 7.44 Find the Dry Media Brushes in the Presets drop-down, and choose the Soft Pastel Large brush.

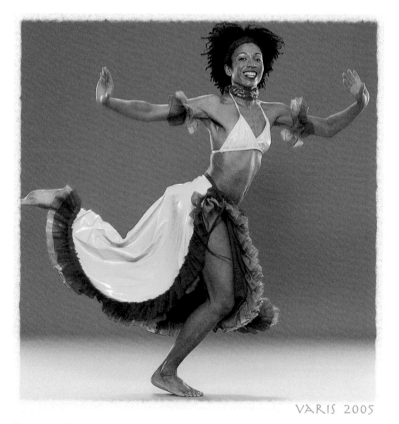

Figure 7.45 The rough-edge look gives the image a hand-made appearance.

To complete the fine-art print look, you can sign the print using the Text tool and a cool font, as I did in the example. The rough-edge look is very popular with portrait photographers, and it looks especially good when the print is done on water-color paper. Figure 7.46 was created using three different brushes to build a more complex edge.

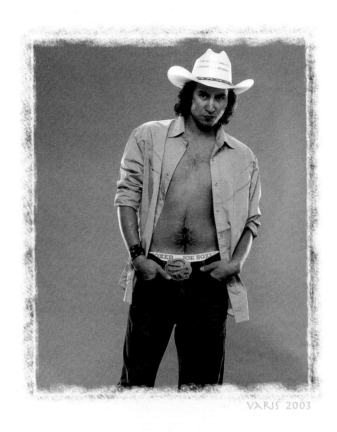

Figure 7.46 Different brushes in a light-dark-light application yield a more complex edge.

A few of the third-party plug-ins offer easy ways to get a wide variety of rough-edge looks, as you can see in the following examples. Figure 7.47 was created using the PhotoFrame Pro plug-in from onOne Software.

I used Extreme Edges, a library of mask images from GraphicAuthority.com, to create the complex edge effect in Figure 7.48.

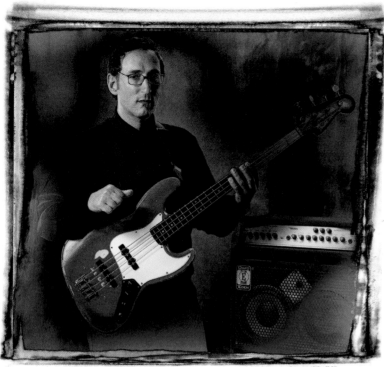

Figure 7.47   Two photo edges were applied to create this effect.

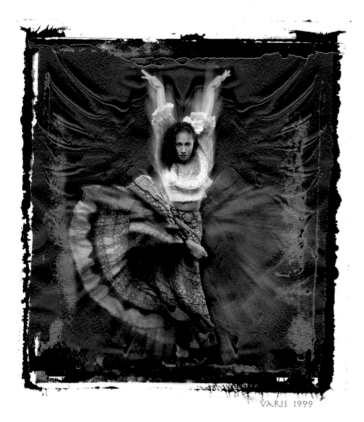

Figure 7.48   Complex shapes used in layer masks created the wet-darkroom edge effect.

Sometimes simple is the best. You can create thin keylines of any color by using the canvas feature with small pixel dimensions. In Figure 7.49, I set a canvas using Relative checked and adding 10 pixels in each dimension with a blue canvas color. Then I added an additional white canvas so I could sign my name under the image.

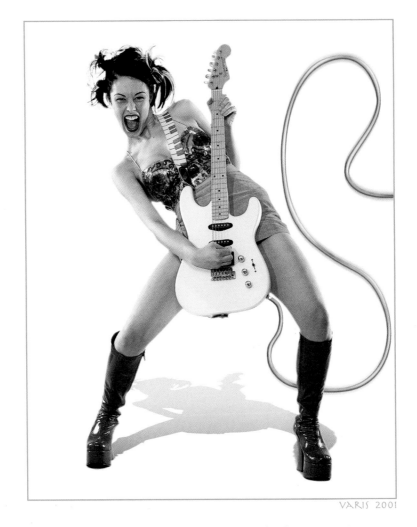

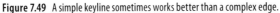

Figure 7.49 A simple keyline sometimes works better than a complex edge.

Edge treatments can do a lot to dress up the presentation of an image, and presentation can be important for portraits and fine-art imagery that will be displayed in a portfolio rather than in a frame on the wall. Explore the possibilities when you start printing your work, even if you decide that the particular image doesn't need anything extra.

Last Minute Fixes

Final tweaking is often necessary before you are happy with a print. Let's step through the final corrections for this image by Aaron Rapoport (Figure 7.50).

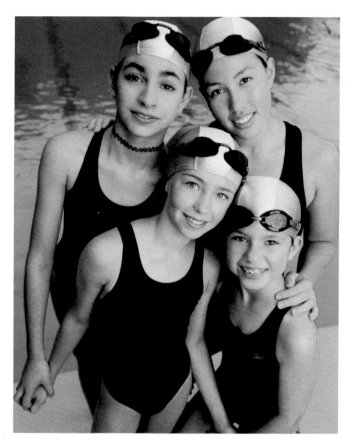

Figure 7.50 The original image directly from Camera Raw (Photo by Aaron Rapoport)

Aaron opted for a lot of contrast and saturation. The bathing suits are very dark, with values down to a level of 5 in some areas. The detail in the suits is not important, so I'll leave them alone and concentrate on the faces. The skin color is not bad, although the highlights read a little on the pink side and the shadows read a tad on the yellow side. The blue water is way out of gamut for CMYK, so we would lose tonal variation when the color clips into CMYK.

First, make some basic Curves and Hue/Saturation adjustments to equalize the skin color and reduce the blue saturation a bit (Figure 7.51).

Next, blend the Luminosity with the Channel Mixer (check Monochrome, set Green to 70 percent, and set Blue to 30 percent) to put some added shape into the skin as shown in Figure 7.52. (You'll remember this technique from your work with the concepts covered in Chapter 4.)

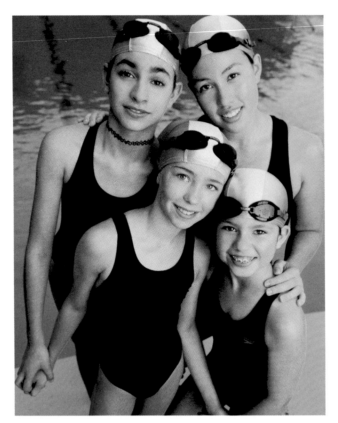

Figure 7.51
The image after Curves
and Hue/Saturation
adjustments

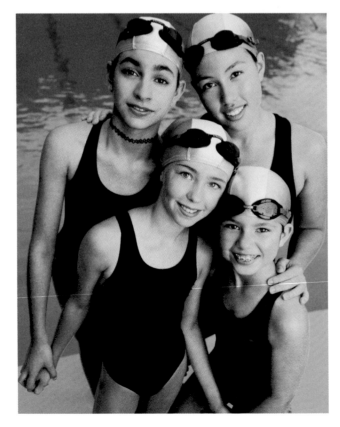

Figure 7.52
Luminosity Blending
adds shape.

Now, add a little sharpening and some High-Pass Overlay Sharpening to further enhance the shape. (Go back to the section titled "Overlay Sharpening and High-Radius Effects" if you need to review this sharpening technique.) As you can see in Figure 7.53, the image is starting to look pretty good.

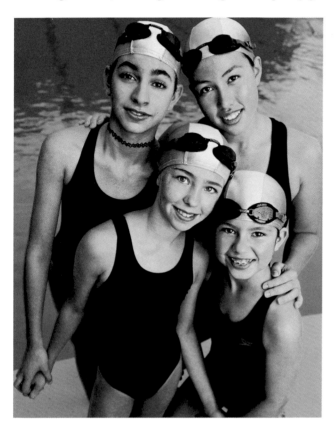

Figure 7.53
Sharpening and a High-Radius High-Pass Overlay layer add some final shape.

There is one last subtle problem. It may be too subtle to see at the print size in this book, but it is a common defect that often appears in inkjet portfolio prints from digital camera files. Look at a close-up of the most offensive areas (Figure 7.54).

The shadow values, which are most noticeable along the arm, have become too saturated. As colors approach black, they should become less saturated, not more saturated. This kind of oversaturated shadow value is quite common in digital camera files that are processed with a saturation boost. The result is often a posterized tone in the dark skin that creates harsh breaks instead of smooth transitions.

Note: The oversaturation problem may or may not be strongly visible in this reproduction, depending on how UCR (under-color removal) is implemented in the separations. The oversaturated shadows often show up worse in inkjet prints that have a greater color gamut than the typical offset lithography press. The saturation is clearly visible in the digital file, so be sure to look at the files (available on the website: www.varis.com/skinbook) as well as the reproductions here.

To remedy the situation, you can employ a little blending options trick. Create a Hue/Saturation adjustment layer and push the Saturation slider all the way to the left; you will end up with a B+W version of the image. Select Blending Options from the Flyaway Layer Options menu and set Blend If Blue sliders, as shown in Figure 7.55.

The oversaturated, dark skin color is first noticeable as a dark tone in the Blue channel, so use that channel to control the blend. Split the Blend slider to smooth the transition, and you'll end up with Figure 7.56.

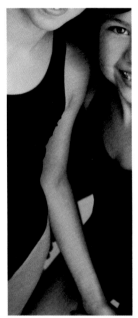

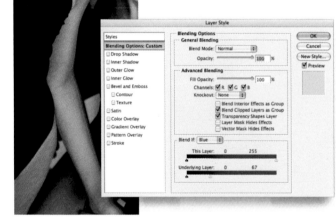

Figure 7.54 Shadow values in the skin tone are too saturated.

Figure 7.55 Blend through a desaturating Hue/Saturation adjustment layer to bring back the color in the lighter areas.

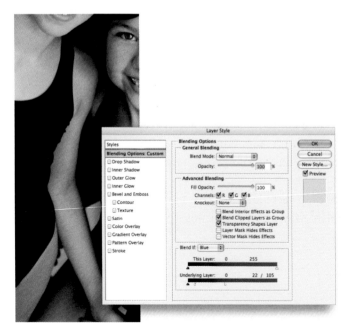

Figure 7.56 Split the Blend slider to soften the transition.

The final image has a more natural look in the shadow areas and is less likely to exhibit ugly posterized transitions in the shadow values of the skin (Figure 7.57).

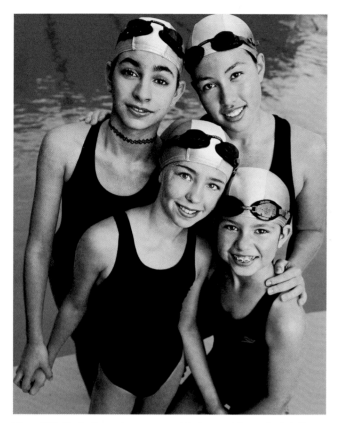

Figure 7.57 The final image has more natural shadow transitions in the dark skin; they are mostly noticeable as less red in the shadows. Compare this to Figure 7.53.

Look back at Figure 7.50. You'll see that we've achieved a more three-dimensional look—the figures have greater presence and better contrast and sharpness. The first version by itself doesn't seem so bad. On the computer monitor, this image may seem to be just fine. The color is vibrant and you won't notice how soft it is. Digital images are so seductive that we often don't push images hard enough, and we settle for less than we could. Sometimes we don't know if we've gone far enough until we've gone too far; when we do, it is a simple matter to reduce a layer's opacity and try another print to find the sweet spot. Often, these subtle tweaks in color, sharpening, blending, and print presentation make the difference between a good image and a great image.

I hope you try some of these techniques on your favorite images and find the hidden treasures that lurk there. May we all create more great images!

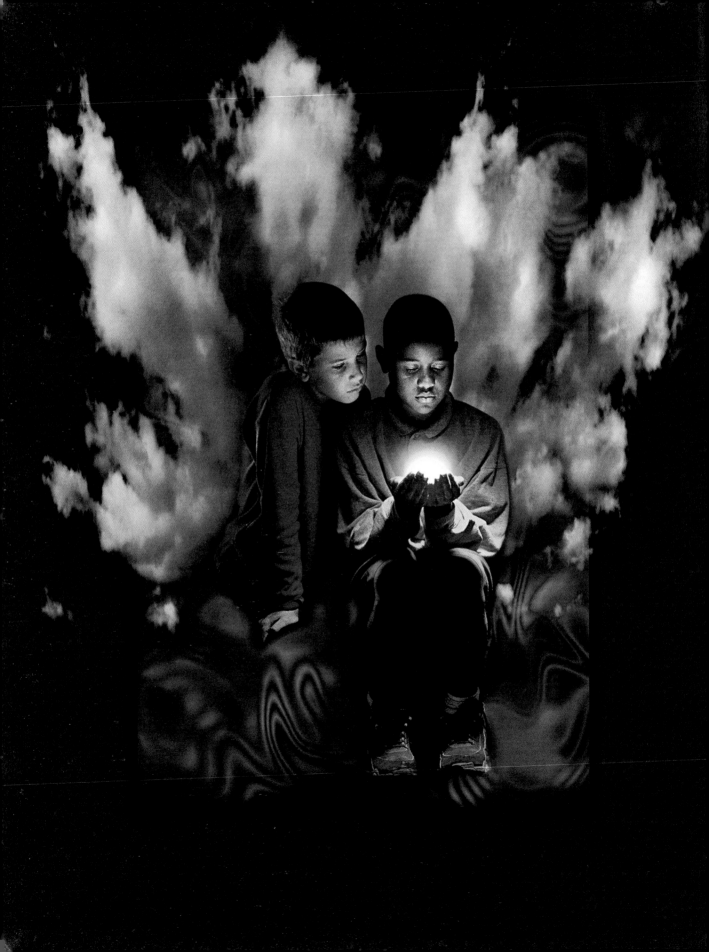

Parting Shots

Digital cameras have given us more control over the images we capture, and they have opened up new possibilities for creative expression. We have explored numerous tools and techniques for capturing and enhancing photographs of the human subject. I hope this material has been a catalyst for your own explorations and that you continue to refine these techniques and develop your own personal approaches to people photography in the digital age. For this final chapter, I will leave you with some additional food for thought.

8

Chapter Contents
The Creative Workflow
Future Developments

The Creative Workflow

Examine the symbolic flow chart in Figure 8.1. This workflow was discussed in detail in Chapter 1, "Digital Imaging Basics, Workflow, and Calibration."

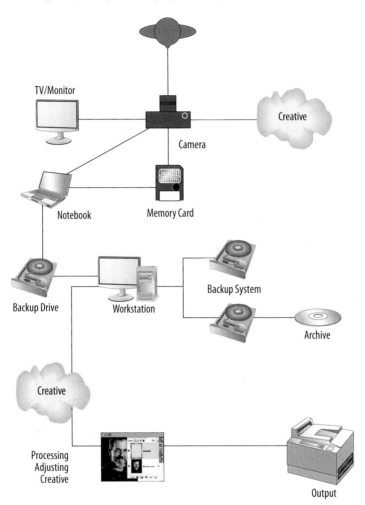

Figure 8.1 Digital photo workflow

Two main areas of creative work in the digital workflow are heavily impacted by digital technology. The first stage, image capture, has been radically altered by the change of the capture medium and instant feedback. The economics and speed of digital capture have also changed the amount of imagery that is typically captured during a shoot. The cost of film and processing used to impose a monetary limit on how many images we could capture. Now, the limiting factor is the amount of storage space available, and it seems like we'll see no end to economies of scale with continuing improvements in density and declining cost of memory. The increased speed at which we can capture, review, and capture again has opened the floodgates to more and more images—we capture more just because we can! As with most changes, there are negative consequences too. More captures encourage the first creative evil: image gluttony. Rather than stop and carefully consider an image, we can be tempted to take the easy way and capture many more images—just in case. Instead of capturing the decisive moment, the undisciplined photographer captures *all* the moments and selects from the multitude. This leads to sloppy thinking, and it is something to guard against.

The second creative stage occurs after the image has been captured and selected. The post-production stage has become just as important as the image-capture stage. The image can be crafted, enhanced, corrected, and "re-imagined" in the digital darkroom in ways that go far beyond Ansel Adams' wildest dreams. These über-photos can be magnificent or grotesque, depending on the sensibilities of the artist. Some photographers succumb to the temptation to Photoshop everything to death, again just because we can. The second creative evil is image vanity. Just how much special trickery does an image deserve? Should we retouch everything to some godly perfection? Should we transform something simple into a Spielberg extravaganza? Sometimes it is hard to know when you've crossed the line until you actually cross it.

It all really comes down to you. The creative artist is the most important part of the process. Not the technology, not the workflow, not the special techniques. They are just tools in service of the vision. These digital tools give you great power. As Spider-Man says, "With great power comes great responsibility." Use the power wisely.

Future Developments

Digital-capture technology is slowly coming out of an early "film emulation" stage of development. The adoption process has focused on making picture-taking familiar to people who have had experience with film-based capture systems. This process is largely complete, and the people who continue to shoot film do so for creative/artistic reasons as the practical benefits of digital capture have been decisively demonstrated. Oddly, we still cling to the past with regard to the form factor of the DSLR. This is changing more slowly. We are just now starting to see experiments with new ergonomic designs unencumbered by the constraints of film-transport mechanisms and large-format film. DSLRs will probably be replaced by direct-view chip designs and cameras will be smaller, lighter, and have sharper optics. Resolutions will continue to climb, but new technology is shifting the emphasis to dynamic range, light sensitivity, and other issues of quality. Radical new optical designs will deliver focus selection after capture, so there will be no need for autofocusing and you'll never miss a shot. These advances are working in prototypes today.

This means that there will continue to be major upheavals in the infrastructure devoted to image making. Support services are changing. The needs of the imaging industry require different services than we've been used to, and the instant delivery of information demands faster and faster turnaround in image capture and delivery. The demand for images will continue to increase, and images will become more and more a commodity, the value dependent on context. Computer-generated imagery will replace many applications for photographic imagery in advertising and commercial areas. Niche markets will rule, and personalized imagery will become more important.

Communication between creative people will demand standards—standard vocabulary, standard tools, and standard file formats. The concept introduced by the digital camera RAW file has major implications for imaging, but new developments will be stifled unless a standard RAW format is adopted. At the moment, the only prospective standard format is DNG and, hopefully, this will be rapidly adopted throughout the industry.

The application of metadata to image files is rapidly producing a standard for metadata-based image editing. We see this in the proliferation of RAW processing applications where edits are separated from the RAW data. Future developments could include just about any kind of image enhancement as a set of instructions that would take up much less space and could be applied to original captured RAW data faster across networks or rendered later at the point of image consumption.

We are standing at the threshold of a whole new way of capturing and experiencing images. Behind us is a short history of photographic processes that were closely connected to the medium of capture for the specific quality of the captured and rendered image. Ahead of us is a new paradigm of imaging that separates the image from the medium of capture and treats it as pure data that can be re-imagined in almost limitless ways. The file has replaced the negative, and images are routinely rendered to multiple different media with a fairly consistent look. The significance of this development is just now beginning to affect how we approach image making. The responsibility for exactly how the image looks now rests completely with the creator of the image!

The one thing that will remain constant is the need for pictures of people. I mean real people, not CGI-rendered illustrations of people (which will be a novelty with narrow applications). People will always respond to pictures of real people in ways that differ significantly from images of other subjects. This means that skill in capturing pictures of people will still be important no matter what other changes occur in image-making technology. We are likely to see improvements in color control and image-enhancement software. The improvements will also likely require more complex skills to apply with any creative integrity.

With these things in mind, be aware that everything in this book will be obsolete in a fairly short time. Certain techniques will still work, but new tools will replace the need for complicated procedures, and new techniques will make things easier and better than ever. The only way to stay competitive is to keep learning. The information in this book will become outdated, so you should be flexible and not take this material to be the ultimate statement on the subject. The concepts introduced here do have value, however, and by mastering the techniques presented here you will be preparing for a future with many rewards.

Thank you for making the effort. May all your future images provide joy beyond your expectations. Live long and prosper.

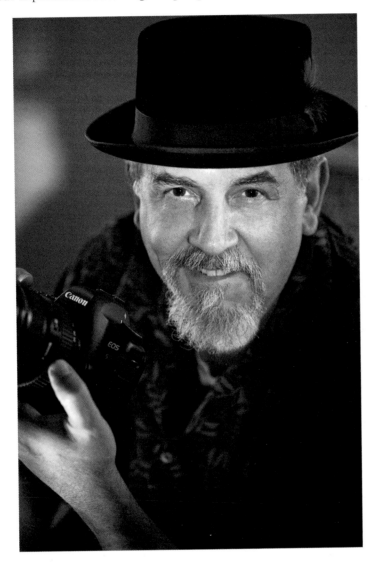

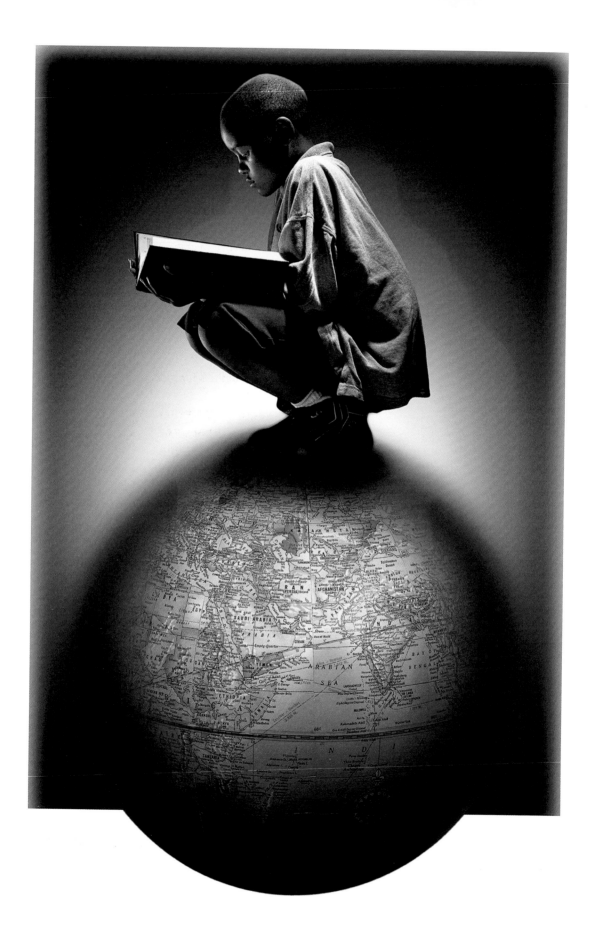

Index

Note to the Reader: Throughout this index **boldfaced** page numbers indicate primary discussions of a topic. *Italicized* page numbers indicate illustrations.

A

Absolute Colorimetric option, 314
ACR (Adobe Camera Raw) format
    calibration for, **34–36**, *34–35*
    exposure evaluation, 21, *21*
    profiles, **31**, *31*
action stopping lighting, **78–79**, *78–82*
ad agencies, retouching for, 215
Adams, Ansel, 10, 14, 89, 93, 128
Add Layer Mask icon, 227
Add Noise filter, 251–253, *253*, 255, *255*
Adobe RGB
    exposure range, 21
    white balance, 51
    zone system values, 89–90, 93
African Americans
    beauty light for, **52–53**, *52–53*
    black and white images for, 150–151, *150–152*
    Luminosity blending for, 136, *136–137*
    skin color values for, **109**, *110*
aim prints, 312
Alien Skin Bokeh interface, 240–241, *240–241*, 248, *249–250*
alpha channels
    creating, 195, *195*
    in depth of field effects, 235
Amount setting
    for noise, 253
    for Smart Sharpen, 291
Anglo-Caucasians
    adjustments, 104–105, *105*
    skin color values, **108**, *109*
artifacts from compression, 5, *5*
artificial light, 42
As Shot option, 36
Asians
    cultural bias with, 113
    skin color values for, **110**, *111*

B

baby oil, 52
background color, 7
Background layers
    for beauty retouching, 182, *183*
    for blur, 238–239, *239*
    for cross-processing, 260, *261*
    for split channels, 125, 134, *135*
Background option for prints, **317**, *317*
backup drives, 9
bags under eyes, **159–160**, *160*
balanced numbers for neutral skin color, **91–93**, *91–92*
    contrast for, **94–99**, *95–98*
    curves for, **93–99**, *93–99*
    Info Panel for, **99**, *100*
bas-relief effect, 303, *304*
BasICColor Display calibrator, 6
Bayer pattern, 3, *3*
beauty light
    for dark-skinned subjects, **52–53**, *52–53*
    description, **48**, *49–50*
beauty retouching, **178–201**, *179–204*
bias in skin color, **113–115**, *114*
bit depth, 4, *4*
bitmap images, 2–3
Black & White adjustment layer, 153
black and white images, **117**
    converting color to, **118–122**, *118–123*
    gradient map colorizing, **145–148**, *145–149*
    for instant tan, **128–131**, *129–131*
    layer blending for, **123–126**, *123–127*
    luminosity blending for, **127–128**, *128*
    power of, **149–151**, *150–152*
    split-toning for, **141–148**, *141–149*
black points
    in skin color correction, **100–108**, *101–107*
    in Zone System, 92–93

black traps, 11
Blade Curvature option, 235
Blend If settings
    for saturation, 326
    for sharpening, 305
    for split channels, 134
    for split toning, 141
    for tattoos, 272
blending and Blending Options
    for black and white, **123–128**, *123–128*
    for dark-skinned subjects, 136, *136–137*
    for HIRALOAM sharpening, 305, *307*
    for prints, 323, *324*, 326–327, *326–327*
    for ramped halos, 295–296
    for Smart Sharpen, 292–293, *294*
    for split channels, 133–134, *133–134*
    for tattoos, 272, *272*
blocky artifacts, 5
blotchy skin, **165–169**, *165–170*
blue color
    filters for, 2
    pixel values for, 3
blur and blur filters
    for beauty retouching, 180–181, *180–182*, 188,
        188, 192, 196, *197*, 201, *203*
    in depth of field effects, **234–241**, *234–241*
    for film grain, 255, *256–257*
    in lens tilt effect, **242–248**, *242–250*
    for overlay diffusion, 230–231, *230–231*
    for screen diffusion, 225–226, *225–227*
    for Smart Sharpen, 291
    in soft focus, 222, *223*
    for wrinkles, 171–176, *172–176*
Blur Focal Distance slider, 246
boards
    for natural lighting, 71–73, *72, 76, 77*
    types, 42
bokeh, 232, *233*, 236, 237, 240–241, *240–241*,
    248, *249–250*
borders for prints, 316, *316*
Boris Karloff lighting, 63, *64*
bounce reflectors
    foamcore, 42, *43*
    for on-camera flash, 60–62, *61–62*

Bounding Box option, 313–314
Boxer, Jeff, 156
brackets for exposure range, **13–16**, *13–16*
brightening eyes, 201, *202*, 204
brightness range, 4, *4*
Brightness sliders for calibration, 35
Brush Density and Pressure setting, 214
brush size
    for retouching, 164
    for spots, 158
    for tummy tucks, 214
brushes for prints, 317–318, *319*
burn in in nighttime shots, 70
butterfly lighting, 48

C

calibration
    color, **51**, *51*
    digital capture, **10–12**
        building, **22**
        camera profiles, **29–34**
        DNG Profile Editor, **22–26**, *23–26*
        exposure evaluation, **17–21**, *17–21*
        exposure range, **13–16**, *13–16*
        lighting, **12–13**
        review, **36**
        testing, **36–37**
        working with, **34–36**, *34–35*
        X-Rite ColorChecker, **26–29**, *27–29*
    monitors, **6–7**, *6*
Camera Neutral calibration preset, 17, *17*
Camera Raw files
    calibration for, **34–36**, *34–35*
    exposure evaluation, 21, *21*
    profiles, **31**, *31*
cameras
    operation of, **2–6**, *2–5*
    profiles. *See* profiles
Canvas Extension option, 317
Canvas Size dialog box, 317, *317*
card readers, 8, *8*
catalogs, Lightroom, **8–10**, *9–10*

catch lights
  benefits, 59–60, *59*
  with on-camera flash, 62, *62*
Caucasians
  adjustments, 104–105, *105*
  skin color values, **108**, *109*
Center Image option
  for desktop printing, 313–314
  for prints, 315
channels and Channel Mixer
  for beauty retouching, 198, *198*
  color, 3
  color to black and white conversion, **119–122**, *120–123*
  in depth of field effects, 235
  for prints, 323
  split, **123–126**, *123–127*
  for tan appearance, 129, *130*
Channels panel, 118
Chart tab, 22, *23*, 25, *25*
Chernus, Ken
  cross-processing use, *264*
  dark-skinned subject portraits, 52, *52*, 136, *136–137*
  Hue/Saturation color repair, **165–169**, *165–170*
  natural lighting use, 73–74, *73–74*, 76, *76–77*
  ring lights used by, 65, *65*
  warm tone image, 139, *140*
children, skin tones for, 108, *109*
China, cultural bias in, 113
chips, **2–4**, *3*
Chlorobromide photographic paper, 139, *140*
CIELAB profiles, 38
clipped-to-white tone, 11
clipping
  in contrast, 95, 97
  in exposure evaluation, 18, *19*
  white point, 33
clipping masks, 184–185, *184*, 188
Clone Stamp tool, 164, *164*
CLUTs (color look-up tables), **309**, *310*
CMM (color management module), 309
CMYK images
  for prints, **308**

sharpening for, 284
for soft proofs, 310, *311*
CMYK numbers, 99, 103–107, *105*
color, **117**
  in beauty retouching, 183
  calibration for, **10–12**, 51, *51*
    building, **22**
    camera profiles, **29–34**
    DNG Profile Editor, **22–26**, *23–26*
    exposure evaluation, **17–21**, *17–21*
    exposure range, **13–16**, *13–16*
    lighting, **12–13**
    review, **36**
    testing, **36–37**
    working with, **34–36**, *34–35*
    X-Rite ColorChecker, **26–29**, *27–29*
  constancy of, 91
  context in, **37–39**
  contrast for, 7, **94–99**, *95–98*
  converting to black and white, **118–122**, *118–123*
  for desktop printing, 312–314, *313*
  digital capture workflow in, **7–8**, *8*
  filters for, 2
  grunge look, 267
  overwhelming, **131–136**, *132–137*
  pixel values for, 3
  for prints, **308–310**, *309–310*
  retouching, **165–169**, *165–170*
  skin. *See* skin color
  in subtle retouching, 204
  for tattoos, 270, 274–276, *275*
  Zone System for, **89–91**, *89*, *93*
color gamut, 38
color look-up tables (CLUTs), **309**, *310*
color management module (CMM), 309
Color Management options, 313–314, *313*
Color Picker, 147, 317, *317*
Color Sampler tool, 100–103, 106
Color Tables tab, 22–24, *23–24*
color temperature, 108
ColorChecker system, 11, 22, **26–29**, *27–29*
ColorEyes Display Pro calibrator, 6

colorizing
    gradient map, **145–148**, *145–149*
    images, **138–139**, *138–140*
Colormatch workspace, 38
ColorSync system, **88**
combination lighting, **68–70**, *68–71*
combo meters, 13
compensation factor for exposure, 18
compression
    file, 5, *5*
    tone, 95, 97
cones, 2
contrast, **117**
    for calibration, 35
    color, 7
    grunge look, 265, 267
    layer blending for, **123–126**, *123–127*
    for neutral color, **94–99**, *95–98*
    in overlay diffusion, 230, *230*
    overwhelming color in, **131–136**, *132–137*
    for prints, 323, *324*
    for tattoos, 270, 274
    in Zone System, **89–91**
converting color to black and white, **118–122**,
    118–123
cross-over shadow colors, 263, *264*
cross-processing, **258–263**, *259–264*
cultural issues in skin color, **108–115**,
    109–112, 114
curves and Curves adjustments
    beauty retouching, 196, *196*
    contrast, **94–99**, *95–98*
    cross-processing, 262, *262*
    multiply diffusion, 228, *229*
    neutral color, **93–99**, *93–99*
    overlay diffusion, 230–231, *230–231*
    prints, 323, *324*
    screen diffusion, 225–226, *225–227*
    soft focus, 222–224, *223–224*
    soft proofs, 312
    tattoos, 272–276, *274–275*
    white/black point correction, 105–106
Custom Proof Setup option, 314

D

D50 light, 309
dark-skinned subjects
    beauty light for, **52–53**, *52–53*
    black and white images for, 150–151, *150–152*
    Luminosity blending for, 136, *136–137*
    skin color values for, **109**, *110*
dark spots, retouching, **157–158**, *158–159*
Darken Blur layer, 176, *176*
Darken group for HIRALOAM sharpening,
    301, *302*
Darken mode for Smart Sharpen, 292–293, *294*
daylight lighting, 12
daylight plus flash lighting, 68–70, *68–71*
Depth Map option, 235
depth of field effects, **232–241**, *232–241*
desktop color, 7
desktop printing, 312–315, *313, 315*
details settings for grunge look, 267
Difference mode for cross-processing, 260, *261*
diffusion. *See* soft focus
digital cameras, **2–6**, *2–5*
digital capture
    calibration for, **10–12**
        building, **22**
        camera profiles, **29–34**
        DNG Profile Editor, **22–26**, *23–26*
        exposure evaluation, **17–21**, *17–21*
        exposure range, **13–16**, *13–16*
        lighting, **12–13**
        review, **36**
        testing, **36–37**
        working with, **34–36**, *34–35*
        X-Rite ColorChecker, **26–29**, *27–29*
    Lightroom catalogs, **8–10**, *9–10*
    workflow in, **7–8**, *8*
Digital Gray Card, 51
Digital Negative (DNG) format, 7
digital photo workflow, **330–331**, *330*
Dissolve mode for beauty retouching, 198
Distort Brush, 279
DNG (Digital Negative) format, 7
DNG Profile Editor, **22–26**, *23–26*, **32–33**, *32–33*

Dodge tool
    for beauty retouching, 185
    for wrinkles, **161–163**, *161–162*
Dr. Doug, skin smoothing for, **170–178**, *171–178*
Dry Media Brushes setting, 318, *319*
Duplicate Merged Layers Only option, 273, *273*
dyes, 38
dynamic range, 4, *4*

E

Edge Glow slider, 265
edges
    creating, **317–322**, *318–322*
    for sharpening, **297–298**, *297–300*
editing profiles, **32–33**, *32–33*
effects, special
    cross-processing, **258–263**, *259–264*
    film grain and noise
        adjusting, **251–258**, *251–257*
        noise patterns in, 258
    grunge look, **265–270**, *265–270*
    soft focus. *See* soft focus
    tattoos
        enhancing, **270–276**, *271–276*
        faking, **276–279**, *277–280*
Emboss filter, 192, *193–194*
Export dialog box, 28–29, *28–29*
exposure
    evaluating, **17–21**, *17–21*
    "exposing to the right", **33**
    grunge look, 267
    overexposed files, 36
    range, **13–16**, *13–16*
external hard drives, 9, *9*
Extreme Edges library, 320
Eye icon, 182
Eyedropper tool
    for blotches, 165–167, *166*
    for neutral color, 100
    for skin color, 91
eyes, 2
    bags under, **159–160**, *160*
    brightening, 201, *202*, 204

catch lights in, 59–60, *59*
retouching, 59–60, *60*
EZYBalance reference cards, 15, *16*

F

f-stops
    for dynamic range, 4
    for exposure range brackets, 15
fabric flags, 42, *44*
Fade Amount setting, 291
Fade command, 192, *194*
Fade Emboss command, 192
Fade Unsharp Mask option, 293
faded color effect, 148
faking tattoos, **276–279**, *277–280*
Faster option for Lens Blur, 235
figure thinning techniques, **210–216**, *211–217*
file format, 5
file size, 5
fill cards
    for natural light, 57–59, *58*, 76, *77*
    in Rembrandt lighting, 56
fill lights
    for action stopping lighting, 78–79, *82*
    in beauty lighting, 52
    flash, 69, *69*
    in Rembrandt lighting, 56
Fill With Overlay-Neutral Color (50% Gray) option
    in beauty retouching, 185
    for film grain, 251
Fill With Soft-Light-Neutral Color option, 161
film, 2
film grain
    adjusting, **251–258**, *251–257*
    noise patterns in, 258
Film Noir image, 84, *85*
filters
    for beauty retouching, 180, *180–182*, 186, 188, *188*
    color, 2–3
    in depth of field effects, **234–241**, *234–241*
    and film grain, 251–252, *255*, *256*
    for sharpening, **284–289**, *285–286*, *288–289*

in soft focus, 221, *221*

for subtle retouching, 204

for wrinkles, 206, *208*

flags, 42, *44*

flash fill lighting, 69, *69*

flash lighting

in action stopping lighting, 78

benefits of, 42

daylight plus flash, 68–70, *68–71*

meters for, 13, *13*

on-camera, **60–62**, *61–63*

radio slaves for, 46, *47*

for studio lighting, 12

umbrellas for, 44, *45*

"flash overpowering daylight" effect, 68

flashlights, 84, *85*

flat images, 95

Flatten Image option, 171, *172*

flattening

files, 126

images, 171, *172*

flow charts for digital photo process, **330–331**, *330*

fluorescent lighting, 13, 42

foamcore cards

for action stopping lighting, 78–79, *78, 82*

for V-flats, 42

focus, soft. *See* soft focus

folders for images, 9, *10*

Foreground To Transparent gradient, 244, *245*

Forward Warp tool

for figure thinning, 212, *215*

for tattoos, 279

free transforms

for tattoos, 277

for thinning, 210, *211*

Full Screen mode, 312

future developments, **331–333**

G

gamma for grunge look, 267

gamut, 38

Gamut Warning, 314

Gaussian Blur filter

for beauty retouching, 188, *188*, 192, 196, *197*, 201

in depth of field effects, 234–235, *234*, 237, *238*, 241, *241*

for film grain, 255, *256*

for Smart Sharpen, 291

in soft focus, 221, *221*

for subtle retouching, 204

Gaussian noise and film grain, 253

General - Zeroed develop preset, 17, *17*

glamour lighting, **48**, *49–50*

global softening effect, **171–178**, *171–178*

goth look, 66, *67*

Gradient Editor, 145–148, *146–147*

gradient map colorizing, **145–148**, *145–149*

Gradient Picker, 145

Gradient tool, 244, *245*

gradients for wrinkles, 206

grain

adjusting, **251–258**, *251–257*

noise patterns in, 258

grass, skin color affected by, 110, *111*

gray cards, **14**

gray color

for desktop, 7

for white/black point correction, 105

Gray Overlay layer, 185, *186*, 198, *200*

Gray Overlay Texture option, 188

gray ramp in Zone System, 90

Gray Texture layer, 188, 190, *191*

grayscale information

in color to black and white conversion, 118–119

splitting, 124

for tone and contrast, 136

green color

filters for, 2

pixel values for, 2–3

Gretag Macbeth ColorChecker Passport system, **26–29**, *27–29*

"group emerging from the darkness" effect, 66, *67*

grunge look, **265–270**, *265–270*

H

hair lights, 48, *50, 53, 54*

halos

in depth of field effects, 238

masking for, 297–298

ramped, **295–296**, *295–296*

with ring lights, 65

with sharpening, 286, 289, 291

hand-held meters, 15

hard drives, external, 9, *9*

hardness of lighting, 47–48

hardware calibration, **6–7**, *6*

Harmel, Mark, 75, *75*

HDR Toning dialog box, 265, *266–267*

Healing Brush, **159–160**, *160*

High Pass filters for wrinkles, 206, *208–209*

High-Pass Overlay Sharpening, 325, *325*

High Pass sharpening

for highlights, 151, *152*

HIRALOAM, 303, 305, *306–307*

for prints, 325, *325*

high-radius sharpening effects, **300–305**, *301–307*, 325, *325*

Highlight setting

for grunge look, 267

for sharpening, 291, *292*

Highlight Fade setting, 292

HIRALOAM sharpening, **300–305**, *301–307*

histograms, 15–16, **33**

holes, background, 182, *183*

Hue/Saturation adjustments

for color repair, **165–169**, *165–170*

in overlay diffusion, 231

for prints, 323, *324*

for skin smoothing, **170–178**, *171–178*

for subtle retouching, 204, *205*

for tone, **138–139**, *138–140*, 143–145, *144*

Hue slider

for blotches, 166–167

DNG Profile Editor, 32, *33*

I

i1Display calibrator, 6

ICC profiles

description, 37

for prints, **308–310**, *309*

importing shots, **17–21**, *17–21*

incandescent lighting, 12

incident meters, 15, *15*

Indians, skin color values for, 114, *114*

indoor lighting settings, 12

Info Panel

for neutral color, **99**, *100*

for opponent colors, 107

for skin color, 91–92, 103–106, *105*

instant tan, **128–131**, *129–131*

interpolation, pixel, 3

inverse S-curve shapes, 230, *231*

Iris option for Lens Blur, 235

ISO values, 12–13, 15, 18

for cross-processing, 258

low light capabilities, 84

in sharpening, 287

J

Jones, Kent, 79, *81*

JPEG (Joint Photographic Experts Group) format, 4–5

artifacts, 5, *5*

LCD previews, **15–16**

K

"K" factor, **14**

Karloff lighting, 63, *64*

keylines for prints, 316, *316*

L

LAB numbers and color space

for prints, **309–310**, *309–310*

for tattoos, **273–275**, *274–275*

in Zone System, **89–91**, *89*

Lastolite EZYBalance reference cards, 15, *16*

Layer Opacity setting, 124–125

Layer Pattern Options menu, 171

Layer Style dialog box

HIRALOAM sharpening, 305, *307*

split channels, 134, *135, 137*

split-toning, 141, *142*

tattoos, 272–273, *272*

wrinkles, 206, *209*

layers and layer blending

    for beauty retouching, 179–186, *182*, 191, *191, 198, 198, 200*

    for black and white, **123–126,** *123–127,* **153**

    for blur, 238–239, *239*

    for cross-processing, 258–262, *259–263*

    in depth of field effects, 238

    for gradient map colorizing, 145–148, *146*

    for lens tilt effect, 246

    for multiple sharpening, **292–293,** *293–294*

    for retouching, 156–157, *157*, 161, *161*

    for screen diffusion, 227–228, *227–228*

    for sharpening, 289, **297–298,** *297–300*

    for Smart Sharpen, 292–293

    for split channels, 134, *135–136*

    for split-toning, 141–145, *142–145*

    for tattoos, 272

    for wrinkles, 171–176, *172, 174*, 206

LCD limitations, **15–16,** *16*

Lens Blur

    in depth of field effects, **235–236,** *235–236*

    in lens tilt effect, 244, *244*, 246–248, *246–248*

    for Smart Sharpen, 291

lens tilt effect, **242–248,** *242–250*

Lensbaby soft-focus lenses, 298, *299–300*

lenses

    in eyes and cameras, 2

    soft-focus, 298, *299–300*

Levels dialog

    for cross-processing, 258

    for wrinkles, 175–176, *175–176*

light meters, 13–14, *13*

light spots, retouching, **157–158,** *158–159*

Lighten Blur layer, 175, *177*

Lighten group for HIRALOAM sharpening, 301, *302*

Lighten mode

    for beauty retouching, 192, *194*

    for Smart Sharpen, 292–293, *294*

    for wrinkles, 175, *175*

lighting, **41**

    in calibration, **12–13**

    portrait. *See* portrait lighting

    technology for, **42–47,** *43–47*

lighting ratios, 76

Lightness slider, 167

Lightroom

    ColorChecker Passport with, 26–29, *28*

    exposure evaluation, **17–21,** *17–21*

    grunge look, **268–270,** *269–270*

    profiles in, **29–30,** *30*

    setting up, **8–10,** *9–10*

Liquify tool

    for tattoos, 279, *279*

    for tummy tucks, 212–216, *214–215, 217*

lithography, 4

Local Adaption method for grunge look, 265

look-up tables (LUTs), **309,** *310*

lossless compression, 5

lossy compression, 5

low key subjects, 228

Low-Radius Unsharp Mask, 300

Luminosity mode

    for black and white, **127–128,** *128*

    for cross-processing, 260, *261*

    for prints, 323, *324*

    for ramped halos, 295–296

    for soft focus, 222, *223–224*

    for split channels, 133, *133*

    for tan appearance, 131

    for Unsharp Mask, 284–285, *285*

LUTs (look-up tables), **309,** *310*

M

magic hour, 73

magic light, 73

main lights in Rembrandt lighting, 56

Manning, Eric, 48, 148

maps for colorizing, **145–148,** *145–149*

Margulis, Dan, 300

markups for retouching, 156, *156*

masks

    for beauty retouching, 182, *182, 198, 198*

for depth of field effects, 238

for layer blending, 125

for lens tilt effect, 246

for screen diffusion, 227–228, *227–228*

for sharpening, **297–298**, *297–300*

for tattoos, 272

Match Print Colors option, 314

mature subjects

beauty retouching, **178–201**, *179–204*

subtle retouching, **204–206**, *205–210*

Max, Peter, 148

megapixels, 3

memory cards, 8

men, wrinkles on, 205–206, *206*

messy edges, 5

metadata, future developments for, 332

midtones, 95, 97, *97*

Minus Eyedropper tool, 165–167, *166*

Mode Change conversion, 119

monitor calibration, **6–7**, *6*

Monochromatic option

in beauty retouching, 186

for film grain, 253, *254*

monochrome images. *See* black and white images

More Accurate option for Lens Blur, 235

Motion Blur

in depth of field effects, 237

for film grain, 255, *257*

for Smart Sharpen, 291

moving subjects

action stopping lighting for, **78–79**, *78–82*

sharpening, **295–299**, *295–299*

multiple memory cards, 8

multiple sharpening layers, **292–293**, *293–294*, **297–298**, *297–300*

Multiply blur, 228, *229*

multiply diffusion, **228**, *229*

Multiply mode for tattoos, 270–272, *271*, *277*, *278*

Munsell charts, 11

N

natural light, 42

controlling, **71–76**, *72–77*

for portraits, **57–60**, *58–60*

neutral gray backgrounds, 7

neutral skin color, **91–93**, *91–92*

contrast for, **94–99**, *95–98*

curves for, **93–99**, *93–99*

Info Panel for, **99**, *100*

New Group From Layers option, 143, 227

New Layer dialog box, 161, *161*

for beauty retouching, *183*, 184–186, *186*, 191, *191*

for cross-processing, *260*

for film grain, 251, *253*

Newton, Helmut, 63, *64*

Nex, Anthony

black and white image by, 150, *150*

depth of field effects by, 232, *233*

lens tilt effect by, 242, *242*

natural lighting use by, 71, *72*

noise and Noise filter

for beauty retouching, 186, *187–188*

and film grain, **251–258**, *251–257*

for Lens Blur, 236

with Unsharp Mask, 287

nose lights, 48

O

octave sharpening, **295**

offset lithography

dynamic range in, 4

sharpening for, 284

older subjects

beauty retouching, **178–201**, *179–204*

subtle retouching, **204–206**, *205–210*

on-camera flash, **60–62**, *61–63*

OnOne Software Focal Point interface, 240, *240*, *250*

opacity

for bags under eyes, 160, *160*

for beauty retouching, 184–186, *187*, 192, 195, 198, *199*, 201, *203*

for film grain, 255, *255*

in gradient map colorizing, 147–148, *148*

in layer blending, 124–125

for ramped halos, 295–296, *296*

for skin smoothing, 177

in soft focus, 222, *222*, 224

for tattoos, 276–277, *279*

for wrinkles, 161–163, *161–162*

opponent colors, 107

out-of-focus image sharpening, 298, *299–300*

outdoor lighting settings, 12

output simulations, **315**, *315*

overexposed files, 36

Overlay blur, 230, *230–231*

overlay diffusion, **230–231**, *230–232*, 248, *249*

Overlay mode

    for cross-processing, 262, *262*

    for film grain, 251–253

    for HIRALOAM sharpening, 303, 305,
        306–307

    for noise patterns, 258

    for wrinkles, 206, *208–209*

Overlay Sharpen technique, **300–305**, *301–307*

Overlay Texture layer option, 185, *187*

oversaturation in prints, 325–326

overwhelming color, **131–136**, *132–137*

P

panels, 42, *43*, 45

Paper White simulation, 311–312, *311*

Patch tool, **163**, *164*

Pattern Fill dialog box, 190–192, *192*

Pattern Name dialog box, 190, *191*

patterns, noise, 258

Pen tool, 317

Perceptual rendering option, 314

PhotoFrame Pro plug-in, 320, *321*

photoreceptors, 2

Photoshop Manages Colors option, 313

pimples, retouching, 165–169, *165–170*

pixel count, 3

pixels, **3–6**

polished reflectors, 44

portrait lighting, **47–48**

    action stopping lighting, **78–79**, *78–82*

    beauty light, 48, *49–50*

combination lighting, **68–70**, *68–71*

experimenting with, **83–84**, *83–84*

natural light, **57–60**, *58–60*, **71–76**, *72–77*

on-camera flash, **60–62**, *61–63*

Rembrandt lighting, **53–56**, *54–57*

ring lights, **65–66**, *65–67*

rule breaking, **63**, *64*

Position option for desktop printing, 313–314

Print dialog box, 312–313, *313*, 315, *316*

Printer Driver dialog box, 314

Printer Manages Colors option, 313–314

prints, 283

    background and canvas options, **317**, *317*

    color for, **308–310**, *309–310*

    desktop, 312–315, *313*, *315*

    edge treatments, **317–322**, *318–322*

    finishing, **315–316**, *316*

    last minute fixes for, **323–327**, *323–327*

    sharpening for. *See* sharpening

    skin color in, 90

    soft proofing, **310–312**, *311*

profiles

    in ACR, **31**, *31*

    ColorChecker Passport system, **27–29**, *27–29*

    description, 37–38

    for desktop printing, 313

    DNG Profile Editor, **22–26**, *23–26*

    editing, **32–33**, *32–33*

    in Lightroom, **29–30**, *30*

    for prints, **308–310**, *309*

    for workspaces, 38

Proof Setup simulations, **315**, *315*

ProPhotoRGB exposure range, 21

Proximity Matching option, **157**, *157*

psychological issues in skin color, **108–115**,
    109–112, *114*

pupils

    enlarging, 201, *202*, 204

    retouching, 59–60, *60*

Q

quality, RAW signals for, 6

R

radio slaves, 46, *47*

radius settings
  for blur, 180, 221, 235, 247
  for edge glow, 265
  High Pass Filter, 206
  high-radius effects, **300–305**, *301–307*
  for ramped halos, 295–296
  Smart Sharpen, 291–292
  Unsharp Mask, 287
  for wrinkles, 171

ramped halos, **295–296**, *295–296*

Rapoport, Aaron
  combination lighting, 68–70, *68–71*
  film grain effect, 255, *255–256*
  prints by, **323–327**, *323–327*
  Rembrandt lighting, 56, *57*
  ring lights lighting, 65–66, *66–67*

RAW files, 4
  calibration for, 10
  exposure range, 21, *21*
  for quality, 6
  standards for, 332

rebuilding skin, **178–201**, *179–204*

receptor sites, chip, 3

Rectangle Path tool, 317

red blotchy skin, **165–169**, *165–170*

red color
  filters for, 2
  pixel values for, 2–3

reference cards, 15

Refine Edge dialog box, 287, *288*, 298

reflectors
  for beauty light, 48, *49–50*
  for natural lighting, 71–73, *72*, 76, 77
  for on-camera flash, 60–62, *61–62*
  types, 42–44, *43*

Relative option for prints, 322

Relative Colorimetric option, 314

Rembrandt lighting
  with natural light, **57**, *58*
  for portraits, **53–56**, *54–57*

Rendering Intent option, 314

resolution, pixels for, 3

retinas, 2

retouching, **155**
  basic image repair, **156–164**, *156–164*
  beauty, **178–201**, *179–204*
  figure thinning techniques, **210–216**, *211–217*
  Hue/Saturation color repair, **165–169**, *165–170*
  pupils, 59–60, *60*
  skin smoothing, **170–178**, *171–178*
  subtle, **204–206**, *205–210*

Reverse-Rembrandt lighting, 56, *56*

RGB images, 3
  exposure range, 21
  grayscale images in, 118
  for prints, **308**

RGB numbers
  for skin color, 91
  for white/black point correction, 103, 105–107
  in Zone System, **89–91**

RGB workspace, 38–39

rim lighting for grunge look, 265, *265*

ring lights, 44, *46*, **65–66**, *65–67*

Robin Myer Digital Gray Cards, 51

rods, 2

Rotation option for Lens Blur, 235

rough proofs, 312

rubber stamp tool, **164**

S

S-curves
  for contrast, 97, *97*
  for overlay diffusion, 230
  for soft focus, 222

Sample: Current & Below option, 159, *159*

Sandberg, Michael Eve, 280, *281*

saturation
  in DNG Profile Editor, 32, *33*
  in HIRALOAM sharpening, 303, *304*
  in neutral color, 99
  for prints, 323–326, *324*
  for separations, 314
  for tattoos, 274

Scale To Fit Media option, 313

Scaled Print Size area, 313

Schewe, Jeff, 89

screen diffusion, **225–228**, *225–228*

scrims, 73–74, *74*

secondary color readout setting, 103

separations

    in contrast, 95

    for desktop printing, **314**

shadows

    in cross-processing, 263, *264*

    for grunge look, 267

    in natural lighting, 76

    for prints, 325, *326*

    for Smart Sharpen, 291–292, *291*

Shape Blur filter, 236, *237*

sharpening, **284**, 325, *325*

    masking for, **297–298**, *297–300*

    multiple layers for, **292–293**, *293–294*

    octave, **295**

    overlay, **300–305**, *301–307*

    ramped halos, **295–296**, *295–296*

    Smart Sharpen for, **289–293**, *290–294*

    Unsharp Mask for, **284–289**, *285–286, 288–289*

    wrinkles, 205–206

Show Backdrop option, 279

shutter speed in nighttime shots, 70, *70*

silks, 73–74, *74*

Simulate Black Ink option, 315

Simulate Paper Color option, 315

simulations

    output, **315**, *315*

    for soft proofs, 311–312, *311*

size

    brush. *See* brush size

    compression for, 5

skin color, 3, **87**

    accuracy of, **88**

    color spaces for, 38

    cultural and psychological issues, **108–115**, *109–112, 114*

    neutral, **91–93**, *91–92*

        contrast for, **94–99**, *95–98*

        curves for, **93–99**, *93–99*

        Info Panel for, **99**, *100*

        white/black point correction, **100–108**, *101–107*

skin shine effect, 53, *53*

skin tone, targets for, 11

sky in natural light, 59

slimming techniques, **210–216**, *211–217*

Smart Radius option, 287

Smart Sharpen, **289–293**, *290–294*

smoothing skin, **170–178**, *171–178*

soft focus, **220**

    basic techniques, **220–224**, *220–224*

    depth of field effects, **232–241**, *232–241*

    lens tilt effect, **242–248**, *242–250*

    multiply diffusion, **228**, *229*

    overlay diffusion, **230–231**, *230–232*

    screen diffusion, **225–228**, *225–228*

soft-focus lenses, 298, *299–300*

Soft Light mode

    for beauty retouching, 185

    for blotches, 169

    for film grain, 255, *257*

    for wrinkles, 161–163

Soft Pastel Large brush, 318, *319*

soft proofing prints, **310–312**, *311*

softboxes, 44, *45*

    for action stopping lighting, 78–79, *78, 80*

    for beauty light, 48, *49–50*

softening effect for skin smoothing, **171–178**, *171–178*

softness of lighting, 47–48

sparkles, 48

special effects, **219**

    cross-processing, **258–263**, *259–264*

    film grain and noise

        adjusting, **251–258**, *251–257*

        noise patterns in, 258

    grunge look, **265–270**, *265–270*

    soft focus. *See* soft focus

    tattoos

        enhancing, **270–276**, *271–276*

        faking, **276–279**, *277–280*

Specular Highlights option, 235–236

split channels, **123–126**, *123–127*
split-toning, **141–148**, *141–149*
Spot Healing Brush, **157–158**, *157–159*
spot meters, 13, *14*, 15
spots, retouching, **163–164**, *164*
spring-frame reflectors, 42
sRGB color space, 21, 38
stacked layers, **123–126**, *123–127*
standard targets, 11, *11*
steps in Zone System, 89–90
Stroke Path option, 318
studio lighting settings, 12
subtle retouching, **204–206**, *205–210*
sun in natural lighting, 59, 71
sunset lighting, 73, *73*
Surface Blur
    for beauty retouching, 180, *180–182*, 186, *201*, *203*
    for wrinkles, 171, *173*

T

tags, color description, 39, 88
tans, instant, **128–131**, *129–131*
tape for on-camera flash, 62, *62*
targets, calibration, 11, *11*
tattoos
    combination of techniques, 281, *281*
    enhancing, **270–276**, *271–276*
    faking, **276–279**, *277–280*
technology, future developments for, 332
test shots, 10
testing calibration procedure, **36–37**
thinning techniques, **210–216**, *211–217*
Threshold setting
    for beauty retouching, 180
    for Lens Blur, 236
    for Smart Sharpen, 292–293, *293*
    for Unsharp Mask, 286–287
    for white/black point correction, **101–103**, *101*
    for wrinkles, 171
tissue paper for on-camera flash, 62, *62*
tonal shape for black and white, 128

tonal transitions, 286
Tonal Width setting, 291
tone, **117**
    compressing, 95, 97
    grunge look, **265–267**, *266–267*
    hue/saturation effects, **138–139**, *138–140*
    layer blending for, **123–126**, *123–127*
    overwhelming color in, **131–136**, *132–137*
    split-toning, **141–148**, *141–149*
    in Zone System, **89–91**
translating RGB images to CMYK, **308**
trimming off edges, **297–298**, *297–300*
tummy tucks, **212–216**, *213–217*
tungsten light, 83
TV monitor calibration, **6–7**, *6*

U

umbrellas
    for beauty light, 48, *50*
    for flash lighting, 44, *45*
under-color removal (UCR) for prints, 325
Uniform option in beauty retouching, 186
Unsharp Mask filter, 255, 257, **284–289**, *285–286*, *288–289*
Unsharp Mask Radius setting, 296
Use Previous Layer To Create Clipping Mask
    option
    for beauty retouching, 184–185
    for cross-processing, 258

V

V-flats, 42, *43*
    for action stopping lighting, 78, *78*
    for combination lighting, 70, *71*
visual center for prints, 316

W

White Balance tool, 17
White layer masks, 279
white points
    for grunge look, 267

in skin color correction, **100–108**, *101–107*
in Zone System, 92–93
wide-angle lenses, 68
workflow
    overview, **330–331**, *330*
    RAW file, 6
Workflow Options dialog box, 21, *21*
workspaces, color, 38–39
wrinkles
    Dodge tool for, **161–163**, *161–162*
    nose lights for, 48

smoothing, **170–178**, *171–178*
in subtle retouching, **204–206**, *205–210*

X

X-Rite ColorChecker, 11, 22, **26–29**, *27–29*

Z

zero sliders for exposure range, 21
Zone System, 10, **89–91**, *89*, **93**